Research in Social Work series

Series Editors: **Anna Gupta**, Royal Holloway, University of London, UK and **John Gal**, Hebrew University of Jerusalem, Israel

---

Published together with The European Social Work Research Association (ESWRA), this series examines current, progressive and innovative research applications of familiar ideas and models in international social work research.

Also available in the series:

Involving Service Users in Social Work Education, Research and Policy
Edited by **Kristel Driessens** and **Vicky Lyssens-Danneboom**

Adoption from Care
Edited by **Tarja Pösö, Marit Skivenes** and **June Thoburn**

Interprofessional Collaboration and Service User Participation
Edited by **Kirsi Juhila, Tanja Dall, Christopher Hall** and **Juliet Koprowska**

The Settlement House Movement Revisited
Edited by **John Gal, Stefan Köngeter** and **Sarah Vicary**

Social Work and the Making of Social Policy
Edited by **Ute Klammer, Simone Leiber** and **Sigrid Leitner**

Research and the Social Work Picture
By **Ian Shaw**

Find out more at:

policy.bristoluniversitypress.co.uk/
research-in-social-work

Research in Social Work series

Series Editors: **Anna Gupta**, Royal Holloway, University of London, UK and **John Gal**, Hebrew University of Jerusalem, Israel

---

Forthcoming in the series:

Social Work Research Using Arts-Based Methods
Edited by **Ephrat Huss** and **Eltje Bos**

The Origins of Social Care and Social Work
By **Mark Henrickson**

Find out more at:

policy.bristoluniversitypress.co.uk/
research-in-social-work

Research in Social Work series

Series Editors: **Anna Gupta**, Royal Holloway, University of London, UK and **John Gal**, Hebrew University of Jerusalem, Israel

International Editorial Board:

Find out more at:

policy.bristoluniversitypress.co.uk/
research-in-social-work

CRITICAL GERONTOLOGY FOR SOCIAL WORKERS

Edited by
Sandra Torres and Sarah Donnelly

First published in Great Britain in 2022 by

Policy Press, an imprint of
Bristol University Press
University of Bristol
1-9 Old Park Hill
Bristol
BS2 8BB
UK
t: +44 (0)117 954 5940
e: bup-info@bristol.ac.uk

Details of international sales and distribution partners are available at
policy.bristoluniversitypress.co.uk

British Library Cataloguing in Publication Data
A catalogue record for this book is available from the British Library

ISBN 978-1-4473-6044-5 hardcover
ISBN 978-1-4473-6046-9 ePub
ISBN 978-1-4473-6047-6 ePdf

Cover design: David Worth
Front cover image: iStock-496492452

Contents

List of figures and tables

Figures

Tables

Notes on contributors

Peter Beresford OBE is Visiting Professor at the University of East Anglia, UK, and Co-Chair of Shaping Our Lives, the national disabled people's and service user-led organisation. He is a long-term user of mental health services and Emeritus Professor at Brunel University London and the University of Essex, UK. He has a long-standing track-record of involvement in the issue of participation as writer, researcher, activist and educator. His latest book is *Participatory Ideology: From Exclusion to Involvement* (Policy Press, 2021).

Suzanne Cahill is Adjunct Professor of Social Work and Social Policy at Trinity College Dublin, Ireland. She holds an honorary professorship in Dementia Care at the National University of Ireland Galway and is an affiliated Professor in Health and Welfare at the Institute of Gerontology in Jönkoping University in Sweden. Most of her academic career has been spent researching and campaigning for the rights of people living with dementia and their family caregivers. Her most recent book is *Perspectives on the Person with Dementia and Family Caregiving in Ireland* (Peter Lang, 2021).

Gemma M. Carney is a critical gerontologist and Senior Lecturer in Social Policy and Ageing at the School of Social Sciences, Education and Social Work at Queen's University Belfast, UK. She is a member of the editorial board of *Ageing & Society* and, with Paul Nash, University of Southern California, is author of *Critical Questions for Ageing Societies* (Policy Press, 2020). She leads a range of interdisciplinary studies of ageing at Queen's and is currently Co-Investigator on an AHRC-funded project, Dementia in the Minds of Characters and Readers.

Sarah Donnelly is Assistant Professor of Social Work in the School of Social Policy, Social Work and Social Justice, University College Dublin, Ireland, and Co-convenor of the European Network for Gerontological Social Work (ENGSW). Sarah's research interests include ageing and dementia, adult safeguarding and capacity and decision making. Sarah is a registered social worker, an active member of the Irish Association of Social Workers (IASW) and a member of the Irish Gerontological Society.

Amanda Grenier is Professor and the Norman and Honey Schipper Chair in Gerontological Social Work at the Factor-Inwentash Faculty of Social Work, University of Toronto, and Baycrest Hospital in Canada. Amanda is an interdisciplinary scholar and critical gerontologist focused on the interface of public policies, organisational practices and older people's lived experience, with a particular focus on ageing and inequality. She currently leads a SSHRC Insight Grant on Precarious Aging. Her recent work includes *Late Life Homelessness: Experiences of Disadvantage and Unequal Aging* (McGill Queens University Press, 2021) and *Precarity and Ageing: Understanding Insecurity and Risk in Later Life*, which she has co-edited with Chris Phillipson and Richard A. Settersten Jr (Policy Press, 2021).

Trish Hafford-Letchfield is Professor of Social Work at the University of Strathclyde, UK. Her research interests are in older people from marginalised communities and their experiences of accessing and using care. Trish has more than 100 publications, with two edited books in a new series on 'Sex and Intimacy in Later Life' (titled *Sex and Diversity in Later Life* and *Desexualisation in Later Life: The Limits of Sex and Intimacy*) with Paul Simpson and Paul Reynolds (Policy Press, 2021). Recent research projects include the impact of COVID-19 on family carers of residents in care homes, and suicide prevention and ageing.

Joan R. Harbison is Adjunct Professor at the School of Social Work, Dalhousie University, Canada. Her scholarship focuses on critical interdisciplinary approaches to ageing in both national and international contexts. Her recent work includes co-editing *New Challenges to Ageing in the Rural North: A Critical Interdisciplinary Perspective* with Päivi Naskali and Shahnaj Begum (Springer, 2019) and, with her interdisciplinary research team from social work, law and sociology, authoring *Contesting Elder Abuse and Neglect: Ageism, Risk and the Rhetoric of Rights in the Mistreatment of Older People* (University of British Columbia Press, 2016).

Paul Higgs is Professor of the Sociology of Ageing at University College London, UK. He has published extensively in gerontology, medical sociology and sociology. He has published 14 books (seven with Chris Gilleard), including: *Cultures of Ageing: Self, Citizen and Society* (Longman, 2000); *Contexts of Ageing: Class, Cohort and Community* (Polity, 2005); *Rethinking Old Age: Theorising the Fourth Age* (Palgrave Macmillan, 2015); and *Social Divisions and Later* and *Life: Difference, Diversity and Inequality* (Policy, 2020). Paul is editor of *Social Theory and Health*. He holds fellowships from the UK Academy of Social Sciences and the Gerontological Society of America.

Alisoun Milne is Professor of Social Gerontology and Social Work at the School of Sociology, Social Policy and Social Research, University of Kent, UK. She is a registered social worker. Alisoun's research interests are in four intersecting areas: social work with older people and their families; mental health in later life; family caring; and long-term care. She is widely published. Her most recent book is *Mental Health in Later Life: Taking a*

Lifecourse Approach (Policy Press, 2020). She is currently co-authoring a book for Emerald Publishing on *Care and Caring*. Alisoun is a member of the Research Excellence Framework 2021 sub-panel for Social Work and Social Policy and a Fellow of the UK Academy of the Social Sciences.

Lorna Montgomery is Senior Lecturer in Social Work in the School of Social Sciences, Education and Social Work, Queen's University Belfast, UK, and is Director of Practice Learning. She practiced as a social worker/ manager in the adult sector for 20 years, and has also worked for five years in a non-governmental organisation in Uganda, East Africa, conducting research on cross-cultural bereavement practices. Her teaching and research interests include adult safeguarding, mental health, parenting and cross-cultural practice. Her latest contributions include articles in *The Journal of Adult Protection* and *Practice*.

Anna Olaison is Associate Professor of Social Work at CESAR Centre for Social Work at Uppsala University in Sweden. Her programme of research aims to investigate how neoliberalism, changing social policies and standardisation of social services influence needs assessment practices. She has published on questions related to decision making and delivery of care and services for older people as well as social workers' abilities to use discretion in assessment meetings and documentation practices. Anna is a social worker and she leads several funded projects on the needs assessment practices of care services for older people.

Mo Ray is Professor of Health and Social Care in the School of Health and Social Care, University of Lincoln, UK. After qualifying as a social worker in 1990, she worked as a social worker/care manager in adult teams, specialising in practice with older people. Her interest in long-lasting relationships and the impact of ill health and disability led to Mo completing a part-time PhD at Keele University, UK, on marriages that last a lifetime. She subsequently secured an ESRC Fellowship which led to a social work lectureship at Keele University. She worked in a number of roles, including Director of Social Work Studies. Mo was awarded a personal Chair in Gerontological Social Work in 2014. Her research interests focus on experiences of ageing, ageing and care and social relationships in older age.

Marjaana Seppänen is Professor of Social Work at the University of Helsinki, Finland. Her background is in social sciences (especially social work) and she has extensively studied and published on questions connected to gerontological social work, ageing, well-being and the living conditions of older adults. Marjaana is part of several international research networks in gerontology and social work.

Tamara Sussman is Associate Professor in the School of Social Work at McGill University in Canada. Her programme of research aims to uncover the ways in which health service systems can exacerbate rather than alleviate distress, exclusion and disadvantage for older persons and their families. Tamara's contributions have been increasingly directed towards examining and improving experiences of living and dying within the context of long-term care, an aspect of the service system fraught with challenges.

Sandra Torres is Professor of Sociology and the Chair in Social Gerontology at Uppsala University in Sweden. Her work as a critical social gerontologist problematises old age-related constructs and deconstructs some of the taken-for-granted assumptions that inform research, policy and practice. Sandra is the President of the Research Committee on Aging of the International Sociological Association and of the Social-Behavioral Section of the International Association of Gerontology and Geriatrics: European Region. She holds fellowships from the (Swedish) Royal Society of Sciences and the Gerontological Society of America, is editor-in-chief of *Ageing & Society*, and author of *Ethnicity and Old Age: Expanding our Imagination* (Policy Press, 2019). At present she is co-editing (with Alistair Hunter) the *Handbook of Migration and Ageing* (Edward Elgar Publishing, 2023).

Paul Willis is Associate Professor of Social Work and Social Gerontology at the University of Bristol, UK. Paul is a registered social worker and researcher in social care, ageing and social inclusion. His current research interests include loneliness, ageing and masculinities; sexuality, gender identity and ageing; and inclusive housing for older adults. Recent funded projects include social inclusion practices in housing with care and support; older men's experiences of loneliness; and health and social care for trans adults in later life. Paul is a Senior Research Fellow of the National Institute for Health Research School for Social Care Research, England.

Acknowledgements

In our Preface we thank everyone who played a role in setting in motion the work that often happens behind the scene prior to a book synopsis being submitted to a publisher. Edited collections are always joint efforts, and sometimes (as is the case for this one) there are colleagues who have played a role in the discussions that sparked the motivation to start a book project, and people who have been specifically instrumental in supporting those who have edited the collection. These acknowledgements are therefore about those who have played a direct role in keeping us committed to managing this project.

Sarah Donnelly would like to thank the School of Social Policy, Social Work and Social Justice at University College Dublin (UCD) for facilitating the sabbatical leave that made the final stages of this project possible. Without this protected time, she would not have been able to commit to this exciting but time-consuming project. In particular, she would like to thank her Head of School, Professor Jim Campbell, and the School Executive and co-director of the Professional Masters in Social Work Programme, UCD, Dr Elaine Wilson, whose ongoing encouragement and support were invaluable.

Sarah would also like to thank her family and friends who have kept her sane and grounded throughout this journey. She would like to send massive thanks to her husband, Marty, who has always kept a smile on her face and helped her to see the big picture in times of stress (which were many!). Her dear parents, Barbara and Michael, brothers and sister and her mother-in-law, Eileen, deserve also a sincere thanks for their unwavering belief in her and their unconditional love and support. Sarah sends also a special word of thanks to the Irish Association of Social Workers 'Change Warrior' colleagues, Sinead Mc Garry, Amanda Casey, Celine O'Connor, Kerry Cuskelly and Cliona Murphy, who inspire her with their advocacy, activism and true commitment to social justice. Last but not least, she thanks her UCD Health Systems buddies Eidin Ní Shé, Carmel Davies and Deirdre O'Donnell for the many debriefs and good times over the last two years.

Sandra is grateful for the intellectual oasis that is the Welfare Research Group at the Department of Sociology of Uppsala University. She co-founded the group in 2012 and feels blessed to count on their constructive feedback on most of the work she publishes. The group is currently led by Professor Hannah Bradby and Dr Clara Iversen and she sends special thanks to them for creating the welcoming and thought-provoking environment that the group offers to those who partake in the seminars they organise every third week. The chapter of which she is the sole author (Chapter 7) benefited greatly from the comments received from the following research group members (besides the group's leaders) who attended the seminar dedicated to this chapter: Professor Ilkka Henrik Mäkkinen, Dr Markus Lundström, Professor Beth Maina Ahlberg, Dr Krisina Engwall, Dr Minoo Alinia, Dr Anna Olaison, Dr Richard Gäddman Johansson, Dr Jan Grimell, Dr Katharina Wesolowski, Dr Jessica Okumu and the inspiring group of doctoral students who contribute to keeping all of us in our toes, that is: Frida Höglund, Aija Duntava and Henrik Daniel Eriksson. Final thanks go to Sandra's darling husband, who is always supportive and never complains about the fact that she spends most of her time in her library.

Last but not least, we thank our contributors for agreeing to work with us in this book project and for attending to various queries and comments as promptly as they did. Their commitment to this edited collection made our journey enjoyable, even though working in the midst of a pandemic.

We dedicate this book to students of social work around the world, whose commitment to the profession will be instrumental to the well-being of the communities they serve. To them we say: never forget that a commitment to social justice and human rights determines whether you will play your part in contributing to creating the caring democracies we all deserve!

Preface

Working on an edited collection, especially in the midst of a pandemic, with all of the professional and personal challenges that we and our contributors have experienced, has been challenging, but also more stimulating than we had anticipated. An edited collection is always a collective effort that is often generated through a series of serendipitous moments, and when one works along with so many scholars who also have a background as social workers one cannot help but feel energised. When reflecting on how this book came to be, we can, however, clearly trace its original conceptualisation back to April 2018 and the European Conference for Social Work Research that took place in Edinburgh. Discussions during the Special Interest Group for Gerontological Social Work (or the European Network for Gerontological Social Work as it later became known as) identified the need for a book that approached gerontological social work from an angle that aimed to empower social work scholars, policy makers and practitioners. As a group we were frustrated about the lack of status and attention given to social work with older people generally, and, parallel to this, we had concerns relating to ageism experienced by older people in our communities and societies stemming from increased neoliberal, reductionist social policies in many countries across Europe. While there were several excellent published texts relating to social work and older people, we felt that there was gap for a book with a critical lens, which would act as a call to arms to the social work profession, encouraging an embracement of the activist and social justice mandate.

Firstly, we must thank Professor Mo Ray and Professor Marjaana Seppänen for their incredible vision and leadership in establishing the Gerontological Social Work Special Interest Group/European Network for Gerontological Social Work in the first place. We would also like to sincerely thank and acknowledge Marjaana, Professor Janet Anand and Dr Anna Olaison for their important contributions to the initial conceptualisation of this book project. Marjaana spent part of her sabbatical at the Department of Sociology, Uppsala University – which houses the Centre for Social Work – with one of us (Sandra) and together they did the thorough inventory of the book market that is always needed when formulating how the book we were planning would differentiate itself from what was already available. That inventory was used when we put together the synopsis for this edited collection, and helped inform how this edited collection would be arranged. We settled on twelve chapters by some of the leading scholars in social work from around the world, and decided that we would aim for two different parts: one about the key concepts in critical gerontology, and another on how these concepts can inform social work policy and practice. Our book project received the support of the European Social Work Research Association (ESWRA) who deemed it interesting enough for the series known as 'Research in Social Work' that they publish. Special thanks must also go to the staff of Policy Press for their unwavering support, particularly Isobel Bainton and Sarah Bird.

It is our sincere hope that this edited collection will introduce social work scholars, policy makers, practitioners and students to critical gerontology and encourage them to deem their unique expertise as pivotal if we are to responsibly address the needs of older people now that population ageing is a societal challenge we all must reckon with. Needless to say, we also hope that this book offers the kind of inspiration necessary to maintain their commitment to continue to better the lives of the older communities that they serve. We have, without a doubt, renewed our commitment while working on this edited collection and look forward to seeing how this work stimulate much-needed discussion about the role of critical gerontology in social work, and the ways in which working with the older segments of our populations enriches our practices.

Sandra Torres and Sarah Donnelly
Stockholm and Dublin
1 May 2021

Social work and critical gerontology: why the former needs the latter

Sarah Donnelly and Sandra Torres[1]

A global transformation is taking place as the world's population is rapidly ageing and, for the first time in history, most people can expect to live into their 60s and beyond. It is therefore understandable that one of the latest reports written by the Population Division of the United Nations' Department of Economic and Social Affairs begins with the following statement:

> According to World Population Prospects 2019 (United Nations, 2019), by 2050, 1 in 6 people in the world will be over the age of 65, up from 1 in 11 in 2019. All societies in the world are in the midst of this longevity revolution – some are at its early stages and some are more advanced. But all will pass through this extraordinary transition, in which the chance of surviving to age 65 rises from less than 50 per cent – as was the case in Sweden in the 1890s – to more than 90 per cent at present in countries with the highest life expectancy. What is

---

[1] **Sarah Donnelly** is Assistant Professor of Social Work in the School of Social Policy, Social Work and Social Justice, University College Dublin, Ireland, and Co-convenor of the European Network for Gerontological Social Work (ENGSW). Sarah's research interests include ageing and dementia, adult safeguarding and capacity and decision making. Sarah is a registered social worker, an active member of the Irish Association of Social Workers (IASW) and a member of the Irish Gerontological Society. **Sandra Torres** is Professor in Sociology and the Chair in Social Gerontology at Uppsala University in Sweden. Her work as a critical social gerontologist problematises old age-related constructs and deconstructs some of the taken-for-granted assumptions that inform research, policy and practice. Sandra is the President of the Research Committee on Aging of the International Sociological Association and of the Social-Behavioral Section of the International Association of Gerontology and Geriatrics: European Region. She holds fellowships from the (Swedish) Royal Society of Sciences and the Gerontological Society of America, is editor-in-chief of *Ageing & Society* and the author of *Ethnicity and Old Age: Expanding our Imagination* (Policy Press, 2019). At present she is co-editing (with Alistair Hunter) the *Handbook of Migration and Ageing* (Edward Elgar Publishing, 2023).

more, the proportion of adult life spent beyond age 65 increased from less than a fifth in the 1960s to a quarter or more in most developed countries today. (United Nations 2019, p iii)

While the demographic shift that we call population ageing started in high-income countries, low- and middle-income countries are experiencing the greatest change now (WHO, 2015). As a demographic transition, population ageing is of interest and concern to scholars, policy makers and practitioners in an array of spheres, since the rapid ageing of populations around the world means that health, labour supply and economic growth-related challenges will arise. This is why population ageing, and the globalisation of international migration, are societal trends that all of us who are involved in gerontological research, policy and practice must reckon with (Lawrence and Torres, 2016; Torres, 2019). Both trends are, of course, cause for celebration, since the fact that more of us are living to reach advanced old age is an achievement for humankind, and increased diversity can expand our imagination in more ways than we can imagine. An array of challenges are, however, posed by these trends, since they affect not only societies and the welfare systems we rely on to provide us with help in difficult times but also the social work profession in particular. However, maximising the health, functional capacity, social security and participation of older people in society is in everybody's interest (Donnelly and O'Loughlin, 2015), which is why this edited collection has this premise as its starting point.

Originally conceived as part of the resources that the European Network for Gerontological Social Work[2] wants to make available to social work professionals and scholars, this edited collection argues that critical gerontology relies on a perspective on old-age diversity and inequality that is particularly auspicious for tackling population ageing. Our core argument is that applying this perspective when formulating policy and practice, and when working with older people, could empower not only the older segments of our populations but also the social work profession. We argue that the key concepts in critical gerontology (such as agency, autonomy, diversity, social justice, inclusion and equality) offer us a gaze that equips us to play a decisive role not only in empowering practitioners to question expectations about their practice that could inhibit them from serving their older clients in person-centred and diversity-informed ways but also in effectively influencing social policy. We are firm in our conviction that

---

[2] Most contributors to this book have met one another through the Special Interest Group on Gerontological Social Work that the European Conference for Social Work Research hosts. The original idea for this edited collection benefited from discussions in this group, which we – as editors – want to acknowledge.

social workers have a unique human-rights expertise, which, combined with evidence-based insight into the diversity of challenges that different segments of our older populations face, offers them a formidable vantage point for advocacy work. Thus, we hope that the critical gerontology perspective this book provides will empower social work students and professionals to engage more actively in the social policy arena in relation to new policies that will most likely impact gerontological social work. The perspective this book presents is, in other words, pro-active in that it aims to both dissect what research, policy and practice could end up meaning to the empowerment (or lack of) of older people, and how to intervene if deemed necessary.

As a sociologist of ageing (Torres), and a former professor in social work as well as in rehabilitation and ageing, and in the capacity of both social work practitioner and academic (Donnelly), we are eager to broaden our focus beyond the skills or the types of practices employed in social work with older people. We believe, namely, that it is in the best interest of the communities we serve (both through our scholarship, practice and the advocacy work we may do on behalf of – and with – older people in order to shape and influence ongoing policy-making debates) if we continue to educate ourselves. This is why this edited collection is about the conceptual and theoretical lenses that critical gerontologists use as they go about the business of making sense of old-age inequalities and the diversity that underlines them. Thus, by focusing on *what* the challenges are, as opposed to having an a priori focus on how we should deal with them, this edited collection aims to expand the horizons of those involved in social work with older people, irrespective of whether they are involved in research, education, policy or practice.

This chapter will therefore set the scene for *how* critical gerontology, with its dual emphasis on macro and micro levels of analysis, embracement of interdisciplinary perspectives and its activist agenda for emancipatory social and economic change offers new ways of approaching social work with older people that strongly align with the underlying values of the profession. The chapter will provide an overview as to where critical gerontology currently sits within social work research, education, policy and practice. We will explore why we need critical gerontology, and outline where we need to go in order for it to be fully adopted by the social work community globally.

Ageing in the midst of health inequalities

Health inequalities provide the backdrop against which the challenges of population ageing can begin to make sense for practitioners and policy makers alike. Older people can experience an increase in disadvantage and vulnerability as they age, meaning that many may require the support and intervention of social work in some capacity. Increased life expectancy has historically meant more years spent in relatively poor health in old age. Although strenuous efforts are being made to reduce levels of morbidity and to extend good health into later life, there is a pressing need for greater attention to the health and social care needs and human rights of today's ageing populations (Ray et al, 2015). This is why gerontological social workers need to be cognisant of the fact that older people can face multiple forms of discrimination not only because of their identities along the age, class, gender, sex, ethnicity, migrancy and disability spectrums but also due to the fact that health-related changes can jeopardise their participation in paid employment and their capacity to fully engage in society (Nazroo, 2017). The ways in which health inequalities at the societal level affect older people's participation must therefore be taken into account when thinking of how active older people can be in various societal spheres.

The notion of health inequalities is best understood in terms of the differences in both objective and subjective health that different groups experience due to social structural variables, such as education, income, gender, class or ethnicity. Older people who experience poverty, for example, especially when it begins very early in life, have lower subjective health and persistent exposure to low socioeconomic status, which increases the prevalence of chronic conditions in mid and later life (Hayward and Gorman, 2004). This is why most health practitioners know that it is members of the middle and upper classes that most likely benefit from so-called health gains, including increased life expectancy (Marmot et al, 2010). Related to this is also the fact that an advantaged lifecourse not only results in a longer life but also a longer healthy life and a shorter period of ill health at the end of life. Lifecourse research demonstrates also that, once embedded, inequalities remain part of an individual's life trajectory; they tend to accumulate and deepen over time (Phillipson, 2013). Social resources, such as social support, interpersonal trust and social cohesion, however, can act as a buffer to the effects of inequality on health for older people (Zang et al, 2019).

The concept of social exclusion is also important to keep in mind when health inequalities are being discussed. This concept can shed light on the individual, structural and societal components of marginalisation and discrimination (Walsh et al, 2017; Prattley et al, 2020). Older adults who have experienced sustained disadvantage over the lifecourse are especially likely to become socially excluded (Jivraj et al, 2016). Social exclusion in later life is associated with a range of adverse health and well-being outcomes (Nazroo, 2017), including long-term illness, disability and psychological distress (Sacker et al, 2017), lower quality of life, unmet social care needs and increased risk of loneliness (Kneale, 2012). Thus, health is both a risk factor and an outcome of social exclusion (Jivraj et al, 2016; Prattley et al, 2020), which is why a discussion on the challenges that population ageing poses cannot disregard the importance of health inequalities and the impact they have as drivers of old-age social exclusion.

Working with older people in the midst of population ageing

Social work with older people operates in a complex, often fragmented policy and practice environment that is characterised by change and uncertainty. Since the turn of the 21st century there has been recognition of the global patterning of care practices and the need to 'transcend' national frameworks (Tronto, 2015, p 21). In spite of this, social policy has increasingly been driven forward by a neoliberalist ideology and its belief in the value of the social care *market* (Nelson Becker et al, 2020). The shift 'towards the private' reflects the influence that this ideology has had on governments' marketisation of care at the expense of the most vulnerable populations. Thus, a number of significant strains over the past decade have impacted on care provision to older people because of cuts to social care budgets imposed by austerity measures and increasing numbers of older people with complex and unmet needs, as well as long-term underinvestment in staff pay, training and retention (Pentaris et al, 2020). Carey (2021, p 6) points out that a 'compelling and seemingly legitimate risk-averse discourse' in relation to older people has emerged from a progressive market hegemony. Therefore, despite the aspirational language of empowerment, well-being and equality for all, bureaucratic health and social care classification systems and risk-averse discourses more often portray older people as a cost, threat or burden (Tomkow, 2018).

Social care systems in many countries are also increasingly characterised by reliance on family members, insufficient availability of health and social care services, an inadequate supply of care workers and long waiting lists with demand vastly outstripping supply. This is especially relevant to care services for older people both in the community and in residential settings and is part of the jigsaw of issues that compromise older people's human rights (Milne, 2020). Decision making also becomes more complex for older people with multiple health and care needs, as the capacity to self-manage is affected by the cumulative effects of long-term conditions (Bunn et al, 2018), as well as the variety of care providers and professionals that older people must sometimes consult with in order to have their health and social care needs met. In addition, and despite a growing recognition of the importance of person-centred, inclusive and integrated approaches to care planning, research in Ireland and Sweden has shown that older people are more frequently excluded from decisions about their future care (Larsson and Österholm, 2014; Donnelly, Begley and O'Brien, 2018). Some of the most concerning impacts of austerity budgets include the premature and unnecessary admission to nursing-home care for people with dementia (Donnelly, Begley and O'Brien, 2018). The challenges of limited or insufficient resources to meet demand have resulted in an increased emphasis on risk-based approaches to social work with older people (Spolender et al, 2014) that have a negative impact on their human rights, autonomy and self-determination. Ironically, there appears to be parallel processes at play between the diminution of older people's voices and human rights and the eroding and undermining of the social work role with older people in some jurisdictions, forming part of a wider ageist picture (Richards et al, 2014). Against this backdrop, it is probably not a surprise to hear that the role and purpose of gerontological social work has always been contested and undervalued when compared with social work with children and families (Lymbery, 2005; Milne et al, 2014).

This is why it is important to note that the consequences of successive neoliberal policies in welfare services over the past 20 years have played a significant role in undermining an already fragile basis for social work with adults generally, and with older people specifically (Lymbery and Postle, 2010; Milne et al, 2014). The impact of regular (re)constructions of gerontological social work has also led to criticisms that it lacks independence and a distinctive identity (Milne et al, 2014). Gerontological social work remains, in other words, profoundly marginalised in many European countries and is at risk of disappearing altogether as a specialist area of social work in many English jurisdictions (Milne et al, 2014). There is therefore a pressing need to reverse this trend and re-establish gerontological social work as an area of expertise that the social work profession cannot relegate to the periphery. In the midst of population ageing, it would be foolish to regard social work with older people as less important than child protection, since some older people must also be protected from the hostile social environment that neoliberalism is creating. Current and future generations of older people and their families need us to remain committed to expanding the imagination of the social work profession as far as ageing, quality of life and the health and social care needs of older people are concerned.

Finally, it is important to acknowledge the devastating impact of the COVID-19 pandemic on our older populations globally. The high incidence of, and death rates from, COVID-19 in older people should be the catalyst for an examination of how we, as social workers, can meaningfully address both systemic and societal ageism, moving forward (Brennan et al, 2020). It has been argued that during the COVID-19 pandemic social workers were well placed, because of the profession's human rights mandate, to advocate for the rights of older people (Pentaris et al, 2020). The crisis should therefore act as a 'call to arms' for social work and further emphasises the need for the adoption of a critical gerontological perspective to social work with older people.

Marrying social work values and critical gerontology

The challenges presented by contemporary demographic trends, and the potential for social work to respond to these, cannot be overestimated (Milne et al, 2014). The values of the social work profession, and its commitment to social justice, place it in an ideal position to promote equality, provide advocacy and uphold older people's human rights to the quality of life, and health and social care that they are entitled to. Since its earliest beginnings as a profession, social work has been divided between those who would emphasise the treatment and cure of individual problems and deficiencies, that is, casework, and those who emphasise structural inequities and the importance of social reform, that is, broader social policy debates (Mendes, 2007). The critical gerontology perspective aligns most comfortably with the latter. Thus, although all social workers are expected to embrace and promote the fundamental and inalienable rights of all human beings while respecting their worth, dignity and diversity, social workers who allow their practice to be informed by the critical gerontology perspective are also prepared to question research, policy and practice that can potentially jeopardise older people's empowerment, autonomy and human rights.

The need to work at both personal (through individual consciousness-raising that connects private troubles with structural sources) and political levels to challenge oppressive and inequitable structures (Fook, 2003) has been repeatedly highlighted by social work scholars, and should not be underestimated by those who would like their research, policy and practice to be informed by the critical gerontology perspective. Social workers have a unique professional responsibility to engage with people and communities in achieving social justice, since this is a

> practice-based profession and an academic discipline that promotes social change and development, social cohesion, and the empowerment and liberation of people. Principles of social justice, human rights, collective responsibility and respect for diversities are central to social work. Underpinned by theories of social work, social sciences, humanities and indigenous knowledge, social work engages people and structures to address life challenges and enhance wellbeing. (International Federation of Social Workers, 2014)

The Global Agenda for Social Work also commits to strengthening the contribution of social work in policy development (Jones and Truell, 2012); a fact that we hope this edited collection could inspire social workers specialising in older people and ageing to do. The agenda in question recognises that global challenges, such as population ageing, require global responses.

The social, economic and professional impact of neoliberalism is therefore one area in which social work has an important role to play (Spolander et al, 2014). This means challenging unjust policies and practices, discrimination and institutional oppression, as well as ensuring access to equitable distribution of resources (International Federation of Social Workers, 2018). While advocating and upholding human rights and social justice is the motivation and justification for social work with older people, it has been argued that failure to engage at a policy level has resulted in the profession (unconsciously or consciously) aiding neoliberal policy reform (Lorenz, 2005; see also Carey 2021). This is the case because, more than any other profession, social work seeks to understand the links between 'public issues' and 'private troubles', and sets out to address both (Jones, 2005). In this regard, it is important to remind social work practitioners that the international definition of social work clearly encompasses practice with both individuals and the wider society (International Federation of Social Workers, 2014). This is the case even though there is relatively little literature that seeks to bridge the two in relation to what social workers might actually accomplish in their practice (Lymbery, 2014). Part of the problem is that considerations about wider social structures and their impact on practice have been overtaken by concerns about each individual (Houston, 2001). This is problematic, because social workers need to address both the individual and the societal systems surrounding him/her, in order to seek transformation (Lymbery, 2014).

Drawing on the implications of the United Nations Madrid International Plan of Action on Aging (2002), the International Federation of Social Work launched its own 'International Policy on Ageing and Older Persons' in 2009. This policy acknowledged social work's strategic position, around the globe, to enable and support the full social integration of older people. Broadly speaking, this includes the promotion of their social, economic and intellectual contributions, and strategic macro- and micro-level advocacy to tackle any social conditions that hinder security, health and well-being (Hokenstad and Roberts, 2011). In this regard, it is important to stress that critical gerontology is concerned with grappling with inequality and oppression while searching for explanations that expose not only the complexities of the challenges that older people face but also the possibilities that empowering them could offer. This is why we firmly believe that this perspective could enrich social work with older people. Embracing critical gerontology means, however, that we accept that social work practice itself might at times be oppressive and aligned to social control, notwithstanding its intentions to provide help to service users (Mendes, 2007; Healy, 2012). This reminds us, of course, that questioning oppressive aspects of systems in which social workers are embedded, along with critiquing discourses about marginalised groups such as older people, is at the very core of what critical social work is characterised by (Duffy, 2017).

Social work activism and research are central to critical social work, and the same applies to critical gerontology. There is, however, some confusion regarding what we mean by critical theory, thinking and approaches in social work with older people. Whereas attention is usually paid to issues of class, redistribution and welfare, we often find a lack of perspectives on gender, ethnicity, lifestyle issues and identity (Hertz and Johansson, 2011). This is not the case when it comes to critical gerontology, which has always aimed to promote scholarship, policy, and practice that is diversity aware and inequalities informed and seeks to empower the older segments of our populations. We need, however, to acknowledge that social work professionals are sometimes derailed from engaging in critiquing social policy because they tend to assume that policy is the realm of policy makers, while practice (and/or the implementation of policy) is what social workers ought to focus on. We believe that nothing can be further from the truth. From our standpoint, policies can be formulated in ways that guarantee the highest level of user-friendly social care only if social workers assist policy makers when policies that will affect older people's lives are being formulated. Pointing out that policies are failing to deliver ought also to be part of what social workers should do. They have, after all, not only the necessary expertise but also the experience necessary to be able to forewarn the authorities that the policies being formulated, and the practices that these will encourage, can do more harm than good to the vulnerable populations whose needs they must meet.

Signs of progress have begun to emerge, however, in the interface between social work practice and social policy formulation. A look at how Irish social workers have mobilised during the COVID-19 pandemic can illustrate what we can accomplish when we work together to raise society's awareness of what older people may need in difficult times such as those we are experiencing as we put the final touches to this edited collection. Throughout the pandemic, front-line social workers and social work academics, in conjunction with the professional body, the Irish Association of Social Workers (IASW), engaged in a successful macro-level advocacy campaign in relation to the human rights of nursing home residents to a private and family life under Article 8 of the European Convention on Human Rights (1950). Social workers fought for nursing home residents' right to communication support so that relationships with family members could be sustained in the context of blanket visiting restrictions, and so that access to end-of-life care and the right to safe family visitation, once permitted by public health guidance, were not jeopardised. Advocacy work also involved the development and piloting of a model for a 'Liaison Social Work Role in Nursing Homes' (McGarry et al, 2020) in order to assist with the vital supports already outlined. Through the sending of letters to key stakeholders outlining problems and providing suggestions for solutions, press releases, a social media campaign on Twitter (#ResidentsHaveRights), a webinar for members of the general public and meetings with, among others, the Minister for Older People and the Health Service Executive, who are responsible for health and social care provision (see IASW, 2021), nursing home residents' situation was improved.

Initiatives like these strengthen our conviction that together we can create change that empowers older people, and the social work profession as well. For us, it seems unrealistic to believe that vulnerable, disenfranchised and marginalised older people can make their voices heard when policies are being formulated and/or need to be revised. This is why we believe that social work professionals have a responsibility to actively engage with policy makers. In other words, we believe that social workers (not just those who specialise in ageing, old age and care of older people), have a unique set of competencies, and a vantage point through their practice, that should inform policy making. We recognise, however, that in order for us to be able to deploy those skills for the benefit of those we serve, we need to understand that our expertise gives us an imitable perspective on the realities of the communities we work with. Our hope is therefore that insight into what the critical gerontological lens offers will provide social workers who work with older people the kinds of epiphanies they need in order to become empowered to such an extent that they can begin to expand their horizons beyond the realm of practice. Critical gerontology raises our awareness of what lifecourse disadvantage means to how we end up ageing. This is why we believe that gerontological social workers should allow this perspective to inform their practice and, in doing so, actively engage in the formulation of social policy that addresses the injustices that different vulnerable groups face throughout their lives. They work, after all, with the aftermath of these injustices once these people seek social services that cater for older people, so advocacy work, and the active critiquing of social policies in the making, can be deemed to be prevention work.

When ageism and neoliberalism get in our way

Something else we would like to focus on now is the concept of ageism. Ageism underpins dominant-negative discourses, language and labels about older people and ageing, and is so entrenched and accepted that it is often denied even when it is made visible (Duffy, 2017). This often leads to the pathologisation of older people's wishes and responses when engaging with health and social care services and can lead to misinformed understandings of who different older people are, and what their needs may be. Conventional social work, while well intentioned, tends to disregard the fact that ageism could get in the way of policy and practice. Critical gerontology, on the other hand, acknowledges that ageism exists and encourages the creation of alternate and positive understandings of ageing and old age, since the emancipation and empowerment of disenfranchised older people can be derailed without them (Duffy, 2017). As social workers, we need to recognise the strengths, resources and resilience of our older citizens, the diversity of their biographies and their potential to contribute to society. We must challenge structural and systemic ageism and discrimination and promote and foster intergenerational solidarity and intergenerational justice. The connection between critique and gerontology rests, namely, on the possibilities for generating a kind of society that better incorporates the diverse needs and interests of older people (Doheny and Jones, 2020) and of the professions that serve them. This is why we urge social workers working with older people to regard critical gerontology as a perspective that could inform their own professional emancipation, at a time when their empowerment is most needed.

Thus, although we recognise the disproportionate influence that austerity has had on many governments, and the fact that the opportunity for social workers to respond positively to the needs of older people has diminished as a result of this (Lymbery, 2014), we believe that the time is ripe for gerontological social workers to begin their own emancipatory journeys. Thus, although we acknowledge the inequality of status and esteem between social workers and other professional groups – namely doctors (Lymbery, 2005) – we believe that the time has come for social work professionals to question the devalued status and esteem that society accords both to older people and to the social workers who cater to their needs. We urge gerontological social workers to start to appropriate other professional identities besides the street-level bureaucrat one (Carey, 2021), and to team up with scholars of critical gerontology who focus on social work practice in order to carve an activist-led space that enables them to not only be critical consumers of policies for older people but also designers of policy interventions that combat societal and institutional ageism.

The time has come for us to reimagine what social work with older people could be about, as opposed to just accepting that this branch of social work is there to implement the often repressive, reductionist policies that others formulate. Social workers who focus on other age groups, and/or vulnerable groups, take their activist and advocacy roles seriously and have therefore been able to effect enormous change in their practices. We need gerontological social workers to become similarly empowered so that they can begin to leave behind their sole focus on administration and case management, in favour of roles that influence and shape social policies and practice. By reframing care and support of older people as a collective responsibility and a public good, we can put in place the policies and resources that we need not only for our current generation of older people but also for when we ourselves are older and need support. Population ageing creates, after all, the conditions necessary to make gerontological social work a priority for the social work profession and a specialisation that policy makers must reckon with. Critical gerontology offers, in turn, the lens needed to uphold and promote the human rights of older people in an environment of neoliberal policies, scarce resources and increasing intergenerational conflict and competition for supports and services.

Outline of the chapters that follow

The chapters that follow are organised into two parts. Part I examines some of the key concepts that the critical gerontology perspective relies on, to dissect the taken-for-granted assumptions that underlie research, policy and practice for older people, while Part II applies them to some of the practice areas that gerontological social workers tend to engage in.

Part I, 'Critical gerontology as guiding principles for social work with older people', is comprised of six chapters that aim to offer presentations of the complexities embedded in the theoretical and conceptual toolbox that social workers who choose to inform their research, policy, practice and education by the critical gerontology perspective must master. Chapter 2, 'The lifecourse and old age', introduces readers to these two concepts and problematises the various ways in which they can be conceived, and discusses the inherent limitations of relying solely on one of these angles. Chapter 3, 'Human rights and older people', offers a critical dissection of the United Nations Universal Declaration of Human Rights and the opportunities it offers to social workers; opportunities that are unfortunately not always seized by practitioners and policy makers. Chapter 4, 'Agency and autonomy', presents these two concepts and the array of challenges that older people with limited autonomy and agency can face. Chapter 5, 'Poverty and late-life homelessness', introduces readers to one of the hidden categories of older people that are seldom acknowledged in social work policy, practice and education. Chapter 6, 'Sexuality and rights in later life', brings attention to another area that is seldom acknowledged in social work discussions focusing on older people – that is, their sexual rights. Last but not least, Chapter 7, 'Ethnicity, race and migrancy', introduces readers to the ways in which these constructs can be approached and the consequences that these approaches have to how these identification grounds are made sense of in research, policy, practice and education.

Part II, 'Applying the critical gerontological lens to social work research, policy and practice', comprised of five chapters, deploys some of the concepts presented in Part I in relation to some of the specific practice areas that are relevant to gerontological social work. Chapter 8, 'Assessment, care planning and decision making', offers readers a critical lens on these areas of practice while problematising the straightforward ways in which practitioner guidelines tend to depict these processes. Chapter 9, 'Elder abuse', makes the case for viewing elder abuse as a societal, rather than purely an individual, problem, with guidance on how practitioners can be more critical in their approach to safeguarding older people from abuse. Chapter 10, 'Dementia: a disability and a human right concern', introduces readers to the dominant narratives and puts forward alternative frameworks for broadening the debate on dementia, improving practice and giving agency, choice and control back to the individual and their family members. Chapter 11, 'User involvement', aims to introduce the notion of user involvement (primarily as it pertains to practice and policy), and the reasons why gerontological social workers should embrace and facilitate this. The final chapter is Chapter 12, 'Opportunities and future prospects for gerontological social work with a critical lens'. This chapter summarises some of the key tenets of the critical gerontological perspective, points to other areas that this perspective could inform and argues that the future of gerontological social work research, policy, practice and education lies in engaging with this perspective.

This edited collection aims ultimately to expand gerontological social workers' conceptual and practice toolbox so that they are able to dissect and interrogate taken-for-granted assumptions in research, policy, education and practice that jeopardise the empowerment of older people by failing to address their diversity and the complexity of needs of our ageing populations.

References

Brennan, J., Reilly, P., Cuskelly, K. and Donnelly, S. (2020) 'Social work, mental health, older people and COVID-19', *International Psychogeriatrics*, 32(10): 1205–1209.

Bunn, F., Goodman, C., Russell, B., Wilson, P., Manthorpe, J., Rait, G., Hodkinson, I. and Durand, M.A. (2018) 'Supporting shared decision making for older people with multiple health and social care needs: a realist synthesis', *BMC Geriatrics*, 18(1): 165.

Carey, M. (2021) 'The neoliberal university, social work and personalized care for older adults', *Ageing & Society*, 1–15, doi:10.1017/S0144686X20001919.

Doheny, S. and Jones, I. (2020) 'What's so critical about it? An analysis of critique within different strands of critical gerontology', *Ageing & Society*, 41(10): 1–21.

Donnelly, S. and O'Loughlin, A. (2015) 'Growing old with dignity: challenges for practice in an ageing society', in A. Christie, B. Featherstone, S. Quin and T. Walsh (eds) *Social Work in Ireland: Changes and Continuities*, Basingstoke: Palgrave Macmillan, pp 230–245.

Donnelly, S., Begley, E. and O'Brien, M. (2018) 'How are people with dementia involved in care planning and decision-making? An Irish social work perspective', *Dementia*, 18(7–8): 2985–3003.

Duffy, F. (2017) 'A social work perspective on how ageist language, discourses and understandings negatively frame older people and why taking a critical social work stance is essential', *The British Journal of Social Work*, 47(7): 2068–2085.

Fook, J. (2003) 'Critical social work: the current issues', *Qualitative Social Work*, 2(2): 123–130.

Hayward, M.D. and Gorman, B.K. (2004) 'The long arm of childhood: the influence of early-life social conditions on men's mortality', *Demography*, 41(1): 87–107.

Healy, K. (2012) 'Critical perspectives', in M. Gray, J. Midgley and S.A. Webb (eds) *The Sage Handbook of Social Work,* London: Sage, pp 191–216.

Hertz, M. and Johannsson, T. (2011) 'Critical social work: considerations and suggestions', *Critical Social Work*, 12(1): 28–45.

Hokenstad, M.C.T. and Restorick Roberts, A. (2011) 'International policy on ageing and older persons: implications for social work practice', *International Social Work*, 54(3): 330–343.

Houston, S. (2001) 'Beyond social constructionism: critical realism and social work', *British Journal of Social Work*, 31(8): 845–861.

International Federation of Social Workers (2009) *International Policy on Ageing and Older Persons*, [online], Available from: www.ifsw.org/ageing-and-older-adults/ [Accessed 10 March 2021].

International Federation of Social Workers (2014) *Global Social Work Statement of Ethical Principles*, [online], Available from: www.ifsw.org/global-social-work-statement-of-ethical-principles/ [Accessed 11 January 2021].

International Federation of Social Workers (2018) *Global Definition of Social Work*, [online], Available from: www.ifsw.org/what-is-social-work/global-definition-of-social-work/ [Accessed 11 January 2021].

Irish Association of Social Workers (2021) *IASW: The Voice of Social Work*, [online], Available from: www.iasw.ie/IASW_TheVoice_SocialWork [Accessed 20 March 2021].

Jivraj, S., Nazroo, J. and Barnes, M. (2016) 'Short- and long-term determinants of social detachment in later life', *Ageing and Society*, 36(5): 924–945.

Jones, D.N. (2005) 'Social work in Europe: time to assert our vision and self-confidence', *European Social Worker*, 2(2): 9.

Jones, D. and Truell, R. (2012) 'The global agenda for social work and social development: a place to link together and be effective in a globalized world', *International Social Work*, 55(4): 454–472.

Kneale, D. (2012) *Is Social Exclusion Still Important for Older People?* London: The International Longevity Centre UK.

Larsson, A.T. and Österholm, J.H. (2014) 'How are decisions on care services for people with dementia made and experienced? A systematic review and qualitative synthesis of recent empirical findings', *International Psychogeriatrics*, 26(11): 1849–1862.

Lawrence, S. and Torres, S. (eds) (2016) *Older People and Migration: Challenges for Social Work*, London: Routledge.

Lorenz, W. (2005) 'Social work and a new social order: challenging new liberalism's erosion of solidarity', *Social Work and Society*, 3(1): 93–101.

Lymbery, M. (2005) *Social Work with Older People: Context, Policy and Practice*, London: Sage.

Lymbery, M. (2014) 'Austerity, personalisation and older people: the prospects for creative social work practice in England', *European Journal of Social Work*, 17(3): 367–382.

Lymbery, M. and Postle, K. (2010) 'Social work in the context of adult social care in England and the resultant implications for social work education', *British Journal of Social Work*, 40(8): 2502–2522.

Marmot, M., Allen, J., Goldblatt, P., Boyce, T., McNeish, D., Grady, M. and Geddes, I. (2010) *Fair Society, Healthy Lives: Strategic Review of Health Inequalities in England Post-2010*, London: The Marmot Review.

McGarry, S., Cuskelly, K., Reilly, P., Coffey, A., Finucane, N., O'Loughlin, A. and Casey, L. (2020) *The Liaison Social Work Role in Nursing Homes and Residential Settings: A Model for Practice*, Dublin: Irish Association of Social Workers.

Mendes, P. (2007) 'Social workers and social activism in Victoria, Australia', *Journal of Progressive Human Services*, 18(1): 25–44.

Milne, A. (2020) *Mental Health in Later Life: Taking a Life Course Approach*, Bristol: Policy Press.

Milne, A., Sullivan, M.P., Tanner, D., Richards, S., Ray, M., Lloyd, L., Beech, C. and Phillips, J. (2014) *Social Work with Older People: A Vision for the Future*, The College of Social Work, [online], Available from: www.cpa.org.uk/cpa-lga-evidence/College_of_Social_Work /Milneetal(2014)-Socialworkwitholderpeople-avisionforthefuture.pdf [Accessed 10 December 2020].

Nazroo, J. (2017) 'Class and health inequality in later life: patterns, mechanisms and implications for policy', *International Journal of Environmental Research Public Health*, 14(12): 1533.

Nelson-Becker, H., Lloyd, L., Milne, A., Perry, E., Ray, M., Richards, S., Sullivan, M.P., Tanner, D. and Willis, P. (2020) 'Strengths-based social work with older people: a UK perspective', in A. Mendenhall and M. Mohr Carney (eds) *Strengths-based Social Work with Older People*, Kansas: The University of Kansas Libraries, pp 327–346.

Pentaris, P., Willis, P., Ray, M., Deusdad, B., Lonbay, S., Niemi, M. and Donnelly, S. (2020) 'Older people in the context of COVID-19: a European perspective', *Journal of Gerontological Social Work*, 63(8): 736–742.

Phillipson, C. (2013) *Ageing*, Cambridge: Polity Press.

Prattley, J., Buffel, T., Marshall, A. and Nazroo, J. (2020) 'Area effects on the level and development of social exclusion in later life', *Social Science & Medicine*, 246: 112722.

Ray, M., Milne, A., Beech, C., Phillips, J., Richards, S., Sullivan, M.P., Tanner, D. and Lloyd, L. (2015) 'Gerontological social work: reflections on its role, purpose and value', *British Journal of Social Work*, 45(4): 1296–1312.

Richards, S., Sullivan, M.P., Tanner, D., Beech, C., Milne, A., Ray, M., Phillips, J. and Lloyd, L. (2014) 'On the edge of a new frontier: is gerontological social work in the UK ready to meet 21st-century challenges?' *British Journal of Social Work*, 44(8): 2307–2324.

Sacker, A., Ross, A., MacLeod, C.A., Netuveli, G. and Windle, G. (2017) 'Health and social exclusion in older age: evidence from Understanding Society, the UK household longitudinal study', *Journal of Epidemiological Community Health*, 71: 681–690.

Spolander, G., Engelbrecht, L., Martin, L., Strydom, M., Pervova, I., Marjanen, P., Tani, P., Sicora, A. and Adaikalam, F. (2014) 'The implications of neoliberalism for social work: reflections from a six-country international research collaboration', *International Social Work*, 57(4): 301–312.

Tomkow, L. (2018) 'The emergence and utilisation of frailty in the United Kingdom: a contemporary biopolitical practice', *Ageing & Society*, 40(4): 695–712.

Torres, S. (2019) *Ethnicity and Old Age: Expanding our Imagination*, Bristol: Policy Press.

Tronto, J. (2015) 'Democratic caring and global care responsibilities', in M. Barnes, T. Brannelly, L. Ward and N. Ward (eds) *Ethics of Care: Critical Advances in International Perspective*, Bristol: Bristol University Press, pp 21–30.

United Nations (2002) *Madrid International Plan of Action on Ageing, 2002*, New York: United Nations, [online], Available from: http://www.un-ngls.org/orf/pdf/MIPAA.pdf [Accessed 10 December 2020].

United Nations (2019) *World Population Ageing 2019 Highlights*, Department of Economic and Social Affairs Population Division (ST/ESA/SER.A/430), New York: United Nations.

Walsh, K., Scharf, T. and Keating, N. (2017) 'Social exclusion of older persons: a scoping review and conceptual framework', *European Journal of Ageing*, 14(1): 81–98.

WHO (2015) *World Report on Ageing and Health*, [online], Available from: www.who.int/ageing/events/world-report-2015-launch/en/ [Accessed 10 December 2020].

Zhang, C.Q., Chung, P.K., Zhang, R. and Schüz, B. (2019) 'Socioeconomic inequalities in older adults' health: the roles of neighborhood and individual-level psychosocial and behavioural resources', *Frontiers in Public Health*, 7: 318.

PART I

Critical gerontology as guiding principles for social work with older people

2

The lifecourse and old age

Alisoun Milne[1]

The lifecourse perspective is a multidisciplinary approach to understanding the mental and physical health of individuals. For older people, it is a particularly helpful lens, as it takes account of what has happened across that person's life and considers how what has happened has affected their health and well-being (Milne, 2020). Old age is, in turn, a social category that may be damaging to a social worker's understanding of age as a lived experience or of differences between a 65- and a 95-year-old. As a 'catch-all' label, this category may also contribute to ageism. During the COVID-19 pandemic, for example, care home residents were effectively ignored until quite late on and many died. The fact that they were marginal to national public health considerations played a key role in their treatment; some commentators would even argue that their human rights were violated – an issue that should be of concern to social workers (Amnesty International, 2020; Anand et al, 2021).

This chapter will argue that gerontological social work needs to (re)connect with the lifecourse and old age as a social category for four reasons: to increase its credibility, to enhance its capacity to be effective, to engage meaningfully with 'what matters' to older people and to challenge ageism in practice.

The lifecourse approach

A lifecourse approach seeks to identify how health outcomes are shaped by biological, personal, psychological, social and historical factors throughout a person's life, as well as those factors that impact on it in old age (Kuh et al,

---

[1] **Alisoun Milne** is Professor of Social Gerontology and Social Work at the School of Sociology, Social Policy and Social Research, University of Kent, UK. She is a registered social worker. Alisoun's research interests are in four intersecting areas: social work with older people and their families; mental health in later life; family caring; and long-term care. She is widely published. Her most recent book is *Mental Health in Later Life: Taking a Lifecourse Approach* (Policy Press, 2020). She is currently co-authoring a book for Emerald Publishing on *Care and Caring*. Alisoun is a member of the Research Excellence Framework 2021 sub-panel for Social Work and Social Policy and a Fellow of the UK Academy of the Social Sciences.

2002). Human development is a lifelong process, and the relationships and events of earlier life stages have consequences for what happens in subsequent stages (Bengston et al, 2012). On the whole, however, issues that damage health – whether they are lifestyle habits such as smoking, socioeconomic issues such as poverty or personal experiences such as childhood abuse – tend to be researched as single issues. As health is an outcome of a range of different lifecourse factors it is most helpful, both for the person and the practitioner, to try to appreciate the impact of these issues in a holistic way: this understanding underpins the lifecourse approach. It is also a lens that tends to fit well with how most of us understand our own needs; our past affects our present and is likely to affect our future.

The lifecourse approach challenges the view that there is such a thing as 'normal ageing' (Phillipson, 2013). Greater fluidity of the lifecourse produces huge variation in later-life trajectories. Increasing diversity is a product of the magnitude and rapidity of social change witnessed during the 20th and 21st centuries; for example, far greater numbers of women in employment (Dannefer and Settersten, 2010). Someone aged 100 will have had a profoundly different lifecourse, lifestyle, health status and family situation than someone of 65. A number of key sociodemographic sources of diversity are important to highlight. A greater number of older people are single, divorced or never married and/or are ageing without children, and there are increasing numbers of people with complex health needs; later life is increasingly socioeconomically unequal, too (Larkin, 2013).

The lifecourse approach fundamentally challenges the biomedical model of ageing. This model tends to dominate the care system, particularly healthcare. It constructs old age as a 'disorder' – or at very least a set of symptoms – to be treated by a health intervention, and regards old age as associated with an inevitable pathological decline in health and increased dependency (Centre for Ageing Better, 2020). This way of thinking permeates our understanding of later life and contributes to a tendency to locate presenting problems – those articulated in a referral to a social worker, for example – as a product exclusively of old age and not linked to lifecourse issues.

Childhood abuse is a prominent example of a personal experience that exerts a powerful lifelong influence on the mental health and well-being of victims. In their 2017 review of the evidence, McCrory and colleagues (2017, p 338) concluded that abuse and neglect in childhood 'represent the *most potent predictor* of poor mental health *across the whole life span*' (emphasis in original). It substantially increases the risk of a wide range of mental health problems developing during both childhood and adulthood (Maschi et al, 2013). An older woman who has suffered from depression throughout her adult life not only needs to be sensitively supported because of her vulnerability to depression, she also needs practitioners to acknowledge that one of the causes of her depression may have been childhood abuse.

A gerontological social worker needs to begin from a place that recognises that depression often has roots earlier in life and to offer support with that appreciation, and empathy, at the forefront of their practice.

It is the linkage between the individual experience of ageing, on the one hand, and the social and historical contexts within which individual ageing occurs, on the other, that differentiates the lifecourse approach from the individual-level life cycle approach (Lloyd, 2012). Being the victim of domestic abuse, for example, was always, and continues to be, a hugely traumatic experience, but how a person who experiences it is offered help is influenced by the historical period in which it occurs. At the turn of the last century, few people considered that older women could be victims of domestic abuse; it was viewed as a 'young woman's issue'. Recent evidence suggests not only that many older women do experience domestic abuse[2] but that much more needs to be done to develop domestic abuse services to meet their needs, including accommodating disabilities (Safelives, 2016). Thus, appreciating the particular nature of domestic abuse in later life is important for social workers supporting older women victims. That the woman is likely to have lived with abuse for many years and, compared to younger women, experienced it for twice as long before seeking help, are important patterns to consider. Also, she is likely to rely on the perpetrator for money and may well be reluctant to give up a lifetime's investment in a marriage, a family and a home. Internalisation of a traditional gendered view that you 'put up with it because it's your duty' may also be an issue, and one related to a time when this was a common attitude (McGarry and Simpson, 2011).

Two other points are important. The first is that – axiomatically – domestic abuse damages women's health and well-being, especially if it is sustained (Women's Aid, 2013). It is linked to premature death and a range of physical health issues, including hypertension and musculoskeletal problems and, for victims of sexual assault, genito-urinary disorders (McGarry and Simpson, 2011). Victims are at significantly increased risk of depression and anxiety, commonly feel angry, frustrated and helpless and have low self-esteem. Long-term abuse, that is, abuse that may have started in childhood and then continued in adulthood, is implicated in a heightened risk of suicide, psychosis, post-traumatic stress disorder and eating disorders (Williams and Watson, 2016).

The second point relates to the systemic response by formal agencies. Constructing domestic abuse as 'a safeguarding issue' or 'elder abuse', which is the current model, not only removes the gendered element but also

---

[2] A study by the domestic abuse charity Safe Lives (2016) estimated that in 2014/15 approximately 120,000 people aged 65+ experienced at least one form of abuse in the UK.

uncouples it from the lifecourse where, for many victims, its roots lie. It also tends to foreground old age as the defining dimension of the abuse, rather than its other dimensions, including gender. Further, it denies older people access to systems developed to support victims of domestic abuse. Ageism is a prominent but largely invisible feature of these patterns, which not only serves to exclude older people, especially older women, from rights-related discourses but also reinforces the separation of abuses experienced in later life from those experienced earlier in life. These are issues that should concern gerontological social workers and highlight the importance of adopting a lifecourse lens (see also Chapter 9).

Old age as a social category

It is important to acknowledge that 'old age' is a contested term. Old age is the only stage(s) of life without a chronologically defined end point; length of life varies hugely. As a differentiating variable conferring a fixed and homogeneous social identity upon *all* older people, this category can obscure differences arising from age, cohort, race, gender and/or disability and individual variation. Old-age stereotypes are also almost universally negative and are associated with ill health, dependency and incapacity to exercise agency, choice or self-determination (Victor, 2010; Swift et al, 2017).

The World Health Organization (2002) notes that in most (developed) countries a person is considered 'old' at 65 years. This simply reflects the age at which many people retire from paid work, although this pattern is not as embedded as it once was. Chronological age is not synonymous with biological age and both the situated and historical context of ageing can be masked by the adoption of a universal definition. It also obscures the importance of issues unrelated to 'age', such as poverty and racism and the complexity and heterogeneity of a large and varied cohort(s) of people (Lloyd, 2012). Data around trends in the prevalence of ill health among 'older people' hides important distinctions and encourages a tendency towards homogenisation.

It is suggested that recent changes to established norms, such as no longer having a state-mandated retirement age, are producing an uneven relationship between chronological age and retirement (Higgs and Jones, 2009). For some older people – those with adequate economic resources and good health – the loosening of traditional constraints offers freedom and choice (Gilleard and Higgs, 2005). But for others a model that assumes personal responsibility for economic and social resources is a risk. Reduced access to welfare benefits and fewer community services threaten those who are vulnerable due to poverty and/or age-related ill health (Centre for Social Justice, 2010). A number of these issues are explored in Chapter 5. Low income and isolation in later life are constructed as a 'personal failure' when, in fact, the major contributors are a change in state pension provision and the withdrawal of community and support services. As Bauman (2000) wryly notes: 'Risks and contradictions go on being socially produced; it's just the duty and the necessity to cope with them which are being individualised' (p 34).

The heterogeneity and diversity of our older populations provide a backdrop to gerontological social work. Users vary in their social, cultural, economic and financial circumstances, and by ethnicity, gender and age cohort too (Ray and Phillips, 2012). The profile and needs of a man aged 75 years with chronic mobility problems who is divorced with no children or friends, and who is dependent on a state retirement pension, is very different to that of a woman aged 98 years with dementia who is widowed, receives an occupational pension and who lives in her own privately owned home next door to her daughter. The differences are not just about age and health issues – although, of course, these are relevant – but are also about age, social class, family situation and resources and strengths. The implications of ageing without children are a key issue, as much age-related policy is predicated on there being a 'supply' of family carers available to care for older relatives when needed (Larkin et al, 2019). Even where there is a family carer, that person could be an older spouse who may have health problems of their own. Not having a family carer and/or local support network threatens an older person's ability to 'age in place', a key policy goal since 2000. The erosion of community infrastructure also threatens the achievement of this goal; this is an important issue for social workers to highlight as a cause of 'need' when developing care plans, including in our elderly man's situation.

Age-related issues

It is important to acknowledge that some needs do emerge in later life. Health problems are more common; 69 per cent of people aged over 75 have at least one illness or disability (Age UK, 2020a). Bereavement is also more likely, as is becoming a long-term carer for a partner. Loss of key relationships, especially the death of a spouse, is implicated in isolation, loneliness and depression (Bartlam and Machin, 2016). The existence of an intimate, confiding relationship is very protective of mental health and can ameliorate the impact of age-related losses, including widowhood and functional disability (Bowling et al, 2002). A larger social network, made up of both friends and relatives, is also protective.

Two points are helpful to highlight. Firstly, most of these issues have a history and are embedded in a lifecourse. A lifelong marriage, for example, is the platform upon which a commitment to provide care for a partner is built; many health problems are caused or amplified by long-term poverty and disadvantage (see following section on 'Health inequalities'). 'New' mental health problems, viewed as 'caused' by bereavement or disability, may have roots in childhood abuse, loss of a child or midlife divorce (Milne, 2020). Confidantes and social networks are developed over a lifecourse. Secondly, while it is important that practitioners recognise the negative impact of common challenges that many older people face, it is also important to recognise strengths and resources (Tanner, 2007, 2010; Nelson-Becker et al, 2020). The role of the social network, for example, can not only bolster an older person's resilience, identity and sense of belonging but can also offer practical and emotional support when they become frail and may need help with activities of daily living (Wild et al, 2013).

Models of health and care

Reductions in time spent by social workers working with older people is one of the most damaging consequences of recent cuts to local government services in the UK and other jurisdictions. Inevitably, this compromises the social worker's potential to build up a trusting relationship and limits their capacity to engage with the older person's lifecourse, biography and concerns (Fawcett and Reynolds, 2010). It is also likely to contribute to an existing tendency to exclude older people from decisions about their care; this is a particular risk when working with people with advanced dementia. That the development of unsustainable support is more likely in contexts where due weight is *not* given to the older person's perspective and preferences underscores the importance of time-rich assessments and relationship-based practice (Richards, 2000; Willis et al, 2021); this is the focus of Chapter 8.

Health inequalities and later life: the lifecourse approach

As stated earlier, one of the key contributions of the lifecourse perspective is making visible links between lifecourse inequalities and later-life health outcomes. Marmot's (2010, 2016) seminal work concluded that 'health inequalities are a product of social inequalities; the range of intersecting factors that shape health and well-being' (p 16). Inequalities in health arise because of inequalities in the conditions of daily life and the fundamental drivers that give rise to them: differential access to power, money, education, opportunities and resources (Wilkinson and Pickett, 2006). Age, social class, gender, ethnicity and disability are therefore all sources of inequality (Allen and Daly, 2016). The cumulative advantage and disadvantage model of health (Prus, 2003) is one of the models utilised to study health inequalities in later life. This model describes processes by which the effects of early economic, educational and other (dis)advantages tend to multiply over the lifecourse (Phillipson, 2013). In proposing a lifecourse approach to understanding variations in health outcomes Kuh and Ben-Shlomo (2004) identify the importance of both the accumulation of disadvantages such as poverty, abuse and levels of exposure, meaning the length of time you are exposed to a disadvantage. At its simplest level, exposure to disadvantages (or risks) will damage health: the more numerous the risks, and the longer the exposure, the greater the level of damage. Conversely, exposure to health-promoting advantages – for example, having a higher income, stronger social network and/or better education – will enhance health (Crystal et al, 2017).

The increased attention paid to the impact of inequality on health outcomes is fuelled, in part, by rapid growth in inequality. For example, since the late 1980s the gap between wealthy people and poor people has been widening across the whole UK population. It is also widening in the older population, reflecting two intersecting trends: the persistence of pre-existing lifecourse inequalities coupled with rising rates of pensioner poverty.[3] In 2019, 1.9 million older people in the UK were living in poverty (Age UK, 2020b). The prevalence of pensioner poverty varies widely across Europe, ranging from 4 per cent in Hungary to 51 per cent in Latvia. Rates are universally much higher among women as a consequence of gendered inequalities across the lifecourse, for example taking time out of paid work to care for children (World Health Organization, 2020). Women are often paid less, too.

Lifecourse inequalities have profound implications for health outcomes (Marmot and Wilkinson, 2005; Ratcliff, 2017). Those who experience persistent exposure to low socioeconomic status (SES)[4] – especially when it begins early in life – have increased prevalence of a range of chronic conditions in mid and later life (Hayward and Gorman, 2004). Five chronic conditions – diabetes, cardiovascular diseases, cancer, chronic respiratory disease and mental health problems – account for an estimated 77 per cent of the disease burden and 86 per cent of the deaths in the European Region. The most disadvantaged groups of older people are the most affected (WHO, 2020).

There is a close relationship between SES and frailty[5] (Tomkow, 2018). Analysis of English Longitudinal Study of Ageing data shows that poorer groups have levels of frailty equivalent to those of their wealthier counterparts who are 10–15 years older. Wealth-related inequalities in levels of frailty widened between 2002 and 2010, a trend that indicates progressively higher levels of frailty over time for the poorest third of the population (Figure 2.1).

---

[3] Defined as living on less than 60 per cent of the national median income.

[4] SES is a total measure of an individual's or family's economic and social position in relation to others; it is reflective of social class.

[5] 8 million + people aged 75+ in England live with three or more long-term conditions: multi-morbidity is increasingly conceptualised as 'frailty' (British Geriatrics Society, 2014).

Figure 2.1: Increase in frailty for different age and wealth groups

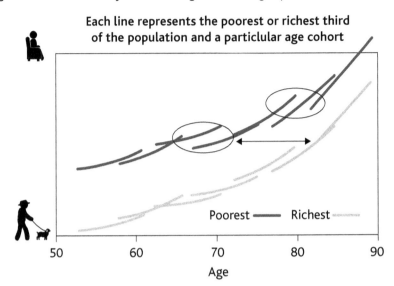

Each line represents the poorest or richest third of the population and a particlular age cohort

Poorest ━━━ Richest

Age

Source: Nazroo, J., Bromley, R. and Pendrill, J. (2017) *The Golden Generation? Wellbeing and Inequalities in Later Life*, Manchester Institute for Collaborative Research on Ageing, [online], Available from: http://hummedia.manchester.ac.uk/institutes/micra/news/2017/golden-generation-report-2017.pdf [Accessed 18 December 2019].

Evidence from European studies specifically identifies low SES in childhood as linked to earlier onset of frailty; interestingly, this risk persists even if people become economically advantaged in adulthood (Wilhelmina et al, 2020).

A fundamental indicator of inequality relates to life expectancy (Marmot, 2005). In 2016–18, men in the least deprived areas of England could expect to live almost a decade longer (83 years) than men in the most deprived areas (74 years) (King's Fund, 2020; Office of National Statistics, 2020). Compared to their wealthier counterparts, people in Europe with low SES are '46 per cent more likely to die early' (Stringhini et al, 2017, p 1233). Data relating to healthy life expectancy is also relevant; healthy life expectancy (HLE) is the average number of years a person can expect to live in good health. There is a gap of 16.5 years for HLE between men living in the most, and least, deprived areas of England; for women the difference is 12 years (Bambra, 2016). This is so because poverty has a direct and indirect impact on health. Being in debt, or on the edge of falling into debt, is anxiety provoking and is associated with shame (Milne, 2020). Being poor is also linked to lower levels of social participation and higher levels of isolation and loneliness (WHO, 2014; Read et al, 2016). Material poverty in childhood is also associated, specifically, with a higher incidence of depression in later life (Scharf et al, 2017).

In 2019, the British Geriatrics Society (2019) estimated that 1.3 million older people in England were suffering from malnutrition and one in five reported denying themselves food to pay for fuel, a choice that is commonly referred to as 'eating or heating'. In Europe, malnutrition is estimated to affect between 13.5 per cent and 30 per cent of older people (PROMISS, 2021). Relevant issues arising from low SES include: poor nutrition, inadequate housing, higher levels of alcohol and tobacco consumption, lower levels of exercise and chronic stress. This evidence challenges the biomedical model referred to earlier, which defines the 'cause' of Alzheimer's disease as exclusively 'old age'. Low SES across the whole lifecourse, and lower levels of education in early life, have been identified as risk factors for dementia, particularly Alzheimer's disease (Livingstone et al, 2017).

Lifecourse and age-related inequalities are issues that a gerontological social worker needs to be cognisant of. As a consequence of tight eligibility criteria regarding access to a social worker in many European countries, older people who do see a social worker tend to be poor, frail, ill and/ or have dementia and have a range of complex needs (Ray et al, 2015). It is important to be aware of the lifecourse nature of many of their needs and of the role inequalities and disadvantage play in creating or amplifying them. Key issues include recognising the challenges that an older person has overcome across their lifecourse and the strategies they use to manage their health – and other – problems and the strengths they retain (Tanner, 2010). As Thompson and colleagues (1990) quite rightly note, 'inequality is one of the fundamental continuities of later life' (p 224).

Understanding the lifecourse-related causes of the older person's poorer physical and mental health also engages gerontological social work with issues of social justice. Reducing poverty for all age groups becomes a priority. Advocacy, seeking rights for all citizens to adequate housing and food, and protecting universal benefits such as the state retirement pension, become part of the social work role alongside front-line practice. This is a goal consistent with the values of social work as a profession. It also echoes the argument made in Chapter 1, that to be effective, critical gerontological social work practice needs to engage with sociopolitical debate and social reform. In this respect, it seems necessary to mention that across Europe there is a great deal of policy emphasis on 'healthy ageing' and, implicitly, on individuals taking responsibility for their own health and well-being (Lloyd, 2012). Poor health is conceptualised in these policies as a product of poor 'lifestyle choices' such as inadequate diet, smoking and lack of exercise, rather than lifecourse disadvantages. The lifecourse approach engages with causative mechanisms rooted in social structures, inequalities and history; a perspective that sits ill with both the biomedical model and the neoliberal narrative of individualism (Holstein and Minkler, 2007). It is important therefore for social workers to retain a critical lens on how policy, often implicitly, informs practice and how terminology used in policy – lifestyle choices, reserving public care for those 'most in need' – can infuse the language of social work in ways that can be experienced by older people as blaming and stigmatising (Hastings and Rogowski, 2015).

Structural inequalities: a note about gender, race and age

Critical gerontologists have also employed the lens of the lifecourse perspective to draw attention to the nature and impact of structural inequalities on the lives of older people. Structural inequality is defined as 'a condition where one group, or category, of people, is attributed an unequal status in relationship to another group(s) of people. This relationship is perpetuated and reinforced by a confluence of unequal relations in roles, access to resources, rights, and opportunities' (United Nations, 2020, p 1). A powerful example of how structural inequalities are reinforced and reproduced is the intersection of ageism with sexism and racism. Ageism is defined as a 'process of systematic stereotyping of older people because they are old, just as racism and sexism accomplish this for skin colour and gender' (Butler, 1969, p 243). Ageism intersects with sexism and racism in ways that compound and amplify its impact (Lee and Turney, 2012). Older women report, for example, feeling 'ignored' and 'sexless', a manifestation of the 'double whammy' of sexism and ageism, and black older women report being exposed to the 'triple jeopardy' of sexism, ageism and racism (Moriarty and Butt, 2004). Discrimination, in all its forms, is profoundly damaging to mental health. Ageism has been identified as contributing to feelings of worthlessness, despair and loneliness and higher levels of depression and anxiety (Sargent-Cox, 2017). Older people refer to 'everyday ageism', for example being talked down to, as 'an assault on their sense of self after self' (Swift et al, 2017, p 204); see Chapter 7.

As anti-discriminatory practice lies at the heart of social work, challenging these embedded practices is pivotal. They both reflect and perpetuate structural inequalities. In front-line practice simply being aware of these contextual issues helps to frame how a social worker supports an older person. Specific ways to call out age discrimination include: challenging budgetary decisions that disadvantage an older person relative to a younger adult; advocating for the right of an older person with dementia to remain in the community when care home admission is a less expensive option, and ensuring that older people have access to talking therapies such as bereavement counselling, not just 'practical services'.

Conclusion

This chapter has explored the nature, and relevance, of two key concepts to gerontological social work: the lifecourse approach and old age as a social category. These are foundational concepts because they significantly influence how we think about, understand and relate to ageing, older people and health; how we conceptualise the causes of ill health; how we address the 'needs' of older people; and the terminology we use (Tanner, 2013). The lifecourse approach encourages engagement with biographical, social, historical and psychosocial needs and with an account of the role played by lifecourse issues in causing, or amplifying, physical and mental health problems (Milne, 2020). It also offers a route into bringing together analysis at the micro level of the older person, such as living alone, with that relating to macro-structural issues such as disadvantage and inequality. Additionally, it engages with issues that persist across the lifecourse; for example, poverty, domestic abuse, trauma and/or chronic ill health. Even when an older person has complex chronic needs, it is important for social work practitioners to resist adopting a deficit approach and an assessment model that is driven by a focus (exclusively) on risk and functional issues. It also requires involvement in advocacy and sociopolitical action to challenge disadvantage and ageism and alignment with the perspectives of older people and their families.

References

Age UK (2020a) *Briefing: Health and Care of Older People in England 2019*, London: Age UK.

Age UK (2020b) *Poverty in Later Life – Briefing*, London: Age UK.

Allen, J. and Daly, S. (2016) 'Briefing paper: older people and the social determinants of health', in P. Kumar, R. Jethwa, G. Roycroft and R. Wilson (eds) *Growing Older in the UK: A Series of Expert-Authored Briefing Papers on Ageing and Health*, London: The British Medical Association, pp 10–22.

Amnesty International (2020) *As if Expendable: The UK Government's Failure to Protect Older People in Care Homes during the Covid-19 Pandemic*, London: Amnesty International.

Anand, J.C., Donnelly, S., Milne, M., Nelson-Becker, H., Vingare, E.M., Deusdad, B., Cellini, G., Kinni, R-L. and Pregno, C. (2021) 'The COVID-19 pandemic and care homes for older people in Europe: deaths, damage and violations of human rights', *European Journal of Social Work*, doi: 10.1080/13691457.2021.1954886.

Bambra, C. (2016) *Health Divides*, Bristol: Policy Press.

Bartlam, B. and Machin, L. (2016) 'Living well with loss in later life', in C. Chew-Graham and M. Ray (eds) *Mental Health and Older People: A Guide for Primary Care Practitioners*, Silver Spring: Springer.

Bauman, Z. (2000) 'Living in the era of liquid modernity', *Cambridge Anthropology*, 22(2): 1–19.

Bengtson, V.L., Elder, G.H. and Putney, N.M. (2012) 'The life course perspective on ageing: linked lives, timing, and history', in J. Katz, S. Peace and S. Spurr (eds) *Adult Lives: A Life Course Perspective*, Bristol: Policy Press, pp 493–509.

Bowling, A., Banister, D., Sutton, S., Evans, O. and Windsor, J. (2002) 'A multi-dimensional model of the quality of life in older age', *Aging and Mental Health*, 6(4): 355–371.

British Geriatrics Society (2014) *Fit for Frailty – Consensus Best Practice Guidance for the Care of Older People Living in Community and Outpatient Settings – A Report from The British Geriatrics Society 2014*, [online], Available from: www.bgs.org.uk/sites/default/files/content/resources/files/2018-05-23/fff_full.pdf [Accessed 20 January 2021].

British Geriatrics Society (2019) *Malnutrition: A Significant Threat to our Health as we Age*, [online], Available from: www.bgs.org.uk/blog/malnutrition-a-significant-threat-to-our-health-as-we-age [Accessed 25 February 2021].

Butler, R.N. (1969) 'Ageism: another form of bigotry', *Gerontologist*, 9(4): 243–246.

Centre for Ageing Better (2020) *An Old Age Problem? How Society Shapes and Reinforces Negative Attitudes to Ageing*, [online], Available from: www.ageing-better.org.uk/publications/old-age-problem-how-society-shapes-and-reinforces-negative-attitudes-ageing [Accessed 25 February 2021].

Centre for Social Justice (2010) *The Forgotten Age: Understanding Poverty and Social Exclusion in Later Life*, London: Centre for Social Justice.

Crystal, S., Shea, D.G. and Reyes, A.M. (2017) 'Cumulative advantage, cumulative disadvantage, and evolving patterns of late-life inequality', *The Gerontologist*, 57(5): 910–920.

Dannefer, D. and Settersten, R.A. (2010) 'The study of the life course: implications for social gerontology', in D. Dannefer and R.A. Setterseten (eds) *The SAGE Handbook of Social Gerontology*, London: SAGE Publications, pp 3–19.

Fawcett, B. and Reynolds, J. (2010) 'Mental health and older women: the challenges for social perspectives and community capacity building', *British Journal of Social Work*, 40(5): 1488–1502.

Gilleard, C. and Higgs, P. (2005) *Contexts of Ageing: Class, Cohort and Community*, Cambridge: Polity.

Hastings, S.J. and Rogowski, S. (2015) 'Critical social work with older people in neo-liberal times: challenges and critical possibilities', *Practice, Social Work in Action*, 27(1): 21–33.

Hayward, M.D. and Gorman, B.K. (2004) 'The long arm of childhood: the influence of early-life social conditions on men's mortality', *Demography*, 41(1): 87–107.

Higgs, P. and Jones, I.R. (2009) *Medical Sociology and Old Age: Towards a Sociology of Health in Later Life*, Abingdon: Routledge.

Holstein, M. and Minkler, M. (2007) 'Critical gerontology: reflections for the 21st century', in M. Bernard and T. Scharf (eds) *Critical Perspectives on Ageing Societies*, Bristol: Policy Press, pp 13–26.

King's Fund (2020) *What is Happening to Life Expectancy in the UK?* [online], Available from: www.kingsfund.org.uk/publications/whats-happening-life-expectancy-uk [Accessed 23 December 2020].

Kuh, D. and Ben-Shlomo, Y.B. (eds) (2004) *A Life Course Approach to Chronic Disease Epidemiology*, Oxford: Oxford University Press.

Kuh, D., Hardy, R., Langenberg, C., Richards, M. and Wadsworth, M.E. (2002) 'Mortality in adults aged 26–54 years related to socioeconomic conditions in childhood and adulthood: post war birth cohort study', *British Medical Journal*, 325(7372): 1076–1080.

Larkin, M. (2013) *Health and Well-Being across the Life Course*, London: Sage.

Larkin, M., Henwood, M. and Milne, A. (2019) 'Carer related research and knowledge: findings from a scoping review', *Health and Social Care in the Community*, 27(1): 55–67.

Lee, H. and Turney, K. (2012) 'Investigating the relationship between perceived discrimination, social status, and mental health', *Society and Mental Health*, 2(1): 1–20.

Livingston, G., Sommerlad, A., Orgeta, V., Costafreda, S.G., Huntley, J., Ames, D., Ballard, C., Banerjee, S., Burns, A., Cohen-Mansfield, J., Cooper, C., Fox, N., Gitlin, L.N., Howard, R., Kales, H.C., Larson, E.B., Ritchie, K., Rockwood, K., Sampson, E.L., Samus, Q., Schneider, L.S., Selbæk, G., Teri, L. and Mukadam, N. (2017) 'Dementia prevention, intervention, and care', *The Lancet Commissions*, 390(10113): 2673–2734.

Lloyd, L. (2012) *Health and Care in Ageing Societies: A New International Approach*, Bristol: Policy Press.

Marmot, M. (2005) 'Social determinants of health inequalities', *The Lancet*, 365(9464): 1099–1104.

Marmot, M. and Wilkinson, R. (eds) (2005) *Social Determinants of Health*, Oxford: Oxford University Press.

Marmot, M. and Bell, R. (2016) 'Social inequalities in health: a proper concern of epidemiology', *Annals of Epidemiology*, 26(4): 238–240.

Marmot, M., Allen, J., Goldblatt, P., Boyce, T., McNeish, D., Grady, M. and Geddes, I. (2010) *Fair Society, Healthy Lives: Strategic Review of Health Inequalities in England Post-2010*, London: The Marmot Review.

Maschi, T., Baer, J., Morrissey, M-B. and Moreno, C. (2013) 'The aftermath of childhood trauma on late life physical and mental health: a review of the literature', *Traumatology*, 19(1): 49–64.

McCrory, E.J., Gerin, M.I. and Viding, E. (2017) 'Annual research review: childhood maltreatment, latent vulnerability and the shift to preventive psychiatry – the contribution of functional brain imaging', *Journal of Child Psychology and Psychiatry*, 58(4): 338–357.

McGarry, J. and Simpson, C. (2011) 'Domestic abuse and older women: exploring the opportunities for service development and care delivery', *The Journal of Adult Protection*, 13(6): 294–301.

Milne, A. (2020) *Mental Health in Later Life: Taking a Life Course Approach*, Bristol: Policy Press.

Moriarty, J. and Butt, J. (2004) 'Inequalities in quality of life among older people from different ethnic groups', *Ageing & Society*, 24(5): 729–753.

Nazroo, J., Bromley, R. and Pendrill, J. (2017) *The Golden Generation? Wellbeing and Inequalities in Later Life*, Manchester Institute for Collaborative Research on Ageing, [online], Available from: http://hummedia. manchester.ac.uk/institutes/micra/news/2017/golden-generation-report-2017.pdf [Accessed 18 December 2019].

Nelson-Becker, H., Lloyd, L., Milne, A., Perry, E., Ray, M., Richards, S., Sullivan, M.P., Tanner, D. and Willis, P. (2020) 'Strengths-based social work with older people: a UK perspective', in A. Mendenhall and M. Mohr Carney (eds) *Strengths-based Social Work with Older People*, Lawrence: The University of Kansas Libraries, pp 327–346.

Office for National Statistics (2020) *Life Expectancies by National Deprivation Deciles, England and Wales: 2016–2018*, London: Office for National Statistics.

Phillipson, C. (2013) *Ageing*, Cambridge: Polity Press.

PROMISS (2021) *Prevention of Malnutrition in Senior Subjects in the EU*, [online], Available from: https://ec.europa.eu/eip/ageing/commitments-tracker/a3/prevention-malnutrition-senior-subjects-eu-and-support-active-and-healthy_en.html [Accessed 20 December 2020].

Prus, S. (2003) *A Life-Course Perspective on the Relationship Between Socioeconomic Status and Health: Testing the Divergence Hypothesis*, Hamilton, ON: McMaster University.

Ratcliff, K.S. (2017) *The Social Determinants of Health: Looking Upstream*, Hoboken: Wiley.

Ray, M. and Phillips, J. (2012) *Social Work with Older People*, Basingstoke: Palgrave Macmillan.

Ray, M., Milne, A., Beech, C., Phillips, J., Richards, S., Sullivan, M.P., Tanner, D. and Lloyd, L. (2015) 'Gerontological social work: reflections on its role, purpose and value', *British Journal of Social Work*, 45(4): 1296–1312.

Read, S., Grundy, E. and Foverskov, E. (2016) 'Socio-economic position and subjective health and well-being among older people in Europe: a systematic narrative review', *Aging and Mental Health*, 20(5): 529–542.

Richards, S. (2000) 'Bridging the divide: elders and the assessment process', *British Journal of Social Work*, 30(1): 37–49.

SafeLives (2016) *Safe Later Lives: Older People and Domestic Abuse*, [online], Available from: https://safelives.org.uk/sites/default/files/resources/Safe%20Later%20Lives%20-%20Older%20people%20and%20domestic%20abuse.pdf [Accessed 20 January 2021].

Sargent-Cox, K. (2017) 'Ageism: we are our own worst enemy', *International Psychogeriatrics*, 29(1): 1–8.

Scharf, T., Shaw, C., Bamford, S.M., Beach, B. and Hochlaf, D. (2017) *Inequalities in Later Life*, London: Centre for Ageing Better.

Stringhini, S., Carmeli, C., Jokela, M., Avendaño, M., Muennig, P., Guida, F., Ricceri, F., d'Errico, A., Barros, H., Bochud, M., Chadeau-Hyam, M., Clavel-Chapelon, F., Costa, G., Delpierre, C., Fraga, S., Goldberg, M., Giles, G.G., Krogh, V., Kelly-Irving, M., Layte, R., Lasserre, A.M., Marmot, M.G., Preisig, M., Shipley, M.J., Vollenweider, P., Zins, M., Kawachi, I., Steptoe, A., Mackenbach, J.P., Vineis, P. and Kivimäki, M. (2017) 'Socioeconomic status and the 25 × 25 risk factors as determinants of premature mortality: a multicohort study and meta-analysis of 1.7 million men and women', *Lancet*, 389(10075): 1229–1237.

Swift, H.J., Abrams, D., Lamont, R.A. and Drury, L. (2017) 'The risks of ageism model: how ageism and negative attitudes toward age can be a barrier to active ageing', *Social Issues and Policy Review*, 11: 195–231.

Tanner, D. (2007) 'Starting with lives: supporting older people's strategies and ways of coping', *Journal of Social Work*, 7(1): 7–30.

Tanner, D. (2010) *Managing the Ageing Experience: Learning from Older People*, Bristol: Policy Press.

Tanner, D. (2013) 'Identity, selfhood and dementia: messages for social work', *European Journal of Social Work*, 16(2): 155–170.

Thompson, P., Itzin, C. and Abendstern, M. (1990) *I Don't Feel Old: The Experience of Later Life*, Oxford: Oxford University Press.

Tomkow, L. (2018) 'The emergence and utilisation of frailty in the United Kingdom: a contemporary biopolitical practice', *Ageing & Society*, 40(4): 695–712.

United Nations (2020) *Economic and Social Commission for Western Asia*, [online], Available from: www.unescwa.org/structural-inequalities [Accessed 26 January 2021].

Victor, C. (2010) *Ageing, Health and Care*, Bristol: Policy Press.

Wild, K., Wilcs, J.L. and Allen, R.E.S. (2013) 'Resilience: thoughts on the value of the concept for critical gerontology', *Ageing & Society*, 33(1): 37–158.

Wilhelmina, B., Van der Linden, A., Sieber, S., Cheval, B., Orsholits, D., Guessous, I., Stringhini, S., Gabriel, R., Aartsen, M., Blane, D., Courvoisier, D., Burton-Jeangros, C., Kliegel, M. and Cullati, S. (2020) 'Life-course circumstances and frailty in old age within different European welfare regimes: a longitudinal study with SHARE', *The Journals of Gerontology: Series B*, 75(6):1326–1335.

Wilkinson, R. and Pickett, K. (2006) 'Income inequality and population health: a review and explanation of the evidence', *Social Science and Medicine*, 62(7): 1768–1784.

Williams, J. and Watson, S. (2016) 'Surviving their lives: women's mental health in context', in D.J. Castle and K.M. Abel (eds) *Comprehensive Women's Mental Health*, Cambridge: Cambridge University Press, pp 1–13.

Willis, P., Lloyd, L., Hammond, J., Milne, A., Nelson-Becker, H., Parry, E., Ray, M., Richards, S. and Tanner, D. (2021) 'Casting light on the distinctive contribution of social work in multidisciplinary teams for older people', *British Journal of Social Work*, doi.org/10.1093/bjsw/bcab004.

Women's Aid (2013) *Statistics about Domestic Violence: Incidence and Prevalence of Domestic Violence*, London: Women's Aid.

World Health Organization (WHO) (2002) *Active Ageing: A Public Policy Framework*, Geneva: WHO.

WHO (2014) *Social Determinants of Mental Health*, Geneva: WHO.

WHO (2020) *Risk Factors of Ill Health among Older People*, [online], Available from: www.euro.who.int/en/health-topics/Life-stages/healthy-ageing/data-and-statistics/risk-factors-of-ill-health-among-older-people [Accessed 15 December 2020].

3

Human rights and older people

Joan R. Harbison[1]

This chapter explores the meaning of human rights for older people, and for the social workers who work with them, within what is often referred to as a human rights and social justice profession (International Federation of Social Workers, 2014). At the outset, it must be understood that although human rights invoke 'moral obligation' (Townsend, 2006, p 166) and 'can provide social workers with a moral basis for their practice' (Ife, 2012, p 1) they are not fixed. Human rights are both dynamic and complex. They pose complicated and difficult questions, rather than providing answers. The challenge for gerontological social work is to both address that complexity and lend its support to the struggles that diverse older people face in gaining access to their rights.

The chapter begins with a discussion of how human rights instruments have failed to serve older people well. It considers the reasons for the limited progress of ongoing international efforts to address this failure. It comments on why older people have not taken charge in these efforts and how constraints on old age identities have combined with those on social work practice to preserve this status quo. It argues that an important task for gerontological social work practitioners is both to respect and to harness the abilities of the older people with whom they work to demand their human rights in the interests of social justice for both themselves and their peers.

---

[1] **Joan R. Harbison** is Adjunct Professor at the School of Social Work, Dalhousie University, Canada. Her scholarship focuses on critical interdisciplinary approaches to ageing in both national and international contexts. Her recent work includes co-editing *New Challenges to Ageing in the Rural North: A Critical Interdisciplinary Perspective* with Päivi Naskali and Shahnaj Begum (Springer, 2019) and, with her interdisciplinary research team from social work, law and sociology, authoring *Contesting Elder Abuse and Neglect: Ageism, Risk and the Rhetoric of Rights in the Mistreatment of Older People* (University of British Columbia Press, 2016).

Older people and the evolution of human rights

Ideas about human rights have evolved in parallel with changing views in societies within a globalising world (Turner, 1993; Ife, 2012). Modern understandings and interpretations of rights have been influenced by what is widely held as the most influential statement of human rights in the modern world (American Bar Association, 2011, 106C): that is, the United Nations Universal Declaration of Human Rights (abbreviated as UDHR) in 1948. The 30 articles of the UDHR are the centrepiece of what in 1966 became a tripartite International Bill of Rights when the International Covenant on Civil and Political Rights and the International Covenant on Economic, Social and Cultural Rights (United Nations, 1966) were adopted by the United Nations General Assembly.

The rights referred to in the UDHR were intended both to address the horrific events of the Second World War and to prevent their recurrence: the Declaration 'is generally agreed to be the foundation of international human rights law … and has inspired a rich body of legally binding international human rights treaties' (Rodríguez-Pinzón and Martin, 2002, p 918). Yet, most of these legally binding instruments, as is the case with the UDHR, have little to say that is specific to older people. References to older people's rights are more often found in instruments that state principles or aspirational 'aims' and 'goals'.

The United Nations answers the question 'What are human rights?' in the following way:

> Human rights are rights inherent to all human beings, regardless of race, sex, nationality, ethnicity, language, religion, or any other status. Human rights include the right to life and liberty, freedom from slavery and torture, freedom of opinion and expression, the right to work and education, and many more. Everyone is entitled to these rights without discrimination. (United Nations, nd)

The United Nations (UN) asserts that human rights are 'universal' and 'the cornerstone of international human rights law'; and, given these characteristics, that 'we are all equally entitled to our human rights'. The UDHR should therefore be understood as including equal rights for older people. However, the circumstances in which those rights can be accessed or removed are often a matter of legal process. And this is a process that is frequently contentious in the case of older people, following both stereotypes of ageing and debates on the decline of their mental capacities (O'Connor, 2010; Ife, 2012).

The UDHR's 'civil and political rights' are also known as negative rights. Civil rights protect the freedoms of individuals, for instance, to express their opinions, in equality before the law, and against discrimination. Political rights include the protection of a person's voting rights, and the right to serve in the governance of their country. In contrast, economic, social and cultural rights (ESCR), known as positive rights, follow from the preamble to the UDHR. This includes the statement that the signatories 'have determined to promote social progress and better standards of life in larger freedom' (United Nations, 1948, Preamble). Hence, Article 22 invokes 'economic, social and cultural rights indispensable to *his* dignity and the free development of *his* personality' (emphasis in original).

ESCR rights occur in the context of, and are limited by, 'the organization and resources of each State' (Rodríguez-Pinzón and Martin, 2002, p 918). Nevertheless, they include rights that are likely to be fulfilled in today's developed economies, including the right to work (Article 23) and the right to education (Article 26). Also included in ESCR are those rights that should be attainable, and yet on account of structural inequalities are not. For instance, Article 25 refers to the right to 'a standard of living adequate for … health and well-being … housing, medical care and necessary social services and the right to security in the event of unemployment, sickness, disability, widowhood, old age or other lack of livelihood'. This specific reference to 'old age' in Article 25 is the only one in the UDHR.

The limitations of rights instruments

The limitations of the UDHR and its associated rights instruments are widely acknowledged. For instance, failure to ratify or implement agreed-upon instruments may flow either from a lack of social and economic resources or from a lack of political will, or both. In addition, the colonising legacy of the association of rights with the European Enlightenment and Western culture is the subject of controversy (Sen, 2006). This includes the UDHR's emphasis on individual as opposed to group rights, and their secularity (Turner, 1993; Ignatieff, 2000; Ife, 2012).

South Asian, East Asian and other countries have criticised the failure to accommodate 'cultural and economic difference'. Western democracies characterise the positions of these critics as 'excuses for repression and authoritarianism'. From the beginning of the 1990s, authoritarianism has increased with the expansion of populist regimes. Yet it is notable that, at the same time, 'worldwide polls on attitudes towards human rights are now available and they show broad support for human rights and international efforts to promote them' (Nickel, 2019).

Today's social workers must engage with these differing interpretations of human rights. Practitioners must ensure that their understanding is attuned to the social, political, cultural and religious locations and values of both their colleagues and those to whom they deliver services. They must also be prepared to mediate intergenerational differences. Yet their decisions should remain focused on supporting human rights and social justice for their older clients.

Existing rights instruments and older people

One of the central questions in considering the rights of older people is whether they should be treated as adults or as a separate group in need of special protections under the law. For some legal scholars, the latter view is inarguable. For them 'the elderly population remains a vulnerable group with no legal instruments tailored to its needs' (Rodríguez-Pinzón and Martin, 2002, p 916; Herring, 2012). This position is the starting point for a comprehensive review of existing international human rights instruments and systems (Rodríguez-Pinzón and Martin, 2002, pp 915–1008). Another key point of their discussion is that, as we have seen, older people's rights are named in treaties protecting ESCR and are based on a state's available resources. So, for instance, although 'the 1988 Additional Protocol to the European Social Charter' appears to confer many rights on older persons that would both provide for their social security and support their full participation in society, these are not necessarily realised. Many states have ratified only portions of the protocol. And the monitoring Committee of Experts does not have powers of enforcement.

Globally, 'coordinated efforts to incorporate elderly concerns into the United Nation's agenda appeared in the early 1980s' (Rodríguez-Pinzón and Martin, 2002, p 948). At the World Assembly on Ageing in Vienna in 1982 the 'International Plan of Action' was adopted. This was followed in 1991 by the United Nations' 'Implementation of the International Plan of Action on Ageing and Related Activities', which includes the 'United Nations Principles for Older Persons' (United Nations, 1991).

A Second World Conference on Ageing in 2002 resulted in the adoption of the Madrid International Plan of Action on Aging (MIPAA) (Rodríguez-Pinzón and Martin, 2002).

Substituting a rhetoric of rights

Many purposes are served by a rhetoric of rights within politics, policy making and the provision of services and care to older people. Governments and other stakeholders claim their support for the rights of older people, especially in the sphere of ESCR. But they do so mostly through measures without specific mechanisms to hold them accountable. The MIPAA is one such measure. It was welcomed by many groups representing older people because it acknowledged older people's contributions to society, as opposed to framing them as a burden, and was intended to support their further development. Hopes that the MIPAA might serve in place of a convention on the rights of older people have not been fulfilled: 'It is evident that, 10 years after its adoption, the Madrid Plan of Action has made only limited headway in national and international development plans' (UN Economic and Social Council, 2013). This disappointment continues.

Even when mechanisms of accountability are available *within* jurisdictions, as is the case with regulations attached to legislation or institutions, rights claims are overridden by those of costs and scarcity prevalent under neoliberal capitalist regimes (Ray et al, 2015; Harbison, 2016). Indeed, there is evidence of the ongoing and publicly acknowledged failure of governments in many countries with well-developed, if shrinking, systems of social welfare to deliver adequate health and social care to older people (Duffy, 2017). With each crisis, promises are made to correct these omissions, but little is done (Carney and Nash, 2020; Lloyd, 2020). Those in favour of a UN convention on the rights of older people argue that such a human rights instrument would bring pressure on governments: to make changes in their treatment of older people, to overcome discrimination and to cease violating their rights as humans (Townsend, 2006).

Further, it has been suggested that the process of rights development itself would have an energising effect on demands that rights be attended to: 'more often than not, it is the process of adopting a treaty and the sort of bottom-up coalition building and soul-searching that it creates that is one of the most enduring legacies of human rights treaty adoption' (Mégret, 2011, p 65). The Convention on the Rights of Persons with Disabilities (CRPD) 'already shows the way by including a much more richly textured mixture of rights, goals, standards and best practices that has contributed to profoundly restructuring rights language' (Mégret, 2011, p 65). Unfortunately, as we shall see, coalition building for a convention on the rights of older people has not been from the 'bottom up'.

The ongoing lobby for a convention on the rights of older people

The Open-ended Working Group on Ageing (OEWG) was established by the United Nations in 2010 in response to the perceived failure of the MIPAA and the growing demand for specific attention to older people's rights (United Nations, A/RES/65/182). The OEWG's purpose was to 'examine how better to protect older people's rights … including the possibility of new human rights instruments' (OEWG, 2010). The Global Alliance for the Rights of Older People (GAROP) was formed in 2011 with the chief intent of lobbying through the OEWG for a convention on the rights of older people (GAROP, 2020). Its nine founding member organisations were affiliated primarily with either professional and academic organisations or non-governmental organisations advocating *on behalf of* older people (Mégret, 2011; Harbison et al, 2016). This leadership remains today. So, although at the request of the OEWG a significant number of civil society groups representing older people have been recruited, the contrast with the grassroots lobby for the Disability Convention is striking (see Chapter 10).

Since its inception in 2010, the OEWG has come under constant pressure, especially from members of GAROP, to bring a proposal for a convention on the rights of older people before the United Nations General Assembly. However, the lobby has not succeeded. Reservations on the part of 'the two key Western players' – the US and the European Union – have been a major ongoing factor in this failure. While they have claimed that their stated objections were based on the lack of success of similar instruments, their hesitation is more likely based on concern about the potential for a repetition of the considerable costs of implementing the CRPD (Harbison et al, 2016).

Enter the WHO campaign against ageism

Just before the OEWG meeting was held on 29 March–1 April 2021, the UN's World Health Organization (WHO) released its *Global Report on Ageism* (WHO, 2021a). The WHO report's definition of ageism is broad based: 'ageism arises when age is used to categorize and divide people in ways that lead to harm, disadvantage, and injustice. It can take many forms including prejudicial attitudes, discriminatory acts, and institutional policies and practices that perpetuate stereotypical beliefs' (WHO, 2021b). Notwithstanding this apparent breadth of scope, the stance appears to be that of a much narrower biomedical positivism. In the UN news release for the report the headline is 'ageism leads to poorer health, social isolation, earlier deaths and costs economies billions: report calls for swift action to implement effective anti-ageism strategies' (WHO, 2021b). The biomedical nature of the approach is underscored in the second slide of a summary of the report. There, the written definition of 'ageism' is illustrated by the outline of an androgynous figure with arrows pointing to the head: 'Stereotypes – how we think'; the heart: 'Prejudice – how we feel'; and more opaquely the hand: 'Discrimination – how we act' (WHO, 2021c). In addition, the emphasis on the costs of ageism underscores the fact that we now inhabit a global society dominated by market values where older people are perceived as high in costs and low in value (Carney, 2021).

The WHO Director-General notes that the report 'offers solutions in the form of evidence-based interventions to end ageism at all stages' (WHO, 2021b). The news release says that already evidence-based studies demonstrate that 'every second person in the world is believed to hold ageist attitudes – leading to poorer physical and mental health and reduced quality of life for older persons' (WHO, 2021b). Such statements engage in positivist certainty, with its emphasis on finding solutions. However, the amorphous definition of ageism leads us to further questions. How can such a massive project work, and are the resources it will consume well placed?

Under the heading 'Combatting ageism' the news release of the report acknowledges 'policies and laws' as well as a range of activities 'addressing ageism'. However, once again the exhortation is that 'All countries and stakeholders are encouraged to use evidence-based strategies, improve data collection and research and work together to build a movement to change how we think, feel and act towards age and ageing, and to advance progress on the UN Decade of Healthy Ageing' (WHO, 2021b). We know that academics and other researchers will engage in this research, but this is unlikely to lead to the building of a 'movement' – especially one from the 'bottom up' through which older people can secure the agency to take charge of their lives (Stammers, 2009).

It is too early to tell what the effects of this new WHO campaign will be. It brings ageism, its measurement and interventions to address it to the forefront of the WHO. Scholars warn that 'holding on to [ageism] as a *key concept* orienting policy, practice or theory will not help us understand the challenges posed by contemporary later life, nor can it serve to underpin local or global policy initiatives designed to address the societal implications of ageing' (Higgs and Gilleard, 2020, p 1267). Yet the appeal of the campaign may be enhanced by the breadth of its proposed scope. It emphasises ageism directed at older people at a time when they are perceived as especially vulnerable in the era of COVID-19. It also includes ageism directed at youth. And it urges better intergenerational relations as an effective means of addressing ageism.

Will this WHO initiative act in collaboration with the international campaign for a convention on the rights of older people? Will it thus strengthen the call for a convention? Or will its focus on an evidence-based positivist approach to ageism at both ends of the age spectrum, serving both to distract attention from those who are old and at the same time undermine the campaign to establish a convention?

How biomedical views of ageing and older people affect their human rights

Concerns about the effects of a biomedical view of older people are long standing in the field of human rights. On this account some scholars have included caveats with their support for an older persons' convention, worrying that it would give priority to rights to 'protections' and might become 'an ageist trap' emphasising 'issues such as "elder abuse and neglect" … mental incapacity … legal guardianship [and] … institutional long-term care' and portraying 'older persons as weak, incapable, and dependent [and therefore incorporating] a "needs-based" rather than a "rights-based" discourse' (Doron and Apter, 2010, p 592).

A clear demonstration of what can happen if a biomedical view of older people, focusing on their physical and mental decay, enters considerations of older people's civil rights is found in the work of lawyer Jonathan Herring. Although he acknowledges that a balance must be struck between an older person's rights to autonomy and 'best interests', he argues that in situations that are defined as 'elder abuse', irrespective of whether older people are 'capable or incapable in law', they should nevertheless be treated as children (Harbison et al, 2016, p 203). He states that 'it is remarkable ... that although local authorities are under an obligation to investigate cases of child abuse and must act to protect children from abuse there is no equivalent obligation in relation to older people' (Herring, 2012, p 186). In support of his position, Herring invokes the European Convention on Human Rights (ECHR, 2010). For instance, he argues that the right to respect for private and family life (Article 8) 'is not just a "negative right" inhibiting state intrusion into a citizen's private life ... [it also] places "positive obligations" on the state to intervene to protect individuals' (Herring, 2012, p 182).

Further, while Herring acknowledges that 'many victims in these cases have conflicting wishes. They want to remain in the relationship, but they want the abuse to stop'; in his view 'it is not possible to respect these two conflicting desires' (Herring, 2012, p 183). Therefore, sometimes older persons should be 'protected' against their will. Herring does not consider that 'it might well be possible [to resolve the conflicts] through negotiations carried out by informed and skilful professionals from a range of disciplines, or indeed engaged members of the community at large' (Harbison et al, 2016, p 204).

However, if the possibility for negotiations in such conflicted situations is to be considered, then those charged with their implementation, often social workers, must first have a sound, alternative understanding of rights that takes us beyond biomedical and legal exactitude. One might anticipate that this would be the case for social worker Jim Ife, author of *Human Rights and Social Work: Towards a Rights-based Practice* (2012), now in its third edition. Yet Ife's brief comments on rights specific to older people begin with a comparison of older people to children. And he likens 'elder abuse' to 'child abuse'. He acknowledges that older people are different from children, for instance in their ownership of property and their financial affairs. More telling are his comments that while children's capacities increase with age 'with many older people ... the capacity to make ... independent decisions decreases over time especially if they are suffering from some form of dementia' (Ife, 2012, pp 83–84). Ife goes on to say that empowerment-based practice, though certainly still possible must take on a rather different set of assumptions about what the older person can realistically be expected to achieve, and it is a case of moving towards greater rather than less dependency ... by working with older people to plan their future realistically.

And he expresses the concern that concentrating on its negative aspects 'can serve to pathologise old age' and foster age discrimination (Ife, 2012, pp 84–85).

Ife is hardly alone in his struggle to come to terms with the complexity of working to secure older people's rights, especially in the context of the increasing diversity of those in old age (Ray et al, 2015). Positions differ dramatically. Take for instance legal scholar Michael Ignatieff's comments that give priority to agency and rights:

> One of the essential functions of human-rights legislation is to protect human beings from the therapeutic good intentions of others. It does so by mandating an obligation to respect human agency – however expressed, however limited – and to desist from any actions, even those intended to help, if these agents refuse or in any other way give signs of a contrary will. ... To be sure, keeping to this rule is hard, but the test of human respect always lies with the hard cases – the babbling incontinent inhabitant of a psychiatric ward or a nursing home. (Ignatieff, 2000, p 39)

There are undoubtedly times when the moral and ethically correct action to take with older clients is to act on their behalf in the interests of their human rights. However, as a social worker one should not readily dismiss opportunities both to inform older people of their rights and to encourage, support and assist them to assert those rights. Doing so may be a first step in overcoming their oppression and re-establishing their agency.

Managerialism, social work and rights practice

The constraints on social work practice, especially those following the advent of managerial approaches in social work organisations, are well documented. The managerial approach leads social workers away from dealing with the complexity of the situations they encounter and toward prescriptions that limit possibilities for meaningful intervention (Ife, 1997). Research by Dunér and Nordström (2006) provides an account of how in Sweden social workers moved older people's rights to service from 'thick' to 'thin' definitions of needs (Geertz, 1973). Leaving aside their professional discretion '[they] allow themselves to be controlled by organizational and administrative guidelines'. And 'meticulous work ... in the needs' assessment' is substituted for responses to the actual needs of the older persons (Dunér and Nordström, 2006, pp 440–441). A study by Ash (2013) of Welsh social workers had similar findings.

The chief purpose of assessment is now not to decide with older people what services will best meet their needs (Bradshaw, 1972). Instead, it is to ensure that those charged with assessing service needs protect the agencies for whom they work by closely following their protocols and guidelines (Warner and Sharland, 2010; Harbison et al, 2016; see also Chapter 8). Older people's rights to service have become the 'right to risk'. How this works in practice is clearly demonstrated in a study by Ann McDonald of social workers' implementation of the Mental Capacity Act 2005 in the English context. She identified 'three distinct types of approach to risk'. A 'legalistic' approach incorporated 'a legal positivist view of the law as a morally neutral system of commands and duties'. An actuarial approach 'tended to conflate capacity assessments with "best interests" decision making and to use persuasion with older people who were rejecting intervention' (McDonald, 2010, p 1236).

The 'rights-based approach' was one of advocacy. 'These workers did not view either the law as neutral or dementia as "an objectively ascertainable medical category". Instead, they used "human rights principles of respect for family life and privacy," were alert to stereotypical constructions of older people with dementia, and privileged the legal capacity to choose over risk' (McDonald, 2010, p 1237; as cited in Harbison et al, 2016, p 137). If human rights are to become central to a transformed gerontological social work practice, social workers and social work students will need to be educated so that they 'relish self-challenge and feel professionally confident to challenge each other and other professionals to take a rights-based approach' (Ash, 2013, p 113).

Old-age identities and older people's demands for their human rights

The acquisition of both individual and group rights is usually the end point of a long period of struggle: 'human rights are seldom given; they have to be seized' (Ife, 2012, p 305). Some critical gerontologists argue that 'agency does not mean acting for oneself under conditions of oppression. It means being without oppression' (Neysmith and Macadam, 1999, p 11). If this is true, where does such a position leave older people? How many will be willing to engage in a struggle for their rights, and how many will be supported to do so?

The increasing numbers of older people surviving well past retirement has led scholars to explore questions about the identities available to those in later life: 'a critical gerontology should include the study of identity as central to understanding the disjunction between ageing from within [the person] and ageing within society' (Phillipson and Biggs, 1999, p 159). With the decline of 'a post-war consensus on welfare' as the organising framework, and in the context of Townsend's critique of its legacy of 'structural dependency', they ask 'what is the moral and existential space to which [older people] are entitled in a world where social integration is achieved through the operation of the marketplace' (Phillipson and Biggs, 1999, pp 163–164; Townsend, 2006). One option for those older people who are relatively well off is to join in consumer culture (Gilleard and Higgs, 2005). Those who become inhabitants of the 'third age' literally and figuratively buy themselves time before their nearly inevitable decline into a 'fourth age' (Gilleard and Higgs, 2009; see Chapter 4).

Third-agers may have seemed well positioned not only to build positive identities for themselves but also through their own actions to insist on positive identities, or at least positive potential for the fourth-agers that they will become. With a few exceptions, this does not seem to be the case (Gullette, 2017). Instead, as we have seen in the demand for a convention on older people's rights, others in positions of power and authority speak *on behalf of* older people. Answers to why this is so may lie in the desire to maintain their position as both active and productive members of society, one that separates them from the problem of the burdensomeness of 'real' old age, where they will encounter 'othering' and societal disapproval (van Dyk, 2014, pp 98–99; Higgs and Gilleard, 2020).

For instance, one might have anticipated that activist groups such as the Raging Grannies would take up the cause of injustices towards their more vulnerable peers and insist on their rights. Instead, with the expressed intent of remaining in the mainstream, they may choose to use their activism in support of the causes focused on younger generations, such as the peace movement, ecology and violence against women and children (Hall, 2005). Other older people knowingly use their energy to deploy strategies that protect them from the assignment of negative identities. They engage in activities sanctioned in the wider society as appropriate for those in late life (Katz, 2005; Formosa, 2014). Those whose struggle to maintain their autonomy is on account of their increasing physical limitations, and the resources to address these, take different measures to protect their positive identities. They reframe the daily events in their lives so that what others see as evidence of frailty becomes just one more thing that the older person manages 'successfully' (Bornat and Bytheway, 2010).

In searching for remedies to global ageism it seems important to better understand the reasons for most older people's reticence to be front and centre in the demand for their human rights. Van Dyk rejects the ideas of many gerontologists that old age is a time of 'uniqueness and difference' that should be celebrated. In comparison to 'the agelessness of midlife … critical gerontology makes only old age into age – therefore unwillingly reinforcing old age as "the other," deviating from the ageless norm' (van

Dyk, 2014, p 99). This 'other' is often one characterised in terms of 'positive age stereotypes' that are in themselves repressive. She asks us to consider Woodward's argument that the conferring of wisdom on older people 'deprives them of their right to feel anger and protest against discrimination' (van Dyk, 2014, p 99). If this is true, can this anger and the energy that comes with it be reignited?

Conclusion

The assault on basic human rights evidenced in the degrading conditions in which older people live, especially in residential care, has once again been placed before the public in the era of COVID-19 (Carney and Nash, 2020). In the short term, there are many circumstances, both in policy responses to these conditions and in practice, in which social work practitioners will have a moral and ethical obligation to give primacy to human rights and social justice in their work with and on behalf of older people. Historically, the initial public outrage about how societies treat their older people fades quickly. And the negation of their rights is reinstated in the face of a lexicon of costs (de Beauvoir, 1970). In the longer term, the search for understandings of why this is so must go beyond narrow investigations, to an exploration of the 'fourth age social imaginary':

> By acknowledging the multiplicity of meanings that 'old age' presents, across the spaces where the state, markets and culture operate, as well as accepting the capacity for age itself to be alienating and oppressive, we are better able to explore its inherent ambiguities and limitations. (Higgs and Gilleard, 2020, p 1627)

Gerontological social work has already demonstrated that the breadth of scope of its knowledge base and in its practice allows it to reach beyond pre-scripted rational and cognitive approaches to old age, and towards understanding the increasingly diverse people who inhabit its territories. Through social work research and practice, and in alliances with older people and their allies, social work is well placed to support the restoration of older people's sense of legitimacy in demanding access to their human rights. Furthermore, social work must act to ensure that older people's rights remain at the forefront of consideration both with policy makers and with the public at large.

References
American Bar Association (2011) *Report to the House of the Delegates* (106C), [online], 8 August, Available from: www.americanbar.org/groups/judical/conferences/administrative_law_judiciary/resources/aba-resolutions/ [Accessed 1 April 2021].

Ash, A. (2013) 'A cognitive mask? Camouflaging dilemmas in street-level policy implementation to safeguard older people from abuse', *British Journal of Social Work*, 43: 99–115.

Bornat, J. and Bytheway, B. (2010) 'Perceptions and presentations of living with everyday risk in later life', *British Journal of Social Work*, 40(4): 1118–1134.

Bradshaw, J. (1972) 'The concept of need', *New Society*, 30: 640–643.

Carney, G. and Nash, P (2020) *Human Rights, Age Discrimination and a Global Pandemic*, [Blog], 15 September, Available from: https://transformingsociety.co.uk/2020/09/15/human-rights-age-discrimination-and-a-global-pandemic/ [Accessed 1 April 2021].

Carney, M. (2021) *Value[s]: Building a Better Life for All*, New York: Public Affairs.

de Beauvoir, S. (1970) *Old Age*, Harmondsworth: Penguin Books.

Doron, I. and Apter, I. (2010) 'The debate around the need for a new convention on the rights of older people', *The Gerontologist*, 50(5): 586–593.

Duffy, F. (2017) 'A social work perspective on how ageist language, discourse and understandings negatively frame older people and why taking a critical social work stance is essential', *British Journal of Social Work*, 47(7): 2068–2085.

Dunér, A. and Nordström, M. (2006) 'The discretion and power of street-level bureaucrats: an example from Swedish municipal eldercare', *European Journal of Social Work*, 9(4): 425–444.

European Convention on Human Rights (2010), [online], Available from: https://www.echr.coe.int/Documents/Convention_ENG.pdf [Accessed 5 April 2021].

Formosa, M. (2014) 'Four decades of universities of the third age: past present and future', *Ageing & Society*, 34(1): 42–66.

Geertz, C. (1973) *The Interpretation of Cultures*, New York: Basic Books.

Gilleard, C. and Higgs, P. (2005) *Contexts of Ageing: Class, Cohort, and Community*, Cambridge: Polity Press.

Gilleard, C. and Higgs, P. (2009) 'The power of silver: age and identity politics in the 21st century', *Journal of Aging and Social Policy*, 21(3): 277–295.

Global Alliance for the Rights of Older People (GAROP) (2020) *Who We Are: GAROP Steering Group*, [online], Available from: www.rightsofolderpeople.org [Accessed 22 March 2021].

Gullette, M.M. (2017) *Ending Ageism, or How Not to Shoot Older People*, New Brunswick: Rutgers University Press.

Hall, F. (2005) *Old Rage and the Issue of Mistreatment and Neglect of Older People*, unpublished MSW thesis, School of Social Work, Dalhousie University, Canada.

Harbison, J. (2016) 'How ageism undermines older people's human rights and social inclusion: revisiting advocacy, agency and need in later life', in P. Naskali, M. Seppänen and S. Begum (eds) *Ageing, Wellbeing and Climate Change in the Arctic: An Interdisciplinary Analysis*, Abingdon: Routledge, pp 11–29.

Harbison, J., Coughlan, S., Karabanow, J., VanderPlaat, M., Wildeman, S. and Wexler, E. (2016) *Contesting Elder Abuse and Neglect: Ageism, Risk and the Rhetoric of Rights in the Mistreatment of Older People*, Vancouver: University of British Columbia Press.

Herring, J. (2012) 'Elder abuse: a human rights agenda', in I. Doron and A.M. Soden (eds) *Beyond Elder Law: New Directions in Law and Aging*, Berlin: Springer, pp 175–195.

Higgs, P. and Gilleard, G. (2020) 'The ideology of ageism versus the social imaginary of the fourth age: two differing approaches to the negative contexts of old age', *Ageing & Society*, 40(8): 1617–1630.

Ife, J. (1997) *Rethinking Social Work: Towards a Critical Practice*, Melbourne: Longman.

Ife, J. (2012) *Human Rights and Social Work: Towards Rights-Based Practice*, Cambridge: Cambridge University Press.

Ignatieff, M. (2000) *The Rights Revolution*, Toronto: Anansi Press.

International Federation of Social Workers (2014) *Global Definition of Social Work*, [online], Available from: www.ifsw.org/what-is-social-work/global-definition-of-social-work/ [Accessed 5 April 2021].

Katz, S. (2005) *Cultural Aging: Life Course, Lifestyle and Senior Worlds*, Peterborough, ON: Broadview Press.

Lloyd, L. (2020) 'Devalued later life: Older residents' experiences of risk in a market system of residential and nursing homes', in P. Armstrong and H. Armstrong (eds) *The Privatization of Care: The Case of Nursing Homes*, New York and London: Routledge, pp 196–208.

McDonald, A. (2010) 'The impact of the 2005 Mental Capacity Act on social workers' decision making and approaches to the assessment of risk', *British Journal of Social Work*, 40(4): 1229–1246.

Mégret, F. (2011) 'The human rights of older persons: a growing challenge', *Human Rights Law Review*, 11(1): 37–66.

Neysmith, S. and Macadam, M. (1999) 'Controversial concepts', in S. Neysmith (ed) *Critical Issues for Future Social Work Practice with Aging Persons*, New York: Columbia University Press, pp 1–26.

Nickel, J. (2019) 'Human rights', in E.N. Zalta (ed) *Stanford Encyclopedia of Philosophy* (Summer 2019 Edition), [online], Available from: https://plato.stanford.edu/entries/rights-human/ [Accessed 1 April 2021].

O'Connor, D. (2010) 'Personhood and dementia: toward a relational framework for assessing decisional capacity', *The Journal of Mental Health Training: Education and Practice*, 5(3): 20–30.

Phillipson, C. and Biggs, S. (1999) 'Population ageing: critical gerontology and the sociological tradition', *Education and Ageing*, 14(2): 159–170.

Ray, M., Milne, A., Beech, C., Phillips, J.E., Richards, S., Sullivan, M.P., Tanner, D. and Lloyd, L. (2015) 'Gerontological social work: reflections on its role, purpose and value', *British Journal of Social Work*, 45(4): 1296–1312.

Rodríguez-Pinzón, D. and Martin, C. (2002) 'The international human rights status of elderly persons', *American University International Law Review*, 18(4): 915–1008.

Sen, A. (2006) *Identity and Violence: The Illusion of Destiny*, New York: Norton.

Stammers, N. (2009) *Human Rights and Social Movements*, London: Pluto Press.

Townsend, P. (2006) 'Policies for the aged in the 21st century: more structured dependency or the realisation of human rights?', *Ageing & Society*, 26(2):161–179.

Turner, B.S. (1993) 'Outline of a theory of human rights', *Sociology*, 27(3): 489–512.

United Nations (1948) *The Universal Declaration of Human Rights*, [online], 10 December, Available from: un.org/en/aboutus/universal-declaration-of-human-rights [Accessed 22 March 2021].

United Nations (1966) *International Covenant on Economic Social and Cultural Rights*, [online], June, Available from: www.ohchr.org/en/professionalinterest/pages,icescr.aspx [Accessed 8 April 2021].

United Nations (1991) *Principles for Older Persons*, [online], 16 December, Available from: www.ohchr.org/en/professionalinterest/pages/universalhumanrightsinstruments.aspx [Accessed 8 April 2021].

United Nations (1996a) *International Bill of Rights* [online], June, Available from: www.ohchr.org/documents/publications/factsheet2rev.1en.pdf [Accessed 8 April 2021].

United Nations (1996b) *International Covenant on Civil and Political Rights*, [online], June, Available from: www.ohchr.org/en/professionalinterest/pages,ccpr.aspx [Accessed 8 April 2021].

United Nations (nd) *What are Human Rights?* [online], 10 December, Available from: https:// www.un.org/en/global-issues/human-rights [Accessed 22 March 2021].

United Nations Economic and Social Council (2013) *Second Review and Appraisal of the Madrid International Plan of Action on Ageing, 2002*, [online], November, Available from: https://undocs.org/E/CN.5/2013/6 [Accessed 22 March 2021].

United Nations Open-Ended Working Group on Older People (OEWG) (2010) *Who Are We*, [online], 21 December, Available from: http://social.un.org/ageing-working-group/index.shtml [Accessed 8 April 2021].

van Dyk, S. (2014) 'The appraisal of difference: critical gerontology and the active-ageing-paradigm', *Journal of Aging Studies*, 31: 93–103.

Warner, J. and Sharland, E. (2010) 'Editorial: special issue on risk and social work', *British Journal of Social Work*, 40(4): 1035–1045.

World Health Organization (WHO) (2021a) '*Global Report on Ageism*', [online], 18 March, Available from: www.int/teams/social–determinants–of–health/demographic–change–and–healthy–ageing–combatting–ageism/global–report–on–ageism [Accessed 20 March, 2021].

WHO (2021b) *Ageism is a Global Challenge: UN*, news release, [online], 18 March, Available from: www.who.int/news/item/18-03-2021-ageism-is-a-global-challenge-un [Accessed 20 March 2021].

WHO (2021c) *Global Report on Ageism [summary slides]*, [online], 29 March, Available from: www.who-int/publications/m/item/summary-slides-global-report-on-ageism [Accessed 30 March 2021].

4

Agency and autonomy

Paul Higgs[1]

The framing of old age has long been regarded as being relatively unproblematic, given that old age and decline appear inextricably linked. This connection helps to explain why concerns of the latter part of the lifecourse are regarded as the province of health and social policy. Old age was a period marked out by 'agedness', something constituted by both physical need and social dependency (Pickard, 2013). Even the most noticeable marker of old age, the state retirement pension, was a product of the widespread recognition that older workers (in the first instance men) needed a substitute income to compensate them for their inability to work, given the physical limitations accompanying ageing (Scheubel, 2013). Similarly, the health problems of the older population were assumed to be intractable chronic conditions that led to institutionalisation of one kind or another (Trattner, 2007; Levene, 2009). The modern welfare state categorically saw older people as a residualised group incapacitated by their social dependency and individual passivity (Carey, 2016).

By the end of the 20th century, this projection of old age was considerably changed. Not only was the reaching of retirement age now an almost universal experience, but high-income nations were now experiencing increased life expectancy as well as increased disability-free life expectancy; the conjunction of both transformed expectations and experiences of later life. While not entirely free from the older narratives of old age, such developments led to discussions of old age as being a potential 'crown of life' rather than 'a tragedy' (Townsend, 1963). Issues of personal agency became more important in later life as the once clear-cut demarcations of old age

---

[1] **Paul Higgs** is Professor of the Sociology of Ageing at University College London, UK. He has published extensively in gerontology, medical sociology and sociology. He has published 14 books (seven with Chris Gilleard), including: *Cultures of Ageing: Self, Citizen and Society* (Longman, 2000); *Contexts of Ageing: Class, Cohort and Community* (Polity, 2005); and *Rethinking Old Age: Theorising the Fourth Age* (Palgrave Macmillan, 2015); and *Social Divisions and Later* and *Life: Difference, Diversity and Inequality* (Policy Press, 2020). Paul is editor of *Social Theory and Health*. He holds fellowships from the UK Academy of Social Sciences and the Gerontological Society of America.

provided by social policy became less easy to maintain. Older people were, in the main, more similar to those who were younger than them, and the cultural distinctions between the working and retired population became more difficult to ascertain (Jones et al, 2008). The period of post-working life seemed to extend and become much more of a lifestyle than being solely an ascribed status.

While old age was still understood in terms of welfare policies, the societies in which older people now lived had become different from the ones that had existed at the dawn of the welfare state in the 1950s. As a number of commentators point out, contemporary societies feature a focus on agency and autonomy, an aspect of social interaction that is very different from the more structured limitations of mid-20th-century Europe (Beck and Beck-Gernsheim, 2002; Bauman, 2013). Agency is a concept used by sociologists to refer to the capacity of individuals to act independently and to make choices. Autonomy is a term used to describe the capacity of individuals to act without significant constraints or coercion. The transformation of society was achieved through the individualising effects of consumer culture; the disembedding of institutionalised forms of life such as the normative nuclear family, and the promotion of lifestyle as an identity (Giddens, 1991; Boltanski and Chiapello, 2005; Rosa, 2013). As a result, the birth cohorts following the Second World War emerged as generations complete with their own dispositions and habits. In particular, those coming to adulthood in the 1960s espoused a cultural approach that rejected ascription and emphasised choice. As this 'baby boomer' generation grew older, it took its own way of life into each age stage that it was passing through (Gilleard and Higgs, 2005). This tendency has been equally true of later life, where the status of retirement has been reworked into the lifestyles of post-working life. One marker of this shift has been the increased wealth and income of older people; something that has made the 'silver' market occupied by older people much more diversified and profitable (Jones et al, 2008; Jones, Higgs and Ekerdt, 2011). Of necessity, this has been an unequal process and is one that has impacted on the heterogeneity of older people in many different ways, reflecting both financial resources and the other assets, such as property held by older people. This has had considerable significance for the nature of old age; a significance that has called into question many of the assumptions of critical social gerontology – ones that see old age as a generalisable social location for all those in later life.

Certainly, it is the case that some approaches to ageing that have sought to identify the components of 'successful ageing' may be more readily able to incorporate the changes in later life into their positions and be happy to endorse them (Rowe and Kahn, 2015). However, as many critics have pointed out, the discourses of successful ageing may themselves have an oppressive quality that insists on a single 'positive' template for ageing, with negative consequences for those unable or unwilling to engage with this ideological formulation for old age (Rubinstein and de Medeiros, 2015). This has left approaches such as critical gerontology in a paradoxical position of both wanting to undermine decline narratives of later life but at the same time not wanting to abandon the framing of old age as a vulnerable or precarious location (Grenier 2012; Grenier et al, 2017; Phillipson, 2021). This dualistic approach creates tensions in what concepts of agency and autonomy mean, as well as where they apply and where they do not. There are many examples of this tension: for example, is the agency and autonomy of using anti-ageing technologies 'transgressive', or is it succumbing to ageist discourses that should be challenged (Vincent, 2009)? Equally, what are the limits on the expression of choice by residents of nursing homes where the person may be harmed by their own choices (Higgs and Gilleard 2016a)?

This chapter addresses these paradoxes and argues that, in and of themselves, the ideas of agency and autonomy play a contradictory role in contemporary ageing, one that should not be sanitised into a decontextualised virtue, freed from analysis or criticism. However, in order to develop this theme in more depth, we need to explore further the bifurcation of the third and fourth ages.

The third age, individualisation and reflexivity

The idea that contemporary later life is best represented as a 'third age' has become an increasingly important concept in understanding contemporary later life. While there are a number of differing interpretations of the concept initially promoted by Peter Laslett (1996) to describe a positive post-work life, Gilleard and Higgs (2005) have argued that it is important to see the third age as operating in a cultural field. A cultural field is where individuals interact using particular repertoires of meaning, which have an unspoken quality but which everyone in such circumstances understands. Differentiation and distinctions between different groups and individuals occur in these cultural fields. Ageing has become an important cultural field where ideas of 'successful' and 'unsuccessful' ageing proliferate (Bülow and Söderqvist, 2014). A key aspect of a cultural field is that it gives rise to combinations of dispositions and practices described as habitus. The third age operates through a habitus where autonomy, choice and 'identity work' play a central role in motivating individual action. Consumerism is often how these actions are realised (Gilleard and Higgs, 2011a). Consumer practices are not confined to any one part of the lifecourse, rather, they have become almost identical with modern society itself. They are also no longer geographically confined to a small set of nations (Hyde and Higgs, 2016). One key vector in promoting these changes is the process of 'individualisation'. As described most clearly by the late German sociologist Ulrich Beck (Beck and Beck-Gernsheim, 2002), individualisation posits the individual as the basic unit of social life. This focus on individualising processes is seen as constituting what he calls 'reflexive modernisation', which is a new form of society that has emerged out of the nation-state-orientated social systems common in the mid-20th century. While modernisation is relatively well understood as the tendency for societies to constantly adapt their institutions and processes to achieve ever-expanding efficiency and growth, reflexivity is the institutional and individual capacity to evaluate and reflect on the choices made. The modernisation of the late 19th and early 20th centuries prioritised the nation-state and was concerned with the 'functional differentiation' of the population. Reflexivity in contemporary times is premised on the individual making their choices in accord with their own priorities. In this new environment, choice and reflexivity are inevitably placed at the heart of social action, leading to what has been described as a 'privatisation' of social problems. Consequently, responsibility for taking action is given to the individual, rather than being placed on society (Calhoun, 2006). In this formulation, the stable social locations that were once associated with class, gender and neighbourhood become disembedded and can no longer be taken-for-granted aspects of people's lives. Occupational structures based on the clear demarcation of tasks, seniority and an interconnection between work and social life have been uprooted by industrial restructuring, flexible working and the destruction of working-class communities. Gender roles that were once ascribed by familial responsibilities and homemaking have similarly undergone a transformation as household forms have become more diverse and less tied to hetero-normative expectations of marriage and child rearing. Health and welfare policies have also shifted from an assumption of universalism towards individualised forms of 'entitlements' that can be modified in accordance with policy objectives or considerations.

While Beck tends to emphasise the decline in 'traditional' modernity and the hollowing-out of its social forms as the features comprising individualisation, he is joined by other major social theorists in seeing individualisation as one of the salient features of contemporary society. Zygmunt Bauman (2013) also accords individualisation a pivotal role in changing society, but attributes it to the rise of a society of consumers rather than producers, with an attendant idealisation of choice as a virtue. Such theoretical approaches often mesh with those of critical gerontologists who would argue that these changes are a deliberate political product of neoliberalism whereby market rationalities become the new normative structures for social life (Polivka, 2011; Polivka and Luo, 2020); however, this latter group see these changes as fundamentally detrimental to older people and needing to be resisted rather than embraced. Whatever its causality, accounts of individualisation and neoliberalism both concur that the contingency of individual action, as well as the imperative of choice-making, are now part of the bedrock of contemporary society.

Consumer culture and agency

Individualisation has not only created the possibility for the emergence of a third-age habitus which is lived through lifestyle consumerism (Gilleard and Higgs, 2011b), but it has also affected the arenas of health and social care. In the context of welfare, this agentic third-age perspective contributes to the growing emphasis placed upon 'the user's voice' – which Chapter 11 in this book touches upon – as well as the creation of opportunities for older people to put forward their perspectives to decision makers (Gilleard and Higgs, 1998). While such developments have been welcomed as a challenge to existing networks of power, offering the prospect of a more responsive welfare system, the fundamental imbalance in power between the public represented as 'users' and public sector providers remains unaltered. The redefinition of older people as 'citizen-consumers' (Clarke et al, 2007) attributes to them a position of agency that often they cannot fill. This is particularly the case in health and social care, given the asymmetry of knowledge between professional service providers such as doctors and service users. This lack of agency is also present in more mundane areas such as utility provision, or in shopping for consumer products, where those who do not voice their choices (or are not prepared to act on them) often find themselves economically disadvantaged. Gilleard and Higgs (1998) have described this development as a 'third age rhetoric' being applied to later life. Again, while the social relationships generated by this emphasis on choice can be seen as aspects of neoliberalism, it should also be noted that the attribution of agency can have real effects, both on those making the attributions as well as on those viewed as agents. This positive dimension was present in a study of Swedish home care services for older people where a majority of respondents appreciated the aspect of choice available in decisions about their care (Duner, Bjälkebring and Johansson, 2019). The cultures surrounding the third age have often projected this attribution of agency and voice, to the advantage of particular sections of the older population. This can be seen in relation to the US advocacy group for retired people AARP (American Association of Retired Persons), and its role in the reform of Medicare and the partial privatisation of social security (Hudson and Gonyea, 2012). Consequently, the issues of agency and choice reflect a particular cultural framing of later life that extends the generational habitus of baby boomers to the field of ageing. It is noteworthy that in so doing the field of ageing is also changed. If consumption practices and a focus on lifestyle have changed the nature of retirement, then so too has the valorisation of autonomy and choice.

The meaning of health in later life has also changed. Unlike previous conceptions centring on the absence of disease, or the minimisation of age-related decline, this newer formulation is interwoven into the 'aspirational science' that makes up much anti-ageing medicine (Gilleard and Higgs,

2014). While a desire to retain youthfulness is present in many myths in many different cultures, anti-ageing medicine in its current form has become a normalised feature of the somatic culture of consumer society. Critical gerontology has often taken a negative stance towards these developments, seeing in them an extension of patriarchal ideals of gendered ageing (Calasanti and Slevin, 2001). The importance of this shift towards anti-ageing techniques can be evidenced by the widespread availability of cosmetic plastic surgery to 'correct' the signs of ageing and the promotion of such ideas in the mass media. Of equal importance are less invasive procedures such as Botox injections and dermabrasion that also seek to achieve an aesthetic anti-ageing effect. Moving beyond gender, the integration of both fitness and dieting practices into an everyday culture of control and aspiration stimulates a discourse of ageing that now identifies it as something that needs to be actively resisted and controlled at all points of the lifecourse (Clarke, 2010; Higgs and Gilleard, 2015). In part, this extension of agency to the body can be understood in terms of Foucault's idea of 'governmentality', where 'the conduct of conduct' of individuals replaces simpler notions of generalised biopolitics resting on mass conformity (Foucault, 1991). The increasing separation of the previously interlinked concepts of 'normal', 'natural' and 'normative ageing' has exacerbated the differences between older people as well as creating a much more contingent environment for the choices older people have to make (Jones and Higgs, 2010). This all adds up to the construction of a culture of ageing where age and the signs of age are to be minimised; where a choice not to decline is viewed as an expression of autonomy and freedom, whereas not doing anything is to embrace giving up and accepting fate. However, all of this focus on agency and autonomy is projected against a backdrop of what has been called 'ageing without agency', the fourth age, to which we now turn.

The fourth age

The term 'the fourth age' has also gained widespread recognition within social gerontology, even if there is still considerable debate about what exactly it represents (Wahl and Ehni, 2020). The term itself is generally attributed to Peter Laslett (1996), where it functioned as a contrast to the more aspirational third age, already discussed. For Laslett, the fourth age is an age 'of dependence and decrepitude' where people become merely 'passengers or encumbrances' (Laslett, 1996, p 194). The significance of this term, therefore, lies in the way that it provides a contrast between a positive conception of later life and a negative one dominated by ill health, impairment and dependency. As we have seen, improvements in health, as well as increases in life expectancy in high-income countries, have given rise to the transformation of retirement from its position as a 'tragedy' (Townsend,

1963) into a potentially desirable post-work stage of life. However, this representation of later life sits uncomfortably with the needs of those whose significant age-related limitations mean that they indeed do need care and do indeed need the intervention of social and health services (Higgs and Gilleard, 2014).

That there needs to be a distinction between a 'vital' old age and a later, more dependent old age was identified in the accounts of Bernice Neugartern (1974) and Matilda White Riley (Suzman and Riley, 1985), two of the key thinkers of 20th-century sociology of ageing. Similarly, explicitly using the distinction between the third and fourth age, Paul Baltes, a gerontologist particularly interested in the plasticity of the older brain, thought that while those in the third age had the capacity to successfully age, those aged over 80 had much poorer prospects. He wrote: 'As demographers celebrate each month gained in the lives of the oldest-old, researchers focused on improving quality of life worry about the associated increase in the gap between longevity and vitality' (Baltes, 2006, p 38).

This view of the fourth age connects with another idea that has come to typify the oldest ages, namely the concept of 'frailty'. This term has emerged as a key concept in the bifurcation of later life, given that it has moved from a 'catch-all' word indicating vulnerability to a clinical measure (Fillit, Rockwood and Young, 2016). The rise of frailty to clinical prominence has led to the development of various scales and indices that differ on whether it is a separate syndrome or is in fact an aggregate condition of vulnerability and risk. Differences aside, what they share in common is an approach that sets those categorised on the terminal trajectory. For Fried, frailty is an age-related syndrome of multi-system failure that is distinct from disease and disability. Critically, it is 'irreversible and presage[s] death' (Fried et al, 2001, p 154). Importantly, frailty as a biomedical construct relates not only to physical weakness (and, increasingly, cognitive decline) but also to individual and social 'failure'. Frailty questions the capacity of the person so categorised to be a competent social actor or have an agentic social identity. It is therefore one of the vectors that Higgs and Gilleard (2015) identify as underpinning the 'social imaginary' of the fourth age. This use of the term social imaginary is important because it draws attention to the fact that categories such as frailty are not merely clinical concepts but also represent a constituent part of a 'feared' old age of dependency and lack. The social imaginary of the fourth age also explains why many older people make considerable efforts to distance themselves from forms of institutionalised care (Gilleard and Higgs, 2017).

The lifestyle identities thrown up by the cultures of the third age seek to separate themselves from the taints of dependency that underpin the fourth age and can be seen to be part of the 'othering' of old age that orientates many contemporary debates on ageism (Higgs and Gilleard,

2020). An example of this has been apparent in aspects of the COVID-19 pandemic. When the quarantining of the 70+ age category was proposed in some European countries to protect them from the virus, there was a noticeable reaction among some sections of older people who resented finding themselves categorised as 'vulnerable' on the basis of their age alone. Some argued that they were fitter than those who might be younger, but who had not adopted healthy lifestyles. On the other side, many societies witnessed the 'fourth ageism' that led to the residents of nursing homes experiencing not only much higher death rates than the rest of the population but also the deeming of their lives to be less important than the availability of hospital beds for other members of the population (Higgs and Gilleard, 2021). We now turn to the idea of 'personhood' and its role in discussions of agency in old age.

Personhood and agency

That personhood is conditional in the fourth age projects one of the important lines of demarcation between later life in the third age and the more bounded experiences brought about by frailty and cognitive impairment. In a culture that puts a high value on agency, autonomy and choice in the construction of individual identities and narratives, the narratives of those defined by the fourth age switch from the first person to the third person (Higgs and Gilleard, 2016b). Assessments and decisions on some of the most important aspects of an individual's life are generally made by others, imputing what is in their 'best interests' and coordinating these with what resources are available (something that will be discussed in Chapter 8). Certainly, while these decisions reflect moral frameworks wishing to provide good care, they are ones that reflect the transformation of agency and autonomy into something that is much more limited. The struggles over agency can be represented as a reflection of character or impairment, but it is the professional or the carer who has the power to frame the narrative to others. Even when the relationship between the older person and the carer is framed as reciprocal there is a fundamental asymmetry that in the presence of frailty or cognitive impairment prevents equal exchange and reciprocity. At its best, reciprocity may be maintained only by the older person ceding power to the carer. The disability movement recognises this lack of real agency and views the ideas of care offered to older people as fundamentally flawed (Kelly, 2020). Consequently, the desire to promote person–centred care in discourses of social care is an attempt to overcome the restrictions to agency brought about by social care itself. Tom Kitwood posited that 'a malign social psychology' excluded those with dementia from society by not accepting their position as persons in their own right. He argued that the dominance of the discourses of autonomy and rationality in contemporary societies undermined the moral recognition of people with mental impairments and should therefore be rejected as the basis for attributions of personhood (Kitwood, 1997). Following on from this, Kitwood argued for the fundamental importance of relationships and moral solidarity in the constitution of personhood. Personhood should be recognised, according to this view, irrespective of the capacities of the individual concerned. This notion of personhood has subsequently become a touchstone in articulating a theoretical basis for health and social care for older people. Unfortunately, policies designed to demonstrate person-centred care have, in time, become markers of 'good' care, while the absence of such indicators indicates 'bad' care. As a result, 'demonstrating' such a policy can come to be more important than actually providing it.

In addition, acknowledging the personhood of older people has also to attend to the problem that the idea becomes meaningful only in the context of its status as a proxy for an unproblematic realisation of personhood. Personhood itself is generally understood in terms of the agency of a person and has an inherent moral dimension. A person is assumed to be able to accept responsibility for their actions, and it is accepted that there is an interrelationship between agency, identity and selfhood (Higgs and Gilleard, 2016a). Where this is missing, in part or in full, as in the case of a person with dementia, there is an implicit assumption that there are 'degrees of personhood' (see Chapter 10). While this may not undermine their rights as a person, it may affect the application of any set of legal rights, or at least make them conditional. The conditionality of personhood as an outcome of negotiation is 'part and parcel' of health and social care; however, it does challenge approaches based on the linking of personhood with an extension of the idea of citizenship (Bartlett and O'Connor, 2010). This view is close to views in critical gerontology, as it identifies those with dementia as representing part of a frail 'precariat' defined by their precarious existence in society (Grenier, Lloyd and Phillipson, 2017). A criticism of this approach is that personhood-centred approaches fail to distinguish between the standing of persons and the capabilities of personhood. One is a moral category of self-hood, with all its connections to personal agency and autonomy, whereas the other is a status rather than having the intrinsic aspect of being a self. Sustaining the personhood of individuals with dementia often then becomes the responsibility of others who have to take on the tasks of creating agency on their behalf. This is often a double-edged sword, given that if the agency imputed to personhood is not evident, it can be seen as creating the 'malign social psychology' described by Kitwood (1997).

While this conundrum is particularly present in the context of the institutional care of people with dementia, it is also present in other fields such as the legal system, clinical practice and the organisation of health and social care. Each of these sectors finds itself engaged in operationalising personhood as well as deciding what constitutes agency, choice or autonomy in the context of criteria of capacity and capability. As a result, while the role of agency and autonomy may be one of the more discussed topics in social care, it is not so often directly connected to debates on reflexivity and agency that feature so highly in discussions of the third age. For critical gerontology, it also poses questions regarding how to facilitate a genuine appreciation of the intent behind person-centred care as well as ensuring that respect for the care of individuals as persons is emphasised rather than being turned into institutionalised procedures.

In the context of the fourth age, what this discussion of personhood illustrates is that different expressions of agency and autonomy operate across the whole field of ageing, sometimes at cross-purposes to one another. Not only do we discover a greater role for personal responsibility in health and personal care services, but it is also the case that there are now many policy inducements encouraging the desirability of both personal and individualised packages of care that can be brought into existence by a diversity of providers. Often there has been a corresponding emphasis on the promotion of 'autonomy' and the benefits of 'self-management'. It is important to be aware that some of the policies put forward under this aegis can lead to negative consequences. The 'responsibilisation' agenda and its impact on older people has been studied by Clotworthy (2020) in terms of what she describes as the shift to the 'competition state', whereby the health and social problems impacting on some older Danes are understood in terms of individualised 're-enablement'. A major issue is the 'intractability' of some of the health-related limitations that older discharged hospital patients experience. This failure of 're-enablement' is problematic for many frail older people and demonstrates the reality of notions of agency and choice in the context of a 'limited' ageing occurring in a reflexive and individualised environment. Policies may appear to be developed to improve the lives of older people, but may instead push them further into situations where their 'agency' is predetermined and oppressive. It could be argued that the processes of individualisation are now being realised through the effects of policy developments in the provision of different welfare services. The replacement of generalised practices of care with more personalised, assessment-based 'care packages' has transformed the experience of old age into one where agency is limited to the role of the 'proxy consumer' rather than the person themselves. The argument that this is allowing for the operation of freedom and choice is undermined by the sheer complexity of these arrangements, as well as the reality of a lack of providers from whom to make real choices. It is therefore ironic that the consequence of the individualisation of care often leads to an increase in the intensity of home-based care, as well as a restriction of institutional care to those with the least ability to look after their own needs.

Conclusion

This chapter has sought to foreground the issues of agency and autonomy in the construction of contemporary ageing. It has been argued that these terms relate to the concepts of reflexivity and individualisation; ones that correspond to key aspects of the cultural field of the third age as well as the social imaginary of the fourth age. This conceptualisation of the changed nature of old age goes beyond seeing this part of the lifecourse as simply heterogeneous; rather, it attempts to understand the impact of social and cultural change on the nature of old age as well as the contribution that successive generations of older people have had on the experience of later life. It also gives us the opportunity to appreciate the role of agency and autonomy. Such an approach differs considerably from the ways that many critical gerontologists have conceptualised later life. The residual status of an old age framed by social and health policy has been a touchstone for many critical gerontologists. The negative status of older people, whether as 'structurally dependent' or in the denial of full rights as citizens, has resulted in many critical gerontologists perceiving old age only as a site of injustice and inequality. This has considerable power in terms of describing aspects of contemporary ageing. However, it does limit awareness of other issues such as the concepts discussed in this chapter in creating the context in which ageing and old age occur. This is not to decry the political ambitions of critical gerontology, but it becomes more and more the case that in order to make the argument for a truly critical gerontology there needs to be a re-evaluation of old age as a more or less unitary category. While there has been much awareness of the differences and divisions among older people, and while there have been attempts to develop an intersectional approach (Holman and Walker, 2021), there is a reluctance to let go of this notional unified category of old age. This ultimately undermines the critical potential of critical gerontology. It cuts itself off not only from considering some of the most important changes to later life that have occurred over the past several decades but also from engaging with the full diversity of experiences and inequalities that are now better understood as intersecting rather than being reducible to one principal cause or with one prefigured outcome. Globalisation, culture, class, gender, household structure, religion, disability and sexuality provide a non-exhaustive list of ways that ageing can be structured in multiply different ways. They also provide more contexts in which the issues of agency and autonomy can be thought about than it is possible to cover in one short chapter. For critical gerontology, the task is to be truly radical in the way that it considers the variety of changes to old age. Doing this may mean being open to the sometimes contradictory nature of aspects of later life; contradictions that can complicate a picture that has sustained much of the critical impulse in gerontology but which now needs updating.

References

Baltes, P. (2006) 'Facing our limits: human dignity in the very old', *Daedalus*, 135(1): 32–39.

Bartlett, R. and O'Connor, D. (2010) *Broadening the Dementia Debate: Toward Social Citizenship*, Bristol: Policy Press.

Bauman, Z. (2013) *The Individualized Society*, Cambridge: Policy Press.

Beck, U. and Beck-Gernsheim, E. (2002) *Institutionalized Individualism and its Social and Political Consequences*, London: Sage.

Boltanski, L. and Chiapello, E. (2005) *The New Spirit of Capitalism*, London: Verso.

Bülow, M.H. and Söderqvist, T. (2014) 'Successful ageing: a historical overview and critical analysis of a successful concept', *Journal of Aging Studies*, 31: 139–149.

Calasanti, T.M., Calasanti, T.M. and Slevin, K.F. (2001) *Gender, Social Inequalities, and Aging*, Oxford: Rowman Altamira.

Calhoun, C. (2006) 'The privatization of risk', *Public Culture*, 18(2): 257–263.

Carey, M. (2016) 'Journey's end? From residual service to newer forms of pathology, risk aversion and abandonment in social work with older people', *Journal of Social Work*, 16(3): 344–361.

Clarke, J., Newman, J., Smith, N., Vidler, E. and Westmarland, L. (2007) *Creating Citizen-Consumers: Changing Publics and Changing Public Services*, London: Sage.

Clarke, L.H. (2010) *Facing Age: Women Growing Older in Anti-aging Culture*, Plymouth: Rowman & Littlefield Publishers.

Clotworthy, A. (2020) *Empowering the Elderly? How 'Help to Self-Help' Health Interventions Shape Ageing and Eldercare in Denmark* (Vol. 20), Bielefeld: Transcript Verlag.

Duner, A., Bjälkebring, P. and Johansson, B. (2019) 'Merely a rhetorical promise? Older users' opportunities for choice and control in Swedish individualised home care services', *Ageing & Society*, 39(4): 771–794.

Fillit, H., Rockwood, K. and Young, J. (2016) 'Introduction: aging, frailty and geriatric medicine', in H.M. Fillit, K. Rockwood and J. Young (eds) *Brocklehurst's Textbook of Geriatric Medicine and Gerontology*, Philadelphia: Elsevier Health Sciences, pp 1–3.

Foucault, M. (1991) *The Foucault Effect: Studies in Governmentality*, Chicago: University of Chicago Press.

Fried, L.P., Tangen, C.M., Walston, J., Newman, A.B., Hirsch, C., Gottdiener, J. and McBurnie, M.A. (2001) 'Frailty in older adults: evidence for a phenotype', *The Journals of Gerontology Series A: Biological Sciences and Medical Sciences*, 56(3): M146–M157.

Giddens, A. (1991) *Modernity and Self-Identity: Self and Society in the Late Modern Age*, Cambridge: Polity Press.

Gilleard, C. and Higgs, P. (1998) 'Old people as users and consumers of healthcare: a third age rhetoric for a fourth age reality?', *Ageing & Society*, 18(2): 233–248.

Gilleard, C. and Higgs, P. (2005) *Contexts of Ageing: Class, Cohort and Community*, Cambridge: Polity.

Gilleard, C. and Higgs, P. (2011a) 'The third age as a cultural field', in D. Carr, K. Komp and S. Kunkel (eds) *Gerontology in the Era of the Third Age: New Challenges and Opportunities*, New York: Springer Publishing, pp 33–49.

Gilleard, C. and Higgs, P. (2011b) 'Consumption and aging', in R.A. Settersten and J.L. Angel (eds) *Handbook of the Sociology of Aging*, New York: Springer, pp 361–375.

Gilleard, C. and Higgs, P. (2014) *Ageing, Corporeality and Embodiment*, London: Anthem Press.

Gilleard, C. and Higgs, P. (2017) 'An enveloping shadow: the role of the nursing home in the social imaginary of the Fourth Age', in S. Chivers and U. Kriebernegg (eds) *Care Home Stories: Aging, Disability and Long-term Residential Care*, Bielefeld: Transcript, pp 229–246.

Grenier, A. (2012) *Transitions and the Lifecourse: Challenging the Constructions of 'Growing Old'*, Bristol: Policy Press.

Grenier, A., Lloyd, L. and Phillipson, C. (2017) 'Precarity in late life: rethinking dementia as a "frailed" old age', *Sociology of Health & Illness*, 39(2): 318–330.

Grenier, A., Phillipson, C., Rudman, D.L., Hatzifilalithis, S., Kobayashi, K. and Marier, P. (2017) 'Precarity in late life: understanding new forms of risk and insecurity', *Journal of Aging Studies*, 43: 9–14.

Higgs, P. and Gilleard, C. (2014) 'Frailty, abjection and the "othering" of the fourth age', *Health Sociology Review*, 23(1): 10–19.

Higgs, P. and Gilleard, C. (2015) 'Fitness and consumerism in later life', in E. Tulle, and C. Phoenix (eds) *Physical Activity and Sport in Later Life*, London: Palgrave Macmillan, pp 32–42.

Higgs, P. and Gilleard, C. (2016a) *Personhood, Identity and Care in Advanced Old Age*, Bristol: Policy Press.

Higgs, P. and Gilleard, C. (2016b) 'Interrogating personhood and dementia', *Aging & Mental Health*, 20(8): 773–780.

Higgs, P. and Gilleard, C. (2020) 'The ideology of ageism versus the social imaginary of the fourth age: two differing approaches to the negative contexts of old age', *Ageing & Society*, 40(8): 1617–1630.

Higgs, P. and Gilleard, C. (2021) 'Fourth ageism: real and imaginary old age', *Societies*, 11(1): 12.

Hudson, R.B. and Gonyea, J.G. (2012) 'Baby boomers and the shifting political construction of old age', *The Gerontologist*, 52(2): 272–282.

Holman, D. and Walker, A. (2021) 'Understanding unequal ageing: towards a synthesis of intersectionality and life course analyses', *European Journal of Ageing*, 18(2): 239–255.

Hyde, M. and Higgs, P. (2016) *Ageing and Globalisation*, Bristol: Policy Press.

Jones, I.R. and Higgs, P.F. (2010) 'The natural, the normal and the normative: contested terrains in ageing and old age', *Social Science & Medicine*, 71(8): 1513–1519.

Jones, I.R., Hyde, M., Victor, C., Wiggins, D., Gilleard, C. and Higgs, P. (2008) *Ageing in a Consumer Society: From Passive to Active Consumption in Britain*, Bristol: Policy Press.

Jones, I.R., Higgs, P. and Ekerdt, D.J. (eds) (2011) *Consumption and Generational Change: The Rise of Consumer Lifestyles*, New Jersey: Transaction Publishers.

Kelly, C. (2020) 'Directly funded home care for older adults', in K. Aubrecht, C. Kelly and C. Rice (eds) *The Aging–Disability Nexus*, Vancouver: University of British Columbia Press, pp 97–112.

Kitwood, T.M. (1997) *Dementia Reconsidered: The Person Comes First*, Buckingham: Open University Press.

Laslett, P. (1996) *A Fresh Map of Life* (2nd edn), Basingstoke: Macmillan.

Levene, A. (2009) 'Between less eligibility and the NHS: the changing place of Poor Law hospitals in England and Wales, 1929–39', *Twentieth Century British History*, 20(3): 322–345.

Neugarten, B.L. (1974) 'Age groups in American society and the rise of the young-old', *The Annals of the American Academy of Political and Social Science*, 415(1): 187–198.

Phillipson, C. (2021) 'Austerity and precarity: individual and collective agency in later life', in A. Grenier, C. Phillipson and R.A. Settersten Jr (eds) *Precarity and Ageing: Understanding Insecurity and Risk in Later Life*, Bristol: Policy Press, pp 215–236.

Pickard, S. (2013) 'A new political anatomy of the older body? An examination of approaches to illness in old age in primary care', *Ageing and Society*, 33(6): 964–987.

Polivka, L. (2011) 'Neoliberalism and postmodern cultures of aging', *Journal of Applied Gerontology*, 30(2): 173–184.

Polivka, L. and Luo, B. (2020) 'From precarious employment to precarious retirement: Neoliberal health and long-term care in the United States', in A. Grenier, C. Phillipson and R.A. Settersten Jr (eds) *Precarity and Ageing: Understanding Insecurity and Risk in Later Life*, Bristol: Policy Press, pp 191–214.

Rosa, H. (2013) *Social Acceleration: A New Theory of Modernity*, New York: Cambridge University Press.

Rowe, J.W. and Kahn, R.L. (2015) 'Successful aging: conceptual expansions for the 21st century', *The Journals of Gerontology: Series B*, 70(4): 593–596.

Rubinstein, R.L. and de Medeiros, K. (2015) ' "Successful aging", gerontological theory and neoliberalism: a qualitative critique', *The Gerontologist*, 55(1): 34–42.

Scheubel, B. (2013) 'Bismarck's Pension System', in B. Scheubel (ed) *Bismarck's Institutions: A Historical Perspective on the Social Security Hypothesis*, Tübingen: Mohr Siebeck, pp 77–104.

Suzman, R. and Riley, M.W. (1985) 'Introducing the "oldest old"', *Milbank Memorial Fund Quarterly*, 63(2): 177–186.

Townsend, P. (1963) *The Family Life of Old People: An Inquiry in East London*, Harmondsworth: Penguin.

Trattner, W.I. (2007) *From Poor Law to Welfare State: A History of Social Welfare in America*, New York: Simon and Schuster.

Vincent, J.A. (2009) 'Ageing, anti-ageing, and anti-anti-ageing: who are the progressives in the debate on the future of human biological ageing?', *Medicine Studies*, 1: 97–208.

Wahl, H.W. and Ehni, H.J. (2020) 'Advanced old age as a developmental dilemma: an in-depth comparison of established fourth age conceptualizations', *Journal of Aging Studies*, 55: 100896.

5

Poverty and late-life homelessness

Amanda Grenier and Tamara Sussman[1]

Responses to poverty, inequality and marginalisation are at the heart of critical approaches to social work and ageing. However, the boundaries being drawn around gerontological social work in education and practice tend to focus on health and on professional issues of assessment and service delivery, with limited connections to either critical gerontology or structural social work. Analysing responses to poverty and late-life homelessness from a critical perspective can explain how these gaps emerged, and situate a more clearly articulated critical gerontological social work approach in research, education and practice.

Homelessness among older people is on the rise across international contexts such as the United States (US), Canada, Europe and Australia (Crane et al, 2005; Gaetz et al, 2016). Some estimates suggest that the numbers of older people who are homeless have grown by 20 per cent in the early 2000s (Crane and Joly, 2014). Although many factors contribute to this rise in late-life homelessness, many of the antecedents can be attributed to service provision, lifelong poverty and social crises such as trauma, family breakdown and mental health/substance challenges (Brown et al, 2016).

---

[1] **Amanda Grenier** is Professor and the Norman and Honey Schipper Chair in Gerontological Social Work at the Factor-Inwentash Faculty of Social Work, University of Toronto, and Baycrest Hospital in Canada. Amanda is an interdisciplinary scholar and critical gerontologist focused on the interface of public policies, organisational practices and older people's lived experience, with a particular focus on ageing and inequality. She currently leads a SSHRC Insight Grant on Precarious Aging. Her recent work includes *Late Life Homelessness: Experiences of Disadvantage and Unequal Aging* (McGill Queens University Press, 2021) and *Precarity and Ageing: Understanding Insecurity and Risk in Later Life*, which she has co-edited with Chris Phillipson and Richard A. Settersten Jr (Policy Press, 2021). **Tamara Sussman** is Associate Professor in the School of Social Work at McGill University in Canada. Her programme of research aims to uncover the ways in which health service systems can exacerbate rather than alleviate distress, exclusion and disadvantage for older persons and their families. Tamara's contributions have been increasingly directed towards examining and improving experiences of living and dying within the context of long-term care, an aspect of the service system fraught with challenges.

Population ageing combined with concerns about growing inequalities between those ageing in poverty or disadvantage and those with more advantageous economic circumstances demands insights from critical social work approaches and active strategies for systematic change.

While there is a strong radical tradition in social work (see Fook, 1993; Leonard, 1997; Healy, 2000), and a related critical feminist focus on social care operating at the peripheries of social gerontology (see Sevenhuijsen, 2003; Baines, 2007; Armstrong and Braedley, 2013), these areas of research and scholarship have seldom been taken up directly in gerontological social work education and practice. Critical social work theories have evolved in child welfare, housing and immigration, but gerontological social work tends to be configured as a medically dominated and professionally defined field with little account for how systems of care and inequality shape the experiences of older people (see Hartford Program and Council for Social Work Education for a North American articulation of gerontological social work).[2] Gerontological social work seems to have replicated the focus on biomedicalised ageing, health issues and/or a professional and applied approach to service delivery that is apparent in the field of ageing (Estes, 1979). In so doing, the boundaries of gerontological social work education and practice, such as those found in the US, mainly overlook structural issues of poverty and homelessness. Yet, social work caseloads include large numbers of older people who are poor and insecurely housed, and much of the research on late-life homelessness is carried out by social work scholars (McDonald et al, 2007; Gonyea et al, 2010; Grenier, 2021). There is, however, a visible gap between the 'gerontological social work' agenda and the lived experiences of older people from marginalised groups. This results in missed opportunities to connect how systems of care and organisational practices unequally impact on the lives of older people who experience poverty and homelessness, as well as the development of a critical social work agenda that would better prepare students for the realities of work in this field.

This chapter argues that addressing the needs of marginalised or underserved populations of older people requires the development of a closer link between knowledge in critical gerontology, radical social work and gerontological

---

[2] The practice of gerontological social work is most clearly defined in the US, where gerontological social work training initiatives emerged primarily from funding through the Hartford Partnership Program for Aging Education, which provides schools of social work with the means to develop specialised field practicums and scholarships in the fields of ageing and health (www.johnahartford.org/about). Aligned with this, the Council on Social Work Gero-Ed Centre leads the development of teaching modules, resources and competence measures for gerontological social work, primarily in the areas of care, health and vulnerability.

social work. First, it examines how social work and allied fields have constructed and approached the problems of ageing, poverty and care and, in doing so, placed these issues outside the peripheries of gerontological social work. Second, it draws on research on late-life homelessness to highlight how poverty, inequality and housing reflect changing conditions and shifting contexts of care that are relatively unaddressed in existing gerontological social work education and practice. Third, it outlines the need to develop a critical gerontological social work agenda that accurately accounts for and advocates for change.

The development of social work and gerontological social work

The history of gerontological social work cannot be separated from the development of social work more generally. Social work is intricately positioned between care and control, particularly for those deemed to be poor and/or from disadvantaged groups. The early development of social work practice responded directly to issues of poverty (and homelessness) through in- and out-of-home care. For example, the starting point for social work in English Canada was poverty relief. Influenced by the Elizabethan Poor Law of 1601, public responses to poverty were considered a last resort, and the idea that poverty was primarily a result of a flawed character prevailed. If families of the poor were not able to care for their own, relief was offered either indoors (poorhouses/almshouses) or outdoors (material support attached to conditions of eligibility and compliance with programme rules). Although programmes were not specifically designed for older people, indoor sites of relief became warehouses for older impoverished people and population groups who were deemed deserving, as they were unable due to mental health challenges or physical disabilities (Katz, 1996; Means and Smith, 1998). The historic tension, clearly exposed by radical social work, is between policy responses framed as 'care' and a means of delivery which was about the control of 'dangerous' or deviant groups, such as those in poverty due to 'deficiencies' (Leonard, 1997). Where ageing and older people are concerned, social work responses reflect tensions between care and control, and 'the problem of ageing' as it is defined through medical expertise is shifting health and social care practices (see Katz, 1996).

Many of the early social work responses of material support for poor and infirm adults ended up being directed to older people. However, older people were not considered a distinct 'population' in social work until geriatric medicine gained ground as a practice (that is, the mid-1940s in the US and 1950s in Britain and other parts of Europe), and ideas about age-based divisions were used in welfare programmes such as public pensions (for example, age 65) (Bruibaker, 2008). Gerontology is considered to have emerged as a discipline in the 1940s (Achenbaum 1995; Katz, 1996) through the development of professional societies (for example, Gerontological Society of America, International Association of Gerontology and Geriatrics), and journals such as *The Gerontologist* and *Ageing & Society* to name but a few. Sub-specialisations such as geriatric medicine and social work began to develop shortly thereafter. Perhaps unsurprisingly, the establishment of ageing as a specialised domain of social work developed from the emphasis on health, function and decline, and was consolidated through assessments of loss of function and eligibility for health and social care services. Although little is documented on how the role of social work shifted alongside policy changes, the shifts from medical and professional care in institutions to the home and community (beginning around the 1970s) (Means and Smith, 1998), and cuts to social programmes (1980s onward) (McDaniel and Gee, 1993), provide a changing landscape against which gerontological social work developed. These historical junctures represent key turning points with regard to poverty and care for older people because they illuminate how the focus on care and health was solidified through responses to older persons, and how issues of poverty, historically associated with social work, disappeared from policy and practice (Struthers, 2013).

As gerontological social work developed alongside medical interpretations of ageing and shifting health and social care programmes, the lens of poverty that was at the heart of early social work fell from the specialist articulation of gerontological social work. Such contextual forces help to explain contradictions that emerge whereby eligibility for public home care services across Canada, for example, is framed around functional decline and the absence of familial support rather than the absence of material goods. This configuration occurs despite the reality that many affluent older persons opt out of the public home care and long-term care system, and hence most older recipients of these public services have limited financial means alongside their needs for care (Tousignant et al, 2006).

Gerontological social work is a terrain shaped by medical and professional debates, and in practice contexts, attention to health, care and individual need (such as the need for assistance with meal preparation) overshadows social, cultural, political and economic understandings of ageing. In this context, gerontological social work typically refers to social work practice in long-term care homes, hospitals, rehabilitation centres and community home care, and is organised around notions of health and function rather than structural issues of poverty or disadvantage. The lens enacted through gerontological social work is medical and professional rather than focused on unmet needs resulting from the inadequacies of public services or neoliberal systems of market-based care. Yet, the failure to link gerontological social work knowledge and practice with insights from the radical tradition in social work and critical gerontology results in oversights with regard to poverty, structural issues and inadequate training for social work practice with older people.

Critical approaches to structure, poverty and care

There are at least three critical sets of literature relevant to gerontological social work as it relates to poverty and homelessness: structural social work, critical gerontology and feminist studies of care. Structural social work developed in response to the power and paternalism in social work responses (care versus control), and drew attention to how personal and social issues are rooted in political, economic, social and cultural conditions and the need to alter processes of inequality and oppression (Healy, 2000). Conveyed through books such as *Structural Social Work* (Mullaly, 1997), *Postmodern Welfare* (Leonard, 1997) and *Radical Casework* (Fook, 1993), critical social work greatly impacted on education, training and studies in the United Kingdom (UK), Canada and Australia, particularly with regard to child welfare. While ageing was often excluded from these discussions, notable exceptions existed. For example, Peter Leonard edited a series including the book *Capitalism and the Construction of Old Age* by Chris Phillipson (1982) (known for critical gerontology). Later, in Canada, Neysmith (1999) wrote *Critical Issues for Social Work Practice with Aging Persons*, and in the UK, Ray (2009) bridged social work and critical perspectives on ageing through the collection entitled *Critical Issues in Social Work with Older People* (see also Ray and Phillips, 2012). These efforts suggest a blurring of boundaries by scholars affiliated with critical gerontology and social work, and a recognisable attempt to expand critical social work to include ageing.

The next strand to offer insight into the inclusion of poverty and homelessness is critical gerontology. Attention to poverty and inequality has long featured in this tradition. For example, landmark studies such as those led by Rowntree (1941) and Townsend (1979) focused on poverty among families and older people in the UK. Writing in the contexts of the US and Europe, Estes and colleagues (2003) outline how the 1980s saw the development of critical gerontology as concerned with the need for a clearer understanding of the 'social construction of dependency' in old age. The development of welfare state services; the financial impoverishment of a large section of older people; the systematic stereotyping of older people (ageism); the dominance of a biomedical model that construes age with decline and illness; and the individual focus on gerontology that paid insufficient attention to social stratification and socioeconomic structures were all illuminated by these scholars. Where critical gerontology provided social work academics with foundations for the analysis of social, cultural, economic and political issues of ageing, the linkages tended to remain at the individual or educational programme level. The professional and educational streams through which gerontological social work knowledge is conveyed and implemented say very little about critical perspectives, nor about examples such as poverty or homelessness. For example, the Social Work Licensure Organization in the US defines Gerontological Social Workers as 'experts at meeting the biopsychosocial needs of older adults' and suggests that such social workers 'may need to assess functional capacity' and should have 'expertise in recognizing the difference between normal and pathological ageing' (SocialWorkLicensure.org).

The third strand of knowledge relevant for understanding the relationship between structures and marginalised experiences of ageing can be found in feminist approaches to care, under the rubrics of social care or the ethics of care. Here, there is some synergy between radical/structural traditions of social work and strong feminist scholarship, particularly in Canada and Nordic countries (Neysmith, 1999; Sevenhuijsen, 2003; Baines, 2007; Armstrong and Braedley, 2013), and similarly, a tendency to overlook ageing. Feminist scholars rendered visible the relationship between the state and the experiences of families and individuals, ethics and philosophical issues of care, the problems of care labour (paid and kin care), contradictions and service gaps and the emotional and economic impacts of providing care. They exposed, for example, how care for older people provided through home care programmes fell outside of the Canada Health Act 1984 because it was not deemed medically necessary, and thus not federally protected by principles such as universality (availability for free to all citizens based on need). Such findings, viewed in combination with the insights of radical social work and critical gerontology, reveal the political weight assigned to medically defined interpretations of ageing, the importance of functional assessments and the implications of care situated in the private and family domain. Although a number of feminist care scholars were located in schools of social work, there was little cross-over between understanding systems that affected older people and their families and the development of a formal gerontological social work agenda of education and practice. A focus on poverty and homelessness reveals the implications of these oversights for the field of gerontological social work and the development of a critical gerontological social work agenda.

Late-life homelessness: intersection of poverty and care

Late-life homelessness is on the rise as a result of population ageing, disadvantage and features such as the rising cost of housing (Crane et al, 2005; Brown et al, 2016). Late-life homelessness exists at the intersection of being older and homeless. It refers to someone who does not have stable, permanent or appropriate housing and is at a later stage of life (typically defined as 50+, due to compressed morbidity and mortality) (Grenier, 2021).

While people who are experiencing late-life homelessness are heterogeneous in terms of gender identity, immigration status, race and ability, two 'groups' have been delineated: those new to homelessness in later life and those who have aged while chronically or cyclically homeless. In all instances, the needs of older people with experiences of homelessness are poorly met – in part because homeless services and programmes have been designed for youth and persons of working age (Cohen, 1999; McDonald et al, 2007; Gonyea et al, 2010; Grenier, Barken and McGrath, 2016; and Grenier et al, 2016).

Most would agree that it is incumbent on social workers to understand and address the needs of older persons with experiences of homelessness. However, the formal configurations of gerontological social work fail to include this group and directions for practice, especially those targeting structural inequalities.[3] Factors such as poverty, unemployment, displacement, a shortage of public support and limited exit options (Gonyea et al, 2010; Grenier, 2021) may sustain and/or cause at-risk groups to fall into homelessness. Yet, the research and practice focus has been on responding to the biomedical issues associated with ageing and homelessness, such as improving access to shelters for persons living with frailty and adapting programmes such as day programmes or permanent housing programmes to better accommodate the intersecting needs of ageing, mental health and substance use. As such, the social work responses have been largely disconnected from critical approaches to gerontology that may call for more attention to structural issues that either propel older persons into homelessness or sustain homelessness for persons as they age.

Considering late-life homelessness in relation to early responses to poverty and care reveals a continuation of ideas expressed through 'indoor' programmes of the workhouse (organised around the capacity to work) and/or the poorhouse (as a warehouse of those without such capacity). In some ways, the shelter reflects an iteration of the indoor relief that is temporary and accompanied by a series of rules and structures, and the ideas of 'deservedness', 'deviance' and 'compliance'. This plays itself out in the myriad of rules governing shelter systems, such as the requirement to leave during the day with the expectation of seeking employment or other more permanent housing options. Hence, the idea of exiting homelessness through work prevails, despite how this reality may become less possible as one ages. Our research with older people, including men and women who had lost employment in mid-life, underscores the difficulty of returning

---

[3] In this text and elsewhere, we employ the term late-life homelessness to denote that homelessness among older people is not an individual issue, but one that has emerged from systems that have left need unmet across the lifecourse and produced and sustained homelessness (see Grenier, 2021).

to work due to age discrimination and from a location of homelessness. The implicit focus on work thus ignores the contemporary conditions of unaffordable housing, ageism and features such as eviction and displacement that are increasingly causing older people to fall into homelessness for the first time in late life. It also overlooks how the need for income security, health/mental health supports and care may alter the needs of marginalised groups of older people as they age – that is, how ageing brings about a precarity related to vulnerability across the lifecourse and the need for care (Grenier et al, 2017). And although pathways to homelessness are wide ranging, late-life homelessness is also expanding through trajectories related to evictions and loss, rising housing costs, incomes that fall below the required thresholds to pay daily bills, combined with needs for care and support (Gaetz et al, 2016).

Of course, as mentioned earlier, there are some distinctions to be made in thinking about late-life homelessness. While a range of pathways and trajectories are considered to lead to homelessness (Piat et al, 2015; Brown et al, 2016), those that have 'aged in situations of homelessness' typically relate to mental health, substance use, colonisation of Indigenous peoples and can be directly connected to changes in the provision of services (Grenier, 2021). That is, they are the same groups of 'dependent' populations (for example, people with disabilities, mental health issues and older people) who were moved into homes for the deaf/blind or disabled psychiaric facilities, and or/homes for the aged in the 1950s and removed from those institutions back into the community in the 1970s. The closure of such institutions through de-institutionalisation meant that such groups began to appear among the homeless, and, arguably, this is the group who have 'aged on the streets' (see Piat et al, 2015). De-institutionalisation and limited community supports meant few available exits from homelessness. This group not only experienced challenges in securing labour, but was also moved into a category of deviance, and blamed for the 'individual failure' to find work once homeless. Furthermore, the shortage of affordable housing amid cuts to housing and social programmes in the 1980s meant that this group continued 'ageing on the streets'. A critical analysis reveals that late-life homelessness is a function of historical policy responses (and the lack thereof). It also reveals the inherent tensions of being both deserving by means of age, undeserving by means of homelessness, and yet 'faulted' for not achieving the stability that is expected in later life.

At the moment, the configuration of late-life homelessness reflects a system whereby responses are organised to prioritise medical issues (for example, the creation of post-acute rehabilitation services for older homeless persons to expedite hospital discharge) or professional responses (geriatric profile). Access configured around medically required needs means that gerontological social workers must employ the appropriate language to advocate for their clients. In our research, for example, shelter and long-term care workers used the concept of the 'geriatric profile' to align this group with 'frail older people' as a means to qualify for public service. Hence, when seeking access to day programmes or housing services, they found ways to emphasise issues such as challenges with ambulation and the need for support with personal care. Here, this example illustrates the convergence of the medical and professional focus as the key to accessing services. Yet, the strategic use of language alone cannot guarantee access. Gaps and barriers to services are widely known to exist for older people with experiences of homelessness, and many are worsened by the age-based eligibility used to assess need and deliver programmes. Services organised around chronological age (which reflect historical approaches to poverty and care outlined earlier in the chapter), and that respond to either the needs of younger homeless people or older people who are housed, create barriers to care. For older people with experiences of homelessness, services are either unavailable or cannot be accessed due to the discrepancy between their complex health and social needs and their age. The only way to address these structural problems is by exposing them and advocating for changes to the policies and practices that exacerbate rather than address or prevent late-life homelessness. Advocating solely by using language to fit client needs into current service configurations sustains approaches that overlook older people in a broader sense, render social needs less visible and leave the structural causes related to disadvantage unrecognised and unaddressed.

Older people with experiences of homelessness are deemed to have 'complex needs' demonstrated through disparities and gaps in service (Warnes and Crane, 2000; McDonald et al, 2007) and are known to have health needs that occur approximately 10–15 years earlier than in the general population. However, a critical analysis reveals that these needs are 'complex' because they fall outside of services organised according to distinct policy domains (for example, income/retirement, labour, housing, care) and/or age-based eligibility. Welfare state structures and institutions deliver responses to poverty and care through distinct programmes such as retirement (Canada and Quebec Pension Plans, Old Age Security), policies geared toward income (disability benefits, Guaranteed Income Supplement) and through corresponding Ministries of Housing (municipal), Health or Long-term Care in the Canadian context.[4] As

---

[4] A review of historical debates suggests policy turning points and the emergence of distinct responses to poverty and care. Analysing the construction of two Canadian special committees, Struthers (2013) found that the 1963–66 and 2006–09 initiatives constructed national dialogues in two different ways, corresponding with the era in which they were written. In the 1960s the problems facing older people were framed in terms of poverty, which resulted in the creation of Guaranteed Income Supplement, implemented in 1967, whereas the 2006–09 subcommittee focused on healthy ageing and a national caregiver strategy.

such, the policy configuration and socially constructed policy divisions shape late-life homelessness, with everyday needs that are experienced in the context of people's lives unmet because they do not neatly fit within separate policy spheres. For example, the majority of services offered to older people presume that they have a home (home care, day programmes), family or can access and afford medical or residential care (long-term care or assisted living) (see Grenier, Barken and McGrath, 2016). A critical analysis gets behind the evidence of health disparities and the claim that older people with experiences of homelessness are poorly served by age and stage-based services, and into an analysis of how current responses replicate unmet need and exclusion. Take how ageing and homelessness have been constructed as separate domains of practice that overlook the possibility of lives that intersect both. This is evident in a description of how workers in long-term care are unprepared to work with formerly homeless persons. As a director of care says, 'We must not forget that the team did not choose to work with this clientele ... we're trained for the little old lady in the knitted sweater' (Sussman et al, 2020, p 1154). This comment speaks to the consequences of age-based services and of framing gerontological social work as a practice that targets older persons with health issues, over-focusing on needs related to poverty and/or marginalisation.

A critical analysis of late-life homelessness reveals contradictions experienced at the intersections of ageing, poverty and care. The limited services and supports, combined with the relegation of social care to the family/private domain means that older people with complex health needs related to homelessness can receive complicated medical treatment without the spaces and supports for rehabilitation and aftercare. Home care is the main programme for older people, and late-life homelessness presents the immediate contradiction of not having a place within which to receive care (Grenier, Barken and McGrath, 2016). So, while older people with experiences of homelessness have access to complicated medical procedures, the lack of home and informal care means that they must return post-medical care either to an institution (hospital, rehabilitation unit or nursing home care) or to the shelter system or the street. This is also the case across a range of international settings (Crane et al, 2005). The shortage of family and friends (who are presumed to step in and take responsibility for care) and the shortage of care services means that older people with experiences of homelessness fall between the cracks of service (Gonyea et al, 2010). This is both a systemic issue and an organisational-level concern because most shelters are not equipped to deal with physical care demands. Yet again, contradictions reveal how the dominant focus on medical and professional issues overshadows the intersections of ageing, poverty and care.

Importance of a critical gerontological social work agenda

Contemporary features such as population ageing, the dismantling of social programmes, precarious lifecourse trajectories, the costs of housing relative to income and unmet care needs signal the need for the development of a stronger critical gerontological social work agenda. Our research on late-life homelessness suggests that deepening inequality will require more thoughtful responses to policy and gerontological social work education and practice. Certainly, the analysis in this chapter echoes the concern about ageing and marginalisation, and the problems of defining gerontological social work through a biomedical, health and professional response at the expense of addressing social, economic and political issues. It has revealed that the attention and response to poverty have gone missing from social work over time, and has highlighted the missed opportunities to link the study of social structures, organisational practices and the lives of older people living at the margins. The current context of COVID-19 has laid bare the challenges that exist at the intersections of ageing and locations such as poverty and homelessness. It has drawn attention to long-existing disparities and gaps in policy, education and practice. Yet, promising initiatives also exist. In recent years, for example, the International Federation of Social Work has pushed for greater attention to inequality and social justice, which holds potential for conversations and practices more closely aligned with the critical focus outlined in this chapter. It has yet to be seen, however, how such macro-level initiatives will trickle down to gerontological social work, education and practice across international contexts.[5]

Our analysis reveals that taking account of disadvantage, poverty and marginalisation experienced by older people is a critical next step. In order to be effective with regard to poverty and homelessness, gerontological social work must include knowledge of how older people living in poverty or with experiences of homelessness are impacted upon by structures and social relations over time. The established literature in radical social work, critical gerontology and feminist social care offers strong foundations to understand and address the social, cultural, economic and political conditions that lead to homelessness. The well-established set of knowledge in these three areas can inform the development of a critical agenda in gerontological social work. The profession of social work is about resilience, empowerment and strengths-based practice. Emphasising 'the geriatric profile' of frailty in an effort to gain access to service for persons

[5] For more information on this agenda see www.ifsw.org/poverty-eradication-and-the-role-for-social-workers/

experiencing late-life homelessness not only stands in stark contrast to the strengths-based, empowering approach purported by the profession but does little to improve the availability of needed services that simply are not there. It also does little to expose and dismantle ideas about control and blame that lie behind service delivery that disadvantage older homeless persons such as limiting access to shelters to those with the physical strength to 'stand in the line' to secure a bed.

The interconnected issues of ageing, poverty and care must take centre stage so that late-life homelessness can be prevented or addressed. Steps that need to be taken include: ensuring the recognition of poverty and late-life homelessness as an important policy issue; developing inter-sectoral collaborations between housing services and ageing services; and building bridges between older persons experiencing poverty and/or late-life homelessness, community groups that advocate on their behalf and decision makers in housing and ageing. Such forms of recognition and alliances hold the potential to work toward joint solutions that promise to improve the circumstances of older persons experiencing homelessness or poverty. We suggest that the foundations already exist and that social workers can be well positioned for leadership in this area. To achieve this, however, requires the commitment and development of a critical gerontological social work vision, agenda and training.

Conclusion

There is much to be done to develop a more critical agenda in gerontological social work education and practice. To date, gerontological social work has focused on outlining the complex health needs of older people and developing professional guidance for functional assessment. We suggest that bodies responsible for the articulation of gerontological social work, such as the Canadian Association for Social Work Education in Canada, the Council on Social Work Education-Gero-Ed Centre in the US and the European Association of Schools of Social Work, engage in activities to redefine the boundaries of a critical gerontological social work that is inclusive of older people, and particularly older people from disadvantaged locations such as poverty and homelessness. At the moment, definitions of gerontological social work are primarily shaped within an American context, thereby missing the relationship with a universal and public welfare state, and the accompanying social and cultural constructs related to deservedness, control and care that operate within and between responses to poverty and care in late life. The failure to link with radical or structural social work, critical gerontology and feminist articulations of social care means that the work of gerontological social work tends to be applied, professional, medically dominated and empirical, rather than concerned with how systems and structures affect the lives of older people, the inclusion of diverse and marginalised voices and relational approaches to poverty and care.

Based on this analysis, and using research on homelessness as an example, we reveal the implications of historical trajectories and decisions in social work, and the missed opportunities for theory building, critical practice and training that are reflective of the realities of older people from marginalised groups. We suggest that the contemporary conditions and the realities of practice, however, necessitate a more detailed focus on ageing and inequality. There is a need for a social work agenda focused on understanding and addressing the relationship between structures, systems and older people's lives. The moment is upon us to change the direction of gerontological social work in order to look beyond individualised notions of health, professional response and blame, and the contradictions that occur for those who are simultaneously older, disadvantaged and living in poverty.

References

Achenbaum, W.A. (1995) *Crossing Frontiers: Gerontology Emerges as a Science*, New York: Cambridge University Press.

Armstrong, P. and Braedley, S. (eds) (2013) *Troubling Care: Critical Perspectives on Research and Practices*, Toronto: Canadian Scholars' Press.

Baines, D. (2007) 'Caring for/caring about: women, home care, and unpaid caregiving', *Resources for Feminist Research*, 32(3–4): 179.

Brown, R.T., Goodman, L., Guzman, D., Tieu, L., Ponath, C. and Kushel, M.B. (2016) 'Pathways to homelessness among older homeless adults: results from the HOPE HOME study', *PloS One*, 11(5): e0155065.

Bruibaker, J.K. (2008) 'The birth of a new specialty: geriatrics', *The Journal of Lancaster General Hospital*, 3(3): 105–107.

Cohen, C.I. (1999) 'Aging and homelessness', *The Gerontologist*, 39(1): 5–15.

Crane, M. and Joly, L. (2014) 'Older homeless people: increasing numbers and changing needs', *Reviews in Clinical Gerontology*, 24(4): 255–268.

Crane, M., Byrne, K., Fu, R., Lipmann, B., Mirabelli, F., Rota-Bartelink, A., Ryan, M., Shea, R. Watt, H. and Warnes, A. (2005) 'The causes of homelessness in later life: findings from a 3-nation study', *The Journals of Gerontology Series B: Psychological Sciences and Social Sciences*, 60(3): S152–S159.

Estes, C.L. (1979) *The Aging Enterprise*, San Francisco: Jossey-Bass.

Estes, C.L., Biggs, S. and Phillipson, C. (2003) *Social Theory, Social Policy and Ageing: A Critical Introduction*, Maidenhead: Open University Press.

Fook, J. (1993) *Radical Casework: A Theory of Practice*, Sydney: Allen & Unwin.

Gaetz, S., Dej, E., Richter, T. and Redman, M. (2016) *The State of Homelessness in Canada 2016*, Toronto: Canadian Observatory on Homelessness Press.

Gonyea, J.G., Mills-Dick, K. and Bachman, S.S. (2010) 'The complexities of elder homelessness, a shifting political landscape and emerging community responses', *Journal of Gerontological Social Work*, 53(7): 575–590.

Grenier, A. (2021) *Late Life Homelessness: Experiences of Disadvantage and Unequal Aging*, Montreal: McGill Queens University Press.

Grenier, A., Barken, R. and McGrath, C. (2016) 'Homelessness and aging: the contradictory ordering of "house" and "home"', *Journal of Aging Studies*, 39(December): 73–80.

Grenier, A., Barken, R., Sussman, T., Rothwell, D., Bourgeois-Guérin, V. and Lavoie, J-P. (2016) 'A literature review of homelessness and aging: suggestions for a policy and practice-relevant research agenda', *Canadian Journal on Aging*, 35(1): 28–41.

Grenier, A., Phillipson, C., Rudman, D.L., Hatzifilalithis, S., Kobayashi, K. and Marier, P. (2017) 'Precarity in late life: understanding new forms of risk and insecurity', *Journal of Aging Studies*, 43(December): 9–14.

Healy, K. (2000) *Social Work Practices: Contemporary Perspectives on Change*, London: Sage Publications.

Katz, S. (1996) *Disciplining Old Age: The Formation of Gerontological Knowledge*, Charlottesville: University of Virginia Press.

Leonard, P. (1997) *Postmodern Welfare: Reconstructing an Emancipatory Project*, London: Sage Publications.

McDaniel, S.A. and Gee, E.M. (1993) 'Social policies regarding caregiving to elders: Canadian contradictions', *Journal of Aging & Social Policy*, 5(1–2): 57–72.

McDonald, L., Dergal, J. and Cleghorn, L. (2007) 'Living on the margins: older homeless adults in Toronto', *Journal of Gerontological Social Work*, 49(1–2): 19–46.

Means, R. and Smith, R. (1998) *From Poor Law to Community Care: The Development of Welfare Services for Elderly People 1939–1971*, Bristol: Policy Press.

Mullaly, R.P. (1997) *Structural Social Work Ideology, Theory, Practice*, Toronto: McClelland & Stewart.

Neysmith, S.M. (ed) (1999) *Critical Issues for Future Social Work Practice with Aging Persons*, New York: Columbia University Press.

Phillipson, C. (1982) *Capitalism and the Construction of Old Age*, London: Macmillan International Higher Education.

Piat, M., Polvere, L., Kirst, M., Voronka, J., Zabkiewicz, D., Plante, M., Isaak, C., Nolin, D., Nelson, G. and Goering, P. (2015) 'Pathways into homelessness: understanding how both individual and structural factors contribute to and sustain homelessness in Canada', *Urban Studies*, 52(13): 2366–2382.

Ray, M. (2009) *Critical Issues in Social Work with Older People*, London: Macmillan International Higher Education.

Ray, M. and Phillips, J. (2012) *Social Work with Older People*, London: Palgrave Macmillan.

Rowntree, B.S. (1941) *Poverty and Progress: A Second Social Survey of York*, London: Longmans.

Sevenhuijsen, S. (2003) *Citizenship and the Ethics of Care: Feminist Considerations on Justice, Morality and Politics*, London: Routledge.

SocialWorkLicensure.org (nd) *Gerontological Social Workers*, [online], Available from: https://socialworklicensure.org/types-of-socialworkers/gerontologi cal-social-workers/ [Accessed 12 March 2021].

Struthers, J. (2013) 'Framing aging through the state: Canada's two Senate Committees on Aging, 1963–1966 and 2006–2009', *Canadian Review of Social Policy*, (68–69): 1–9.

Sussman, T., Barken, R. and Grenier, A. (2020) 'Supporting older homeless persons' positive relocations to long-term care: service provider views', *The Gerontologist*, 60(6): 1149–1158.

Tousignant, M., Dubuc, N., Hébert, R. and Coulome, C. (2006) 'Home-care programmes for older adults with disabilities in Canada: how can we assess adequacy of services provided compared with needs of users?', *Health and Social Care in the Community*, 15(1): 1–7.

Townsend, P. (1979) *Poverty in the United Kingdom: A Survey of Household Resources and Standards of Living*, Berkeley: University of California Press.

Warnes, A. and Crane, M. (2000) *Meeting Homeless People's Needs: Service Development and Practice for the Older Excluded*, London: King's Fund.

6

Sexuality and rights in later life

Paul Willis and Trish Hafford-Letchfield[1]

Social work is a human rights-based profession. Advocating and upholding human rights is a core activity embedded in the international definition of social work (IFSW, 2014). In the context of supporting older people, this intersects with the United Nations (UN) Principles for Older Persons (United Nations, 1991), which sets out independence, participation, self-fulfilment and dignity as principles integral to supporting older people to fully participate in society. Missing from discourses both on ageing and on human rights is an understanding of *sexual rights*. The World Association for Sexual Health (WAS) (2014) identifies 16 sexual rights as 'grounded in universal human rights'; however, social and cultural discourses compound the invisibility of older adults' sexual rights and inhibit discussion about the sexual well-being of older adults in social work practice contexts.

In this chapter we identify through a critical lens the sexual and gender discourses that limit recognition of sexual well-being in later life. As discussed in Chapter 1, critical gerontology grapples with and seeks to challenge sources of inequality, exclusion and oppression experienced by older people; sexuality is one such source of social exclusion that can

---

[1] **Paul Willis** is Associate Professor of Social Work and Social Gerontology at the University of Bristol, UK. Paul is a registered social worker and researcher in social care, ageing and social inclusion. His current research interests include loneliness, ageing and masculinities; sexuality, gender identity and ageing; and inclusive housing for older adults. Recent funded projects include social inclusion practices in housing with care and support; older men's experiences of loneliness; and health and social care for trans adults in later life. Paul is a Senior Research Fellow of the National Institute for Health Research School for Social Care Research, England. **Trish Hafford-Letchfield** is Professor of Social Work at the University of Strathclyde, UK. Her research interests are in older people from marginalised communities and their experiences of accessing and using care. Trish has more than 100 publications, with two edited books in a new series on 'Sex and Intimacy in Later Life' (titled *Sex and Diversity in Later Life* and *Desexualisation in Later Life: The Limits of Sex and Intimacy*) with Paul Simpson and Paul Reynolds (Policy Press, 2021). Recent research projects include the impact of COVID-19 on family carers of residents in care homes, and suicide prevention and ageing.

manifest in acts of discrimination, expressions of hostility and discourses of shame and silencing. In line with this critical lens, we integrate messages from recent research on older people's sexual lives to broaden social work's understanding of the diversity of sexual experiences across older age, gender, ethnicity and sexuality. An intersectional approach underpins our discussion. Age, gender, ethnicity and sexuality are interconnecting social structures for organising social life that generate inequalities in the ways in which older people from different social backgrounds are represented, understood and supported (King et al, 2019). These intersections can generate further forms of inequality, exclusion and shame for people with care and support needs. We conclude with suggestions for gerontological social workers on how to affirm and support the sexual rights and well-being of older adults.

Sexual well-being and rights: key frameworks

The World Health Organization (WHO) (2021) asserts that sexuality 'is a central aspect of being human throughout life' and that it 'encompasses sex, gender identities and roles, sexual orientation, eroticism, pleasure, intimacy and reproduction' (WHO, 2021). Furthermore, good sexual health comprises of 'a state of physical, emotional, mental and social well-being in relation to sexuality' (WHO, 2021). Across research, sexual well-being is measured in different ways. Lorimer et al (2019) identify three overarching domains: cognitive affect (for example, self-reports on sexual self-esteem and anxiety), interpersonal (such as satisfaction with sexual relationships and communication) and sociocultural (for instance, understanding well-being in relation to gender norms and stereotypes). From a critical gerontological perspective, we are interested in the *sociocultural dimensions of sexual well-being*, namely how socially endorsed notions of ageing, gender, ethnicity and older age filter contemporary understanding of older people's sexual expressions, agency, identity and relationships.

The development of sexual rights is rooted in international lobbying for greater recognition of women's reproductive rights and protection from sexual violence. The 1994 UN International Conference on Population and Development acknowledged reproductive rights and sexual health as areas for global action (Altman and Symons, 2016) alongside the WAS Declaration of Sexual Rights. Like human rights, sexual rights are universal and integral to the maintenance of health and well-being. While age is mentioned in the context of equality and non-discriminatory treatment, there is no discussion of how ageing processes and structures complicate sexual agency and how to support older people's sexual desires, expressions and identities. Richardson (2000) identified three prominent strands of discourse on sexual rights: (1) rights to participate in sexual activities and practices; (2) rights to self-define, claim and express individual identities, inclusive of lesbian, gay, bisexual and queer (LGBQ)[2] identities; and (3) rights recognised by public and social institutions and the state recognition of stigmatised relationships. All three represent areas often denied to or disassociated from older people's lives, particularly older adults with care and support needs or perceived as vulnerable. Accordingly, we next discuss key concepts and theories for developing a critical understanding of discourses that confound a more affirming understanding of older people's sexual rights.

Ageism and ageist erotophobia

Age as a social construction shapes the ways in which we understand and approach the sexual subjectivity of different age groups. Children are often represented as needing protection from sex and sexual desires, while for older people sex is deemed to be no longer relevant – or people become 'post-sexual' (Moore and Reynolds, 2016). Perceiving older people as sexually inactive, in sexual decline or beyond sexual desire, both as subjects of desire and as experiencing desires, is common (Simpson et al, 2017). Ageist expressions convey negative, dismissive or degrading beliefs and attitudes about older people and are expressed in covert and subtle ways (Gendron et al, 2016). In the context of sex and sexuality, older people in Global North societies are either denied sexual agency or the subjects of ridicule and disgust. Another ageist belief is the presumption that frailty and disability prevent the enjoyment of sexual activity. Further, the lack of attention to sexual health problems or access to sexual health information and treatments reinforces attitudes of shame and disgust (Hafford-Letchfield, 2008; Nash et al, 2015).

Ageist erotophobia, or expressions of 'disgust at the thought of ageing body-selves as sexual' (Simpson et al, 2017, p 244), can manifest through everyday cultural mediums such as the disparaging representation of older people's sexual libido on birthday cards, through to degrading practices such as the withdrawal of support to vulnerable older adults who express desires and experience arousal. Gewirtz-Meydan et al (2019) reviewed research that examined sexuality from the perspectives and personal sexual experiences of older people themselves. They found that older people internalised these ageing stigmas and spoke about the challenges they experienced with expressing their sexuality within the constraints of social conventions that inhibited them from doing so. These included the lack of professional support and the hegemony of penetrative sex. Older people's personal accounts of sex also

---

[2] We have used different abbreviations where we are discussing specific pieces of research that may or may not include trans people (LGBQ and LGBTQ). This is so we accurately reflect who is included in the research and do not misleadingly indicate that trans people were the focus of the study when this is not always the case.

convey psychological and physical benefits, including self-reports on higher quality of life (Freak-Poli and Malta, 2020). Placing older people's voices at the centre of any analysis is therefore essential for recognising the meaning of sexuality in later life. In practice, this translates to upholding their agency and applying therapeutic skills to provide a safe and sex-positive environment for older adults to express and explore key aspects of their sexual life-stories and current issues and concerns impinging on their sexual, and general, well-being.

Lifecourse perspectives on LGBQ ageing

The concept of *heteronormativity* locates heterosexuality as a normative marker of socio-sexual relationships and captures the 'myriad ways in which heterosexuality is produced as a natural, unproblematic, taken-for-granted, ordinary phenomenon' (Kitzinger, 2005, p 478). Heteronormative assumptions in social care practice render older LGBQ adults' sexual and romantic relationships, and circles of support, invisible to service providers (Almack et al, 2019). In turn, this limits older people's rights to express sexual identities outside the heterocentric norm. A commonly voiced expression by those providing care to diverse groups of older adults is that equal treatment is achieved by 'treating everybody the same'; this pervasive discourse shuts down recognition of older people's sexual lives and histories that fall outside heteronormative markers and life events (Willis et al, 2016).

Older LGBQ people's lives diverge from the life experiences of other older people because of the socio-legal history of marginalisation experienced by LGBQ citizens in the UK and many other European nations. Consequently, older LGBQ people may harbour concerns about 'risky visibility' in care environments and anticipate homophobic or biphobic expressions from care providers (Westwood, 2016). Social workers need to champion the rights of LGBQ service users in these settings and work with providers to create inclusive environments, staff practices and agency policies. This includes being attuned to the unique life histories of older LGBQ individuals if they are to build a holistic understanding of the person they are supporting. To facilitate these personal discussions a safe, affirming environment should be provided that explicitly signals to LGBQ service users that their life experiences are valued.

The concept of *accumulative disadvantage* enhances social work understanding of how historical experiences of homophobia, biphobia and sexuality-based discrimination[3] impact on LGBQ people's concerns,

---

[3] The term homophobia typically denotes hostility in attitudes, expressions and actions towards lesbian and gay people (Herek, 2004). The term biphobia captures the unique oppression bisexual people experience, which can include their sexual attractions and desires not being acknowledged or being dismissed (Obradors-Campos, 2011). We also acknowledge that many LGBQ-identifying people experience transphobic attitudes and actions based on their gender and gender identity differing from the sex assigned to them at birth.

expectations and well-being in later life. The work of Crystal and Shea (1990) identifies processes across the lifecourse by which social advantages and disadvantages accumulate and shape the material, economic and cultural resources available to people in later life. For older LGBQ people, social stressors experienced in earlier life, and associated negative coping practices (for example, smoking and alcohol consumption), can exacerbate health inequalities between LGBQ and heterosexual older people (Kneale et al, 2019). Experiences of historical marginalisation are associated with lower identity affirmation and poorer mental health (Fredriksen-Goldsen et al, 2017). A study from the Netherlands indicates that older lesbian, gay, bisexual, queer and trans (LGBTQ) people's openness about their sexual identity and life history improved the perceived quality of the relationship with formal caregivers (Pijpers, 2020). However, respondents from the same study also reported experiences of discrimination from caregivers. For older LGBQ people, previous and current experiences of discrimination from health and social care professionals deplete their trust and confidence in care providers and inhibit them from, first, accessing services and, second, disclosing their identity.

The criminalisation of homosexual acts during the 20th century has permeated the life stories of some older LGBQ people. In the UK, partial decriminalisation of sex between men was first achieved in 1967 in England and Wales (an unequal age of consent remained in place for those engaged in same-sex activity until 2001). Similar legal reforms were enacted post-Second World War in other Western European nations over different decades, such as the Swiss decriminalisation of homosexual acts in 1942 (Delessert, 2005).[4] In the UK the sexual lives of lesbians and bisexual women were not outlawed in the same way as those of men; however, the social environments in which they lived were extremely hostile to their relationships and social affiliations (Wilkins, 2015). Older LGBQ people belonging to Black ethnic minority groups will have experienced a lifetime of institutional racism and may look to members of their ethnic community for psychological support. This generates additional stressors in having to privilege racial identities over sexual identity or risk homophobic experiences across multiple communities (Seelman et al, 2016; Kum, 2017).

The personal histories of older LGBQ adults were also overshadowed by the medical classification of homosexuality as a mental disorder.

---

[4] Despite legal advances for equality across nations, a 2020 EU report reminds us that public attitudes towards LGBQ (and trans) people continue to vary considerably in levels of acceptance across member states (European Parliament, 2020). Indeed, in some member states such as Poland anti-LGBTQ measures have been recently introduced in public law; experiences of institutional oppression are not a feature of history alone.

Homosexuality was listed as a disorder under the International Classification of Diseases until 1990. Some older adults will have experienced conversion therapies to 'cure' homosexual desires – psychological therapies and treatments aimed at 'curing' same-sex attractions (King, 2019). These traumatic experiences severely cripple trust in health and public authorities, including social workers, perceived as representing the interests of the state rather than the best interests of the individual. Experiences may also vary according to ethnic background, as illustrated by findings from the UK Government Equalities Office (2018) survey of LGBTQ people (with 108,000+ respondents). Among those reporting experiences of conversion therapy, older respondents were more likely to report this (10 per cent of those aged 65+ years) than younger age groups. Furthermore, respondents identifying as Black, Asian and minority ethnic were more likely to report this than White respondents, casting light on the additional heteronormative pressures and institutional racism experienced by LGBQ people within these groups.

Queer perspectives on identity and ageing

Sexual identity categories do not reflect the diversity of older LGBQ people's lived experiences (King and Cronin, 2013). Experiences of health, well-being, social support and caring vary according to intersections across gender, ethnicity, disability and, of course, age. There is a danger that helping professionals, including social workers, attribute common features to older LGBQ people's social and intimate relationships that may, at best, disregard areas of commonality shared with other older adults or, at worst, lose focus on the individuality of older people's life-experiences (King and Cronin, 2013). Equally, identity categories do not tell us much about the sexual practices of older LGBQ adults, a topic we know little about, and how sexual experiences differ across gender, social environments and power dynamics.

Queer theory is a nebulous cluster of social and linguistic perspectives from across the humanities, education and social sciences. These perspectives are rooted in postmodernist and post-structural approaches to social identities as discursive – identity categories are understood through language and available discourse (Hicks and Jeyasingham, 2016). Queer theory 'demonstrates a concern with language and sexuality as a form of knowledge' (Hicks and Jeyasingham, 2016, p 2359). Through a queer lens, essentialist ideas about sex, gender and sexual orientation as being innate and predetermined are rejected in favour of performative approaches where, instead, these subject positions are sustained through iterative social and cultural practices (Butler, 1990). Foucault's (1998) historical analysis of the ways in which medical and legal institutions construct and perpetuate sexual types illustrates the binary between heterosexual and homosexual identities; a ubiquitous Western understanding of sexuality that serves to separate homosexual identities and desires as inferior and often invisible (Sedgwick, 1990).

Social gerontology has been slow to engage with these ideas, with some exceptions such as the work of King and Cronin (2013) and Hughes (2006). Queer perspectives invite us to consider and interrogate how other binaries that separate 'young/old' operate in parallel with the heterosexual/homosexual binary to marginalise older people's expressions of sexual desire and intimacy (Hughes, 2006). An additional binary is the cultural distinction between sexual/post-sexual that accompanies assumptions about appropriate age, sex and youthfulness. Thinking critically about these pervasive ideas facilitates a deeper awareness of 'the erotic in old age' (Hughes, 2006, p 57), expanding recognition of and support for non-penetrative expressions of sexuality between people of same and different genders in later life. While queer perspectives help to trouble ageist and normative assumptions about older age and sex, Moore and Reynolds (2016) argue that a subversive politic does not take into account corporeal dimensions to sexual agency and the ways in which issues of frailty, disability and physical decline may prevent a 'reinvention of the sexual self' (p 7). Social workers supporting older people will be familiar with the ways in which changes in physical function alter older people's everyday agency, identity and relationship experiences. The impact on older adult's sexual agency is another critical consideration.

Heterosexuality and gender in older women and men

Trends observed in later-life relationships have similarly challenged aspects of those institutions that shore up heterosexuality. UK demographic trends show that older people in England and Wales are getting married and divorced in greater numbers (taking into account the ageing population) (Office of National Statistics, 2017). These are in the context of increasing divorces and single living across the globe (Eurostat, 2020). Data from the cross-national panel database Survey of Health, Ageing and Retirement in Europe (Becker et al, 2019) demonstrated a strong positive association of being married/having a partner to well-being and mental health, in that people are seeking to maintain or extend their relationships across different network structures. Similarly, Clouston et al (2014) found that individuals in marital partnerships had higher physical function than those who remained single or were divorced. Rising trends such as cohabitation, living alone together and singlehood operate as alternatives to marriage for older adults and are increasingly replacing remarriage following divorce or widowhood (Brown et al, 2017). Identifying the consequences of these different trends is significant for gerontological social work when assessing and designing support. This includes access to caregivers, given that spouses historically have been the primary source of care (Brown et al, 2017).

Research into the sexual health and well-being of men and women in later life in the UK (Lee et al, 2016) shows increasing expectations concerning sexual fulfilment. At the same time, there are dominant if not restricted ways of thinking about the sexual pleasure of heterosexual older people, framed by gender stereotypes. The sexuality of older women may become constrained by biological changes, understood through cultural pathology as decline and loss of attractiveness, and the moral constraints of being a good wife/partner and/or mother/grandmother. This is beginning to change for those of the baby boomer generation. They will have encountered the countervailing influences of feminism (Bassnett, 2012) in politics, education and work experience and loosening social attitudes towards sex, particularly outside of marriage (Gilleard and Higgs, 2007). While it is encouraging to see these social scripts being reinvented for older women, double standards persist whereby women face moral censure for transgressing an approved ageing femininity (Gewirtz-Meydan et al, 2019). Those heterosexual men and women wishing to continue with penetrative sex but experiencing challenges may need sensitive information about erectile dysfunction and vaginal dryness (as well as physical health, for example, cardiology and respiratory complications) and require support for the impacts on their psychological and social well-being (for example, loneliness and depression) (Hughes et al, 2015).

Older women who lack power in sexual relationships experience less sexual self-efficacy and partner negotiation, impacting on their practice of safe sex (Meyer et al, 2020). Poor engagement of care professionals with their issues and concerns makes the situation more complex and discriminatory (Hafford-Letchfield, 2008). Lee et al's (2016) research showed that a significant proportion of older men remain sexually active into their 70s and 80s. However, when men do experience difficulties, for example with erectile dysfunction, medical and pharmaceutical interventions are typical, focusing on restoring penetrative sexual activities (Gledhill and Schweitzer, 2014). Sexual decline is considered more challenging for men, given fears of loss of status and their greater reluctance than women to seek help, putting their sexual health at risk (Gewirtz-Meydan et al, 2019).

There is a higher incidence of sexual health problems reported among Black and minority ethnic older women (Asiedu et al, 2017). In the UK those of Black African ethnicity carry a disproportionate percentage of HIV, with 38 per cent of new diagnoses among heterosexual Black African men and women (Public Health England, 2019). Within the European Union, in 2015, migrants (including refugees) represented 27 per cent of people newly diagnosed with HIV in the region (18 per cent were non-European migrants), providing evidence on inequities for these groups related to their state of health and the accessibility and quality of health services available to them (WHO, 2017).

Experiencing a sexual difficulty can be a source of distress and relationship disruption, and depression has been reported by people experiencing sexual difficulties in mid-to-late adulthood (Hinchliff et al, 2018). Self-reports of poorer mental health are associated with declines in desire and the frequency of sexual activity among older people, highlighting how physical health and sexual well-being are intertwined and are therefore important to address in social work practice (Jackson et al, 2019). Social workers must assess how changes or fluctuations in mental and sexual well-being impact on the intimate relationships of older service users and must be prepared to explore what these difficulties may be. Older heterosexual people will benefit from discussion of alternatives to penetrative sexual practices, helping to resolve accompanying feelings of disappointment and self-blame (O'Brien et al, 2012). Many older persons have learned to approach sex in a more sensual way, and intimacy can become more important, for example, through kissing, touch and physical closeness (previously regarded as 'foreplay' but now central to the sexual/intimate repertoire).

Older adults increasingly have expectations that care and nursing homes will accommodate couples and sexual intimacy, including private bedrooms, shared beds and access to safer sex materials (Nash et al, 2015; Rahn et al, 2020). While care homes are communal environments, the need for separate and comfortable spaces that uphold the privacy and dignity of residents and their intimate partners of all sexual and gender identities is a core requirement. One Spanish study highlights barriers to upholding privacy for sexual activity in care facilities – these included the design of facilities and lack of individual bedrooms and bathrooms, and the standardised structure of daily routine and communal activity across homes (Villar et al, 2014).

Intimate partnerships can be deeply valuable to people at the end of their lives, where many physical and emotional changes are occurring and may influence individuals' and couples' attitudes about sexuality (Bridget, 2014). The sense of emotional connection derived from sexual activity can take on new significance in the context of a terminal illness. The sense of specialness from being close to someone physically and emotionally, desiring another and being desired in return, can be a life-affirming act to those who are dying (Taylor, 2014).

All of these nuances and sensitivities in the interactions of gerontological social workers with older people themselves, their partners and lovers, and being able to support individuals in negotiating their sexual rights in the face of ignorance, paternalism and denial, are highly significant. The following case study illustrates some of these dynamics.

Case study

Doreen, an 80-year-old White heterosexual woman has been widowed for 12 years. She lives alone in supported housing, has mild emphysema and diabetes and, more recently, her memory has deteriorated quite rapidly. Doreen has two children, Tony aged 58 and Marina aged 48, who live a couple of hours away. They see her every two weeks or so. Three months ago, Doreen met Ted, a Black Caribbean man aged 68 years, at a community group for falls prevention. Ted recently moved in with Doreen. Doreen tells Tony and Marian of her intention to marry Ted and to use her savings to take Ted on a luxury cruise. Tony contacts the local adult safeguarding team, stating that Doreen is at risk. He states that Doreen has 'always been a conservative and deeply religious woman'. Tony is very concerned whether Doreen is capable of consenting to 'all what's happening' and refers to Ted as a 'lecherous old man'.

Key questions to consider:

1. What do you think might be Tony's main concerns?
2. What might be some of the assumptions informing Tony's response?
3. What are the issues that you would want to explore in relation to Doreen's sexual rights and well-being?

Negotiating intimate relationships for trans older people

The experiences of trans people in negotiating intimate relationships have been overlooked in research on sexuality and ageing. Riggs et al's (2018) work identified four themes in research: (1) the effects of cisgenderism,[5] (2) the effects of gender dysphoria upon some people's capacity to negotiate intimate relationships, (3) the impact of medical aspects of transitioning and (4) the importance of recognising and valuing the unique and positive ways that many trans people negotiate relationships (pp 86–87). Riggs et al stress the importance of paying attention to the holistic accounts of trans people's lives, which includes acknowledgement of their intimacy needs and expressions. Social workers and other professionals must work much better with trans people to develop alternative ways of understanding and working with their own bodies. This might include being more aware of

[5] Cisgenderism denotes a dominant social hierarchy around gender and self-definition and associated attitudes and beliefs. Individuals self-defining their gender are perceived as inferior or lacking validity in comparison to those whose sex assigned at birth aligns with their gender identity (Ansara, 2012).

physical or psychological safety when meeting potential new partners, and in their relationships with existing ones. Some trans people may adopt a celibate or asexual identity upon transitioning and, as with any major life change, may reprioritise or take pragmatic decisions around their sexuality or sexual expression (Riggs et al, 2018). For some individuals, social and medical transitioning will commence in mid-to-later life (Willis et al, 2020) and hence these decisions are of equal concern to older adults.

Conclusion

Throughout this chapter, we have identified a range of critical perspectives and concepts for enhancing gerontological social work in this subject area (the rights to person-centred care; sexual autonomy; expression of sexual and gender identities and other marginalised identities; access to sexual health and human rights advocacy). In practice, these perspectives provide the theoretical foundations for enabling older service users to exercise sexual agency, with support where needed. Social workers as human rights advocates are well placed in older people's care and support services, including healthcare settings, to promote the sexual rights and agency of older individuals. This requires facilitating challenging and sensitive conversations with service users, their significant others and other professionals. However, this is familiar territory to gerontological social workers. Social workers should recognise and critically explore the discourses of shame, guilt and recrimination that some older people will hold about this subject and have held on to throughout their lives. Silence can inhibit these conversations and sustain these internalised discourses. Equally, religious beliefs and values held by others, including staff providing care, about sex and sexuality across the lifecourse require exploring and questioning. Opening up critical dialogue about these oppressive and often ageist discourses is an integral activity in putting critical gerontology into practice.

From a critical gerontological perspective, there are many ways in which social workers can exercise affirmative practice and promote older people's sexual rights and well-being:

- Place older people's voices at the centre of any analysis and recognise the meaning of sexuality in later life to each individual. This includes being attuned to the unique lifecourse experiences, histories and sexual stories of older individuals, including those experiencing LGBTQ ageing.
- Gaining the trust and confidence of the older service user is the first priority before initiating conversations about sex and intimacy – this will take time and does not lend itself to single meetings.
- Assess how changes or fluctuations in mental and sexual well-being may impact on the intimate relationships of service users and explore what

these difficulties and stressors may be. Reluctance to address issues or problems or being overcautious can deny older people autonomy in the form of ageist erotophobia.

- View sexuality from a broad perspective, addressing its biological, psychological and social aspects and the diverse range of sexual desires, attractions and intimacy needs of people in later life.
- Explicitly consider how sex and intimacy may be a part of planning care and support, particularly for those at the end of life. Family members or close friends may play a critical role in supporting their loved one and providing them with the opportunity to enjoy intimate moments at the end of life.
- Working with gender diversity must include the person's experiences of intimacy as part of a broader psychosocial assessment to support people to live fulfilling and meaningful intimate lives as they determine them to be.

References

Almack, K. (2019) '"I didn't come out to go back in the closet": ageing and end-of-life care for older LGBT people', in A. King, K. Almack, Y.-T. Suen and S. Westwood (eds) *Older Lesbian, Gay, Bisexual and Trans People: Minding the Knowledge Gaps*, Milton Park: Routledge, pp 158–171.

Altman, D. and Symons, J. (2016) *Queer Wars: The New Global Polarization over Gay Rights*, Cambridge: Polity Press.

Ansara, Y.G. (2012) 'Cisgenderism in medical settings: challenging structural violence through collaborative partnerships', in I. Rivers and R. Ward (eds) *Out of the Ordinary: LGBT Lives*, Cambridge: Cambridge Scholars Publishing, pp 102–122.

Asiedu, G.B., Hayes, S.N., Williams, K.P., Bondaryk, M.R., Halyard, M.Y., Parker, M.W., Balls-Berry, J.E., Pinn, V.W. and Breitkopf, C.R. (2017) 'Prevalent health concerns among African American women belonging to a national volunteer service organization (The Links, Incorporated)', *Journal of Racial and Ethnic Health Disparities*, 41(1): 19–24.

Bassnett, S. (2012) *Feminist Experiences: The Women's Movement in Four Cultures*, London: Routledge.

Becker, C., Kirchmaier, I. and Trautmann, S.T. (2019) 'Marriage, parenthood and social network: subjective well-being and mental health in old age', *PLoS One*, 14(7): e0218704, https://doi.org/ 10.1371/journal. pone.0218704.

Bridget, T. (2014) 'Experiences of sexuality and intimacy in terminal illness: a phenomenological study', *Palliative Medicine*, 28(5): 438–447.

Brown, S.L. and Wright, M.R. (2017) 'Marriage, cohabitation, and divorce in later life', *Innovation in Aging*, 1(2): igx015, https://doi.org/10.1093/geroni/igx015.

Butler, J. (1990) *Gender Trouble*, New York: Routledge.

Clouston, S.A., Lawlor, A. and Verdery, A.M. (2014) 'The role of partnership status on late-life physical function', *Canadian Journal on Aging*, 33(4): 413–425.

Crystal, S. and Shea, D. (1990) 'Cumulative advantage, cumulative disadvantage, and inequality among elderly people', *The Gerontologist*, 30(4): 437–443.

Delessert, T. (2005) 'Entre justice et psychiatrie: l'homosexualité dans le projet de Code pénal suisse (1918)', *Gesnerus*, 62(3–4): 237–256.

European Parliament (2020) *Briefing: The Rights of LGBTI people in the European Union*, [online], Available from: www.europarl.europa.eu/RegData/etudes/BRIE/2020/651911/EPRS_BRI(2020)651911_EN.pdf [Accessed 17 February 2021].

Eurostat (2020) *Marriage and Divorce Statistics: Statistics Explained*, [online], Available from: https://ec.europa.eu/eurostat/statistics-explained/index.php/Marriage_and_divorce_statistics [Accessed 25 February 2021].

Foucault, M. (1998) *The History of Sexuality (Vol. 1: The Will to Knowledge)*, Harmondsworth: Penguin Books.

Freak-Poli, R. and Malta, S. (2020) 'Sex and intimacy in later life: from understanding and acceptance to policy', *Australasian Journal on Ageing*, 39(S1): 16–21.

Fredriksen-Goldsen, K.I., Kim, H.J., Bryan, A.E., Shiu, C. and Emlet, C.A. (2017) 'The cascading effects of marginalization and pathways of resilience in attaining good health among LGBT older adults', *The Gerontologist*, 57(s.1): S72–S83.

Gendron, T.L., Welleford, E.A., Inker, J. and White, J.T. (2016) 'The language of ageism: why we need to use words carefully', *The Gerontologist*, 56(6): 997–1006.

Gewirtz-Meydan, A., Hafford-Letchfield, T., Ayalon, L., Benyamini, Y., Biermann, V., Coffey, A., Jackson, J., Phelan, A., Voß, P., Geiger Zeman, M. and Zeman, Z. (2019) 'How do older people discuss their own sexuality? A systematic review of qualitative research studies', *Culture, Health and Sexuality*, 21(3): 293–308.

Gilleard, C. and Higgs, P. (2007) 'The third age and the baby boomers', *International Journal of Ageing and Later Life*, 2(2): 13–30.

Gledhill, S. and Schweitzer, R.D. (2014) 'Sexual desire, erectile dysfunction and the biomedicalization of sex in older heterosexual men', *Journal of Advanced Nursing*, 70(4): 894–903.

Government Equalities Office (2018) *National LGBT Survey*, [online], Available from: www.gov.uk/government/publications/national-lgbt-survey-summary-report [Accessed 18 December 2019].

Hafford-Letchfield, T. (2008) 'What's love got to do with it? Developing supportive practices for the expression of sexuality, sexual identity and the intimacy needs of older people', *Journal of Care Services Management*, 2(4): 389–405.

Herek, G.M. (2004) 'Beyond "homophobia": thinking about sexual prejudice and stigma in the twenty-first century', *Sexuality Research and Social Policy*, 1(2): 6–24.

Hicks, S. and Jeyasingham, D. (2016) 'Social work, queer theory and after: a genealogy of sexuality theory in neo-liberal times', *The British Journal of Social Work*, 46(8): 2357–2373.

Hinchliff, S., Tetley, J., Lee, D. and Nazroo, J. (2018) 'Older adults' experiences of sexual difficulties: qualitative findings from the English Longitudinal Study on Ageing (ELSA)', *The Journal of Sex Research*, 55(2): 152–163.

Hughes, A.K., Rostant, O.S. and Pelon, S. (2015) 'Sexual problems among older women by age and race', *Journal of Women's Health*, 24(8): 663–669.

Hughes, M. (2006) 'Queer ageing', *Gay and Lesbian Issues and Psychology Review*, 2(2): 54–59.

International Federation of Social Workers (2014) *Global Definition of Social Work*, [online], Available from: www.ifsw.org/what-is-social-work/global-definition-of-social-work/ [Accessed 4 January 2020].

Jackson, S.E., Firth, J., Veronese, N., Stubbs, B., Koyanagi, A., Yang, L. and Smith L. (2019) 'Decline in sexuality and wellbeing in older adults: a population-based study', *Journal of Affect Disorders*, 15(245): 912–917.

King, A. and Cronin, A. (2013) 'Queering care in later life: the lived experiences and Intimacies of older lesbian, gay and bisexual adults', in T. Sanger and Y. Taylor (eds) *Mapping Intimacies: Relations, Exchanges, Affects*, London: Palgrave MacMillan, pp 112–119.

King, A., Almack, K. and Jones, R.L. (2019) *Intersections of Ageing, Gender and Sexualities: Multidisciplinary International Perspectives*, Bristol: Policy Press.

King, M. (2019) 'Stigma in psychiatry seen through the lens of sexuality and gender', *British Journal of Psychology International*, 16(4): 77–80.

Kitzinger, C. (2005) 'Heteronormativity in action: reproducing the heterosexual nuclear family in after-hours medical calls', *Social Problems*, 52(4): 477–498.

Kneale, D., Henley, J., Thomas, J. and French, R. (2019) 'Inequalities in older LGBT people's health and care needs in the United Kingdom: a systematic scoping review', *Ageing & Society*, 41(3): 493–515.

Kum, S. (2017) 'Gay, gray, black, and blue: an examination of some of the challenges faced by older LGBTQ people of color', *Journal of Gay and Lesbian Mental Health*, 21(3): 228–239.

Lee, D.M., Nazroo, J., O' Connor, D., Blake, M. and Pendleton, N. (2016) 'Sexual health and wellbeing among older men and women in England: findings from the English Longitudinal Study of Ageing', *Archives of Sexual Behavior*, 45(1): 133–144.

Lorimer, K., DeAmicis, L., Dalrymple, J., Frankis, J., Jackson, L., Lorgelly, P., McMillan, L. and Ross, J. (2019) 'A rapid review of sexual wellbeing definitions and measures: should we now include sexual wellbeing freedom?' *The Journal of Sex Research*, 56(7): 843–85.

Meyer, S.R., Lasater, M.E. and García-Moreno, C. (2020) 'Violence against older women: a systematic review of qualitative literature', *PLoS ONE*, 15(9): e0239560, https://doi.org/10.1371/journal.pone.0239560.

Moore, A. and Reynolds, P. (2016) 'Against the ugliness of age: towards an erotics of the ageing sexual body', *Interalia: A Journal of Queer Studies*, 11a: 88–105.

Nash, P., Willis, P., Tales, A. and Cryer, T. (2015) 'Sexual health and sexual activity in later life', *Reviews in Clinical Gerontology*, 25(1): 22–30.

Obradors-Campos, M. (2011) 'Deconstructing biphobia', *Journal of Bisexuality*, 11(2–3): 207–226.

O'Brien, K., Roe, B., Low, C., Deyn, L. and Rogers, S.N. (2012) 'An exploration of the perceived changes in intimacy of patients' relationships following head and neck cancer', *Journal of Clinical Nursing*, 21(17–18): 2499–2508.

Office for National Statistics (2017) *Census Data*, [online], Available from: www.ons.gov.uk/ons/guide-method/census/2011/census-data/index.html [Accessed 2 December 2019].

Pijpers, R. (2020) 'Experiences of older LGBT people ageing in place with care and support: a window on ordinary ageing environments, home-making practices and meeting activities', *Sexualities*, [online first], 20 June, https://doi.org/10.1177/1363460720936471.

Public Health England (2019) 'Prevalence of HIV infection in the UK in 2018', *Health Protection Report*, 13(39): 1–6.

Rahn, A., Jones, T., Bennett, C. and Lykins, A. (2020) 'Baby boomers' attitudes to maintaining sexual and intimate relationships in long-term care', *Australasian Journal of Ageing*, 39(S1): 49–58.

Richardson, D. (2000) 'Constructing sexual citizenship: theorizing sexual rights', *Critical Social Policy*, 20(1): 105–135.

Riggs, D., von Doussa, H. and Power, J. (2018) 'Transgender people negotiating intimate relationships', in P. Dunk-West and T. Hafford-Letchfield (eds) *Sexuality, Sexual and Gender Identities and Intimacy Research in Social Work and Social Care: A Lifecourse Epistemology*, London: Routledge, pp 86–100.

Sedgwick, E.K. (2008, reprint of 1990 edition) *Epistemology of the Closet*, California: University of California Press.

Seelman, K.L., Adams, M.A. and Poteat, T. (2016) 'Interventions for healthy ageing among mature Black lesbians: recommendations gathered through community-based research', *Journal of Women and Aging*, 29(6): 530–542.

Simpson, P., Horne, M., Brown, L.J., Wilson, C.B., Dickinson, T. and Torkington, K. (2017) 'Old(er) care home residents and sexual/intimate citizenship', *Ageing & Society*, 37(2): 243–265.

Taylor, B. (2014) 'Experiences of sexuality and intimacy in terminal illness: a phenomenological study', *Palliative Medicine*, 28(5): 438–447.

Villar, F., Celdrán, M., Fabà, J. and Serrat, R. (2014) 'Barriers to sexual expression in residential aged care facilities (RACFs): comparison of staff and residents' views', *Journal of Advanced Nursing*, 70(11): 2518–2527.

Westwood, S. (2016) ' "We see it as being heterosexualised, being put into a care home": gender, sexuality and housing/care provision among older LGB individuals in the UK', *Health and Social Care in the Community*, 24(6): 155–163.

Willis, P., Maegusuku-Hewett, T., Raithby, M. and Miles, P. (2016) 'Swimming upstream: the provision of inclusive care to older lesbian, gay and bisexual (LGB) adults in residential and nursing environments in Wales', *Ageing & Society*, 36(2): 282–306.

Willis, P., Raithby, M., Dobbs, C., Evans, E. and Bishop, J. (2020) ' "I'm going to live my life for me": trans ageing, care, and older trans and gender non-conforming adults' expectations of and concerns for later life', *Ageing & Society*, 1–22, [online first], 19 May, doi:10.1017/S0144686X20000604.

Wilkins, J. (2015) 'Loneliness and belongingness in older lesbians: the role of social groups as "community"', *Journal of Lesbian Studies*, 19(1): 90–101.

World Association for Sexual Health (2014) *Declaration of Sexual Rights*, [online], Available from: https://worldsexualhealth.net/resources/declaration-of-sexual-rights/ [Accessed 28 November 2019].

World Health Organization (WHO) (2017) *Action Plan for the Health Sector Response to HIV in the WHO European Region*, [online], Available from: www.euro.who.int/en/health-topics/communicable-diseases/hivaids/publications/2017/action-plan-for-the-health-sector-response-to-hiv-in-the-who-european-region-2017 [Accessed 25 February 2021].

WHO (2021) *Definitions: Sexual Health*, [online], Available from: www.who.int/health-topics/sexual-health#tab=tab_2 [Accessed 7 December 2020].

7

Ethnicity, race and migrancy

Sandra Torres[1]

This chapter draws attention to three identification grounds that social workers are expected to consider and that policy makers see as a priority, that is, ethnicity, race and migrancy. One of the reasons why this is the case is that the globalisation of international migration is one of the greatest challenges many societies have been facing in recent decades (Torres and Lawrence, 2012; Lawrence and Torres, 2016; Torres and Karl, 2016). As a result of this, social workers must now address the challenges that increased diversity can pose. In the case of those who specialise in ageing and older people, referred to in this book as gerontological social workers, it is important to note that population ageing has also increased the number of older people who need eldercare services. Thus, gerontological social workers have to deal with both the challenges that population ageing poses and the ones that the globalisation of international migration presents. Their work is therefore impacted upon by two major societal trends that most societies are facing these days, which is why this book proposes that critical gerontology could offer a valuable tool to advance research and increase the user-friendliness of social work policy and practice as far as our ageing populations are concerned.

Gerontological social work practice needs to accommodate and respond to greater heterogeneity among older people and it is in this context that this book introduces the critical gerontology lens to social workers. This is, after all, a lens that is particularly helpful when one wants to engage in research, policy and/or practice in a heterogeneity-informed way. Thus,

[1] **Sandra Torres** is Professor in Sociology and the Chair in Social Gerontology at Uppsala University in Sweden. Her work as a critical social gerontologist problematises old age-related constructs and deconstructs some of the taken-for-granted assumptions that inform research, policy and practice. Sandra is the President of the Research Committee on Aging of the International Sociological Association and of the Social-Behavioral Section of the International Association of Gerontology and Geriatrics: European Region. She holds fellowships from the (Swedish) Royal Society of Sciences and the Gerontological Society of America, is editor-in-chief of *Ageing & Society* and the author of *Ethnicity and Old Age: Expanding our Imagination* (Policy Press, 2019). At present she is co-editing (with Alistair Hunter) the *Handbook of Migration and Ageing* (Edward Elgar Publishing, 2023).

this chapter deals specifically with the source of heterogeneity that ethnicity, race and migrancy bring to the table, and does so because demographic data is clearly showing that ethnic, racial and migrant minorities are slowly but surely increasing in numbers across the world, with subsequent implications to population ageing. According to the Migration Data Portal (2021), there are, for example, 258 million international migrants in the world, and 11 per cent of them are 65+ years old. If one lowers the age threshold to 60+ – which is what the United Nations recommends when designing policy to address the needs of ageing populations – one can establish that 12 per cent of them are considered older migrants. The same source also states that the vast majority of the international migrant stock can be found in Oceania, North America and Europe. In regard to ethnic and racial minorities, it is interesting to note that the American Administration for Community Living and the Administration on Aging (which are operating divisions of the US Department of Health and Human Services) write the following in an attempt to raise awareness of the fact that services to older people must nowadays meet the needs of an increasingly heterogeneous population:

> Racial and ethnic minority populations have increased from 7.2 million in 2007 (19% of the older adult population) to 11.8 million in 2017 (23% of older adults) and are projected to increase to 27.7 million in 2040 (34% of older adults). Between 2017 and 2040, the white (not Hispanic) population age 65 and over is projected to increase by 36% compared to 135% for older racial and ethnic minority populations. (Administration for Community Living and Administration on Aging, 2018, p 3)

How ethnic and racial minorities are defined differs across the world, as minorities are always distinguished in relation to the majority population, and the ethnic and racial composition of societies differ for a variety of reasons. The same holds true for how migrants are defined, which is why this chapter will introduce readers to what ethnicity, race and migrancy actually mean. The terms ethnic and racial minorities and the term migrant are not, in other words, as clear cut as they may seem at first glance. Irrespective of what these terms mean in different parts of the world, it is statistics such as those presented here that have led social work scholars, practitioners and policy makers to want to build capacity to best serve these populations. The same holds true in other disciplines and professions that focus on the health and social care sector. A recent editorial published by the *British Journal of Medicine* draws attention to the lack of updated UK data on older ethno-racial communities, and does this while also urging policy makers and practitioners to keep in mind that poor health may characterise these populations:

The UK has not collected any survey data specifically on older ethnic minority populations, but data from 2004, the last year when the Health Survey for England oversampled ethnic minority people (over 15 years ago), found that the proportion of people aged 61–70 reporting fair or bad health was 34% for white English people but 86% for Bangladeshi people, 69% for Pakistani people, 63% for Indian people, and 67% for black Caribbean people. (Bécares, Kapadia and Nazroo, 2020, p 368)

It is clear that there is an increased awareness that the older segments of our populations who are defined as ethnic, racial and/or migrant minorities are growing in numbers, and that we do not currently have enough evidence-based knowledge about these groups. Ethnicity, race and migrancy are slowly but surely becoming constructs on which most of us in gerontological social work research, policy and practice need expertise. In light of all of this, it is perhaps not surprising that there are scholars in social work who fervently argue that the curriculum for gerontological social workers needs to include ethnogerontology, which is the sub-field of gerontology that specifically deals with the intersection between old age/ageing and ethnicity, race and migrancy. Their arguments include the notion that without this expertise one cannot offer user-friendly social work to diverse older populations (Edmonds Crewe, 2005), and neither can one develop models for culture-competency (Min, 2005). Irrespective of what one thinks of these arguments, it is an unrefuted fact that increased diversity among the older segments of our population merits capacity-building efforts in social work.

This chapter sets out to increase the expertise of social work researchers and practitioners as far as ethnicity, race and migrancy is concerned, since understanding the complexity associated with these identification grounds is a prerequisite to utilising a critical gerontological approach to empower one's research and professional practice, and to ultimately being able to contribute to enhancing the lives of older people. Thus, this chapter will not bring attention to what older ethnic, racial and migrant minorities need or how services to these minorities should be designed. Instead, it offers insight into *how* a critical understanding of different approaches to ethnicity, race and migrancy could inform (and misinform) gerontological social work research, policy and practice. The rationale for this focus is the fact that social workers need to be wary of the evidence that is available about older ethnic, racial and migrant groups, since scholarship, practice and policy focusing on these minorities are unfortunately sometimes characterised by unsophisticated ways of making sense of ethnicity, race and migrancy (Karl and Torres 2016; Lawrence and Torres 2016; Torres 2019). This chapter, therefore, starts from the premise that focusing on the needs of the growing numbers of older segments of our populations that are deemed to be ethnic and racial minorities, and/or to have a migrant background, could distract us from questioning the taken-for-granted assumptions we tend to have about these populations. The key to developing a critical gaze in gerontological social work lies in expanding our own imagination about what ethnicity, race and migrancy actually mean before we can begin to discuss how to best meet the needs of ethnic, racial and older minorities.

Ethnicity, race and migrancy: elusive constructs

Although research on ethnicity, race and migrancy is extensive, most scholars agree that different sociocultural contexts utilise these constructs for different purposes, depending on how value laden they have been throughout history. There are, however, a couple of clarifications about how these experts distinguish these constructs from one another that need to be spelt out. Let us begin with ethnicity and race, which are sometimes regarded as synonymous even though they allude to very different presumed commonalities. Both are used as classificatory devices to single people out, and to denote the social group to which people are believed (or claim) to 'belong' on the basis of their sharing (or being presumed to share) phenotypical characteristics (such as skin colour, body structure and/or hair texture); the fact that they share (or are presumed to share) national and regional backgrounds, historical circumstances, language and/or ethnocultural values, as well as the fact that (as a result of this) they share (or are presumed to share) behavioural patterns (Isaac, 1975).

Experts on ethnicity and race use these constructs in different ways: ethnicity is most often associated with the notion of attachments, while the construct of race is most often used today to denote the sharing of phenotypical characteristics, as the basis for presumed genetic distinctiveness has long been abandoned because genetic differences among humans are 'inconsistent and typically insignificant' (Cornell and Hartmann, 1998, p 21; see also the entry on genotype in Cashmore, 2004). In this respect, however, it must be noted that

> the use of the expression 'race' in the law, census, and in official documents, may appear to give government sanction to a classification which is no longer of explanatory value in zoology, and to keep alive a pre-Darwinian belief that it is important to the understanding of differences which are now known to be of social, cultural, and economic character. (Banton, 2004, p 334)

Thus, although race is sometimes used by laypersons as a synonym for ethnicity (as well as by scholars of ageing and old age who do not have ethnicity and race as their specialisation; see Torres 2019), they are in fact different constructs. Worth noting, however, is that scholars have urged us to not lose sight of the fact that although 'race as biology is fiction, racism as a social problem is real' (Smedley and Smedley, 2005, p 16). This is why Elias and Feagin (2016) argued that, as long as institutional and systemic racism exists, we cannot disregard the importance of race, even though we must remain clear as to what the difference between ethnicity and race is.

In this respect, it is alarming to note that a scoping review of 20 years of research on older ethnic and racial minorities showed that studies that measure the impact of racism on ageing are extremely rare (Torres, 2020a), which suggests that one of the experiences that may potentially affect the lifecourse of vulnerable minorities is not an experience that scholars have tended to take into account, let alone measure the effects of. Thus, because research on ageing and old age that brings attention to ethnicity and race tends to be informed by conceptualisations and theories in gerontology rather than those that ethnicity and race experts rely on (Torres, 2020b), there are huge knowledge gaps regarding the impact (if any) that ethnicity and race potentially have on ageing and old age. In this respect, it seems appropriate to quote Weber (1961, p 306), who described ethnic groups as 'groups that entertain a subjective belief in their common descent' and warned us that 'ethnic membership does not constitute a group; it only facilitates group formation of any kind' (Weber, 1978, p 389). The same could be claimed regarding race and migrancy, which are also constructs that can be used to categorise people and that swiftly, but often erroneously, facilitate the assumption that commonalities between them exist and that differences between them and us are a given. Hughes (1994) argued, for example:

> An ethnic group is not one because of the degree of measurable or observable difference from other groups: it is an ethnic group, on the contrary, because the people in it and the people out of it know that it is one; because both the ins and outs talk, feel and act as if it were a separate group. This is possible only if there are ways of telling who belongs to the group and who does not, and if a person learns early, deeply, and usually irrevocably to what group he belongs. (Hughes, 1994, p 91)

Thus, scholars who specialise in ethnicity and race do not necessarily regard these constructs as important because they are always relevant to people's lives but, rather, because we (for example, laypersons, scholars who are non-experts on these constructs, practitioners and policy makers alike) have been socialised into thinking of ourselves (and others) in those terms, and because we therefore sometimes insist on interacting with one another on the basis of group membership, as if that membership both was a given and had significance.

At this juncture, it seems necessary to mention that when we categorise people as non-members of a group that we ourselves think that we belong to, we are automatically drawing a boundary between the 'us' with whom we identify and the 'them' whom we regard as different. Once we have drawn that boundary, it is relatively easy to assume that deviance is more common among 'them' than the 'us' that we most often associate with what we deem to be 'normal'. Thus, the drawing of boundaries that is at stake when we use ethnicity, race and migrancy to classify people facilitates the 'feeling' of 'otherness and sameness' in relation to those we categorise using these boundaries. Of interest in this respect is that social work scholars have established that once we – in our practice – classify people as either similar or different from us because of ethnicity, race or migrancy, we are more inclined to culturalise their problems and/or needs (Eliassi, 2015). This can cause us to disregard the possibility that racism may underlie the problems that ethnic, racial and migrant communities face, because, once we determine that they 'are' different from us, we begin to shift our attention away from us and unto them (Eliassi, 2017). This is why this chapter argues that the ways in which we approach ethnicity, race and migrancy have consequences for how we perceive the boundaries that we draw between ourselves and the older segments of our populations that we identify as ethnic, racial and/or migrant communities, as well as the boundaries that we draw when differentiating between clients and/or when deciding which policies and practices are relevant when addressing their needs.

In terms of migrancy, it is important to note that the demarcation between migrants and non-migrants is context bound. In the UK, for example, this construct is often used when alluding to people who are about to, and/or have just, migrated from one sociocultural context to another. In Sweden, migrant is the term used to denote those of non-native descent, and who are therefore deemed to be different from the ethnic majority (Eliassi, 2015), sometimes irrespective of whether they are citizens and/or how long they have lived in the country. Irrespective of how common it is to utilise the term migrant in Sweden to draw a boundary between the ethnic majority and those who are deemed to 'belong' to minority groups, the term migrant in this part of the world is not a temporary label used to refer to people's mobility but, rather, a label used to delineate a boundary to the ethnic majority group. Regarding older migrants specifically, it is important to stress that a thorough review of the Swedish literature found that older migrants are assumed to have special needs, even though there is no evidence that this continuously perpetuated assumption is relevant, because no representative study of this population has been conducted (Torres, 2006).

By alluding to the nuances required when using the constructs in question, this chapter is trying to encourage the reader to interrogate what terms such as older ethnic, racial and/or migrants actually accomplish in both policy-making debates and practitioners' discussions. The critical gerontological lens is, after all, one that questions taken-for-granted assumptions, and in doing so exposes how debates and practices unnecessarily homogenise certain groups along demarcation lines that may or may not have any explanatory power. Worth mentioning is that part of the reason why ethnicity, race and migrancy are deemed to be elusive constructs – that can get in the way of rather than enhance social work policy making and practice – is that it is not only that these constructs are always contextually and historically determined, but that there is almost always a tension between ascribed and assigned identities as far as these identification grounds are concerned. In other words, there can be a difference between *how* ethnicity, race and migrancy are made sense of by those who are identified as being either ethnic and racial minorities or migrants, and how those who identify them as such make sense of this identification. This is probably one of the reasons why Gelfand (2003) – an American specialist on ethnicity and old age – referred to the three components of these constructs as being about self-identification, others' identification and the specific behaviours we associate with these labels.

Approaches to ethnicity, race and migrancy and their implications

Having established what the constructs in focus actually mean, it is now time to offer a brief summary of the ways in which debates about ethnicity and race have evolved. Cornell and Hartmann (1998) label the three approaches that scholars have relied on as primordialism (which is also referred to as essentialism), circumstantialism (which is, in turn, referred to as structuralism) and social constructionism. Worth mentioning is that although these specialists focus solely on ethnicity and race, these approaches can also be used to make sense of migrancy. Table 7.1 describes what characterises these approaches.

Table 7.1: Different approaches to ethnicity, race and migrancy

Primordialist approach	Circumstantialist approach	Social constructionist approach
Focuses primarily on what people *are*	Focuses primarily on what people *have*	Focuses primarily on what people *do*
Regards them as a *background*	Regards them as a *social position*	Regards them as an *identification ground*
Concerned with *what*	Concerned with *when*	Concerned with *how*
Focuses primarily on *minorities* (who 'belongs' inside the boundary)	Focuses primarily on *minorities* (who 'belongs' inside the boundary)	Focuses on *majorities and minorities* (not just who 'belongs' inside the boundary, but also how the boundaries are drawn)

The first thing to note is that the original approach that was utilised a century or so ago – primordialism – has been deemed obsolete by experts on ethnicity and race for decades (hence the use of grey in one column of Table 7.1). This does not mean that non-experts no longer rely on this approach. In fact, most laypersons make sense of ethnicity, race and migrancy in primordialist ways, which is why it is not uncommon for both ethnic and racial minorities, as well as migrants, to constantly be asked 'where do you come from originally?' – as if the answer to this question provides the inquirer with valuable information about who the person being asked the question may be, what his/her background may be characterised by and what value-orientations and behavioural preferences he/she may rely on. This is why this approach is associated with the 'the idea that ethnicity is fixed, fundamental, and rooted in unchangeable circumstances of birth' (Cornell and Hartmann, 1998, p 48), even though 'there is simply too much change and variation in ethnicity and race around the world to support the primordialist account' (Cornell and Hartmann, 1998, p 52). Thus, although the pull of this approach lies in its claim that it can explain how people come to feel connected to other people on the basis of common ancestry, this is an approach that has long been deemed obsolete by scholars specialising in ethnicity, race and migrancy.

Regarding gerontological social work, the notion that having insight into older people's ethnic, racial and migratory backgrounds is a prerequisite for high-quality and user-friendly services is an example of a primordialist understanding. Thus, although culture-appropriate social work models may seem to propose an inclusive way of addressing ethnocultural diversity among older populations, there is always a risk that, in presupposing that people care about 'their' culture, one is actually assuming that one understands exactly why it is that 'their culture' may matter to them. It is for this reason that specialists on ethnicity, race and migrancy, as well as critical gerontologists, tend to be wary of the one-size-fits-all approach that culture-appropriate models urge us to utilise, and argue instead that one can gain insight into an older person's needs and preferences only if one is curious about his/her personal biography (Hollinsworth, 2013).

Social constructionist approach to ethnicity, race and migrancy

The social constructionist approach is the one that experts in ethnicity and race most heavily rely on. One of the things that distinguish this approach is the notion that the meanings that people attach to ethnicity, race and migrancy emerge in the interaction between what others claim about them and/or what they claim they have, and who they themselves claim to be and/or have. Thus, when ethnicity, race and migrancy are understood from the social constructionist perspective, the focus shifts *from what* these social positions mean, *and when* they matter, *to how* they come to matter. This is why it is common to refer to ethnicity, race and migrancy as *identification grounds* when one relies on the social constructionist approach, and why constructionists urge us to shift our attention to how non-minorities create the boundaries that circumscribe the social positions that ethnic, racial and migrant minorities can end up being accorded. Thus, social constructionists regard the area of scholarship to which they contribute, the policies that are formulated and the practices professionals engage in as more important than the actual groups being studied and/or targeted by policy and practices.

In this respect, it is important to note that there is a major difference between the social constructionist approach and circumstantialism, as 'identities are made in the circumstantialist account, but not by the groups involved. On the contrary, circumstances do the work' (Cornell and Hartmann, 1998, p 73). Social constructionists are instead more interested in teasing out *how* different people's efforts (including policy makers and practitioners) shape, reinforce or transform ethnic, racial and migrant minorities' identities, and the meanings we end up attaching to them. This is why they are interested in discovering who the identifier is, and how the identification has been accomplished, as opposed to just being interested in who minorities are claimed to be and/or what they are claimed to have as far as resources are concerned. Hence the argument that

> construction involves both the passive experience of being 'made' by external forces ... and the active process by which the group 'makes' itself. The world around us may 'tell' us we are racially distinct, or our experiences at the hands of circumstances may 'tell' us that we constitute a group, but our identity is also a product of the claims we make. (Cornell and Hartmann, 1998, p 80)

This quote draws attention to one of the issues that the circumstantialist approach sheds light on, and that is the 'practical uses' (Cornell and Hartmann, 1998, p 56) that different groupings/classifications make possible for those who end up making claims about certain identities. It is for this reason that the circumstantialist approach regards ethnicity, race and migrancy as malleable and pragmatically utilised categories, and why it is not uncommon for circumstantialists to regard ethnic and racial groups as interest or lobby groups (Glazer and Moynihan, 1963). Social constructionists accept this proposition, which is why critical gerontologists tend to be wary when so-called stakeholders are treated by policy makers and practitioners as spokespersons for specific groups of older people who may, or may not, identify with the groups they are claimed to belong to, or the stakeholders' views of what these groups are characterised by and/ or need. Thus, a critical gerontological approach stresses that there is a fine line between using stakeholders' expertise to orient oneself about how to approach so-called 'vulnerable' groups and allowing them to dictate which needs come to be identified as 'legitimate' for these groups. The latter runs the risk of getting in the way of achieving person-centred social work, as one can easily begin to mistakenly assume that one knows what a specific client needs without actually asking relevant questions to this effect. Critical gerontologists want us therefore to remain vigilant so that the assumptions about groups that stakeholders claim characterise these groups never replace understanding clients' own views on their actual needs, preferences and circumstances.

Thus, the notion that people can choose to accentuate and/or undermine the importance of their own (and others') ethnic, racial and migratory 'backgrounds', depending on the context in which they find themselves, in an attempt to access the resources associated with certain *social positions* is central to the circumstantialist approach, because

> individuals and groups emphasize their own ethnic and racial identities when such identities are in some way advantageous to them. They emphasize the ethnic or racial identities of others when it is advantageous to set those others apart or to establish a boundary between those viewed as eligible for certain goods and those viewed as ineligible. ... Similarly, they ignore ethnic and racial bonds when circumstances change and other interests, poorly served by an ethnic or racial boundary, come to the fore. (Cornell and Hartmann, 1998, p 58)

Thus, one of the things that distinguish the circumstantialist approach from the primordialist one is that this is a perspective that shifts attention away from our attachments and origins and towards the ever-changing array of circumstances in which we find ourselves, and the strategies we use to manage those circumstances. This is why circumstantialists regard ethnicity, race and migrancy as *social locations/positions* that are fluid, malleable and instrumentally deployed, as opposed to regarding them as fixed, determined and inevitable. Social constructionists acknowledge, in turn, that some ethnic, racial and migrant groups can be accorded a certain position within a sociocultural context, but propose that regarding these positions as such can blind us to the very fact that it is not just minorities' own practices that tend to determine the positions that they end up occupying, but that the practices of dominant and powerful groups matter as well. It is for this reason that agency is important to constructionists and critical gerontologists alike, and why one must never lose sight of the fact that both what ethnic, racial and migrant minorities *do* and what majority and dominant groups *do* contribute to how we make sense of these *identification grounds*.

Put differently, constructionists are not particularly interested in the actual claims minorities make about who they and others *are* (because they do not regard these constructs as designations that a person can be forced into), nor are they interested in solely establishing what people have (or lack). Instead, they propose that we focus on what people *do* to accomplish certain identities and not others in specific circumstances and through specific practices. This is why constructionists focus on *how* ethnicity, race and migrancy are accomplished by groups of people, policies and practices, and why they argue that ethnicity, race and migrancy matter only if we ourselves (both those who claim these identities and those who identify them as relevant to people's lives) let them matter. The raises a question: does gerontological social policy and social work practice let ethnicity, race and migrancy matter, and, if so, through which practices are these identification grounds accomplished? This is another way of saying what Table 7.1 shows in the bottom right-hand corner when stating that the social constructionist approach encourages scholars, policy makers and practitioners alike to turn their magnifying glass unto themselves and address *how their own* practices per se shape the realities of ethnic, racial and migrant minorities vis-à-vis what these communities themselves do.

Conclusion

This chapter has argued that if we want to formulate social work policy and implement practice that meets the needs of older people who are deemed to be ethnic, racial and/or migrant minorities, we need to 'turn our analytic gaze back upon ourselves' so that we can become aware of 'the hidden presuppositions that shape our thought' (Emirbayer and Desmond, 2012, p 574). The reason why this chapter has argued this is that a critical gerontological lens on policy and practice encourages us to downplay the focus on who older ethnic, racial and/or migrant people 'are' so that we can shift our attention to what we ourselves contribute to differentiating clients from one another when we use labels that may not mean much to them, and that easily obfuscate what all clients need, namely a person-centred approach to their situations so that appropriate services can be implemented to meet their needs.

In this respect, it is important to draw attention to Cornell and Hartman's (1998) notion that identities are constructed differently depending on the *construction sites* in which they are identified. They propose that the political sphere (including policy debates and documents), the labour market, neighbourhoods, social institutions, the cultural sphere and daily experience are the construction sites where assumptions about ethnicity, race and migrancy take shape. Thus, the ways in which those in positions of power within these sites perceive ethnic, racial and migrant minorities, and the manner in which they handle these minorities' claims on resources, contribute to the meaning-making that surrounds these identification grounds. These bases for identification, in turn, end up becoming 'fixed as givens' in relation to minorities, and therefore get in the way of recognising the heterogeneity within groups and the uniqueness of those whose very needs social work scholarship, policy and practice are meant to address. A critical gerontological lens on ethnicity, race and migrancy (which would entail implementing the social constructionist approach when serving these communities) offers a way to regard social work scholarship, policy and practice as construction sites where stories about who older ethnic, racial and migrant minorities are, and what their needs may be, are told and reproduced (Torres, 2019). In other words, the stories we tell ourselves about other people (and about ourselves) set the parameters and expectations for the policies we formulate, and the practices we employ to address their needs. Moreover, when we tell stories about ourselves and others along ethnic, racial and migrancy lines, we end up singling out people along identification grounds that may not, in fact, make much sense to them. In proposing this, this chapter is not suggesting that ethnicity, race and migrancy do not affect older people. Instead, it urges us to think about the notion that these things matter because 'more powerful and encompassing social structural realities in many societies and globally' (Elias and Feagin, 2016, p 93) have allowed them to matter and that social work should be very careful when it allows these identification grounds to matter without making sure that they matter to the people they are meant to serve.

Related to this is 'the increasing unwillingness among dominant groups to accept responsibility for the problems of racism' (Essed, 1991, p 28), not to mention the fact that racial tensions around the world have continued to intensify over the past decades, and social work has unfortunately been slow in embracing an anti-racist agenda as one of its core professional values (Lavalette and Penketh, 2014). Dominelli (1989) was one of the first to question whether the social work profession could be deemed to be caring enough, considering that it sometimes seemed oblivious to the marginalisation and discrimination that ethnic and racial minorities tend to face at the mercy of the welfare state. It is the posing of such uncomfortable questions that this book encourages gerontological social workers to do once they have begun to utilise the critical lens. We must, however, be aware that institutions and professions 'think' in terms of categories, which is why it seems necessary to mention that – in societal settings and policy discussions that deem ethnicity, race and migrancy to be relevant – there is a heightened risk for social work practice to be formulated as if these identification grounds per se have practice-related significance. This reminds us of the ideas of Prottas (1979), who was one of the first to note that one of the main tasks 'grassroots bureaucrats' perform entails matching potential clients' characteristics with the rules that exist within the welfare institutions whose resources these clients would like to access. He argued also that the ways in which clients are categorised are mainly determined by how institutions can 'treat' them. Institutional categorisation is, in other words, one of the ways in which *clientisation* occurs or constitutes the processes through which an older person in need of help and support ends up receiving that help and becoming a client of these services. From this it follows that critically inclined scholars of social policy recognise the following:

> there is at least a prima facie case for seeing 'integrative' institutions of Europe as locked into processes of discrimination and marginalization. When questions of gender, race, class and colonialism are applied to the institutions of the political and economic subsystems, it becomes clear that these institutions are infused with cultural and historical identities, statuses and expectations. Exclusion, it can be argued, is not a by-product of system malfunction, it is woven into the fabric of those institutions – the labour market and the welfare state – that are offered as the means to resolve the problem of exclusion. (O'Brien and Penna, 2008, p 89)

Thus, when we urge gerontological social workers to view ethnicity, race and migrancy through the lens that social constructionism offers, we are urging them to look at their own practices, as well as the policies that have informed them, with the same agency that they would use to regard the older people whose circumstances they wish to improve. Social workers trained in critical gerontology understand that there is great variation *within* ethnic, racial and migrant groups, which is why boundary making – which is about identifying differences between groups – could blur this within-group variation. Thus, if 'we can recognize ethnicity (and, as argued here, race and migrancy as well) as a way of making up people, we can examine the social effects of this way of making up people yet not lose sight of the fact that (these identification grounds are) simply a way of making up people' (Carter and Fenton, 2010, pp 9–10). The uniqueness of the older individuals whose lives and needs we wish to impact upon in constructive ways, and whose agency and autonomy we wish to foster, is not preserved when we reduce them both to the groups we assume they belong to and to the various taken-for-granted assumptions we make about them.

References

Administration for Community Living and Administration on Aging (2018) *Profile of Older Americans*, [online], Available from: https://acl.gov/sites/default/files/Aging%20and%20Disability%20in%20America/2018OlderAmericansProfile.pdf [Accessed 15 March 2021].

Banton, M. (2004) 'Race: as classification', in E. Cashmore (ed) *Encyclopedia of Race and Ethnic studies*, London and New York: Routledge.

Bécares, L., Kaparia, D. and Nazroo, J. (2020) 'Neglect of older ethnic minority people in UK research and policy', *British Medical Journal*, 2020: 368, https://doi.org/10.1136/bmj.m212.

Carter, B. and Fenton, S. (2010) 'Not thinking ethnicity: a critique of the ethnicity paradigm in an over-ethnicised sociology', *Journal for the Theory of Social Behaviour*, 40(1): 1–18.

Cashmore, E. (ed) (2004) *Encyclopaedia of Race and Ethnic Studies*, London and New York: Routledge.

Cornell, S. and Hartmann, D. (1998) *Ethnicity and Race: Making Identities in a Changing World*, Thousand Oaks; London; New Delhi: Pine Forge.

Dominelli, D. (1989) 'An uncaring profession? An examination of racism in social work', *Journal of Ethnic and Migration Studies*, 15(3): 391–403.

Edmonds Crewe, S. (2005) 'Ethnogerontology', *Journal of Gerontological Social Work*, 3(4): 45–58.

Elias, S. and Feagin, J.R. (2016) *Racial Theories in Social Science: A Systemic Racism Critique*, New York and London: Routledge.

Eliassi, B. (2015) 'Constructing cultural otherness within the Swedish welfare state: the cases of social workers in Sweden', *Qualitative Social Work*, 14(4): 554–571.

Eliassi, B. (2017) 'Conceptions of immigrant integration and racism among social workers in Sweden', *Journal of Progressive Human Services*, 28(1): 6–35.

Emirbayer, M. and Desmond, M. (2012) 'Race and reflexibility', *Ethnic and Racial Studies*, 35(4): 574–599.

Essed, P. (1991) *Understanding Everyday Racism*, Newbury Park: Sage.

Gelfand, D.E. (2003) *Aging and Ethnicity: Knowledge and Services* (2nd edn), New York: Springer Publishing Company.

Glazer, N. and Moynihan, D.P. (1963) *Beyond the Melting Pot: The Negroes, Puerto Ricans, Jews, Italians, and Irish of New York City*, Cambridge: MIT Press.

Hollinsworth, D. (2013) 'Forget cultural competence; ask for an autobiography', *Social Work Education*, 32(4): 1048–1060.

Hughes, E.C. (1994) *On Work, Race and the Sociological Imagination* (ed L.A. Coser for The Heritage of Sociology Series), Chicago: University of Chicago Press.

Isaac, H. (1975) *Idols of the Tribe: Group Identity and Political Change*, New York: Harper and Row.

Karl, U. and Torres, S. (eds) (2016) *Ageing in Contexts of Migration*, London and New York: Routledge.

Lavalette, M. and Penketh, L. (2014) *Race, Racism and Social Work: Contemporary Issues and Debates*, Bristol: Policy Press.

Lawrence, S. and Torres, S. (eds) (2016) *Older People and Migration: Challenges for Social Work*, London and New York: Routledge.

Migration Data Portal (2021) *Older Persons and Migration*, [online], Available from: https://www.migrationdataportal.org/international-data?i=stock_old_perc&t=2020 [Accessed 15 March 2021].

Min, J.W. (2005) 'Cultural competency: a key to effective future social work with racially and ethnically diverse elders', *Family in Society: The Journal of Contemporary Family Services*, 86(3): 347–358.

O'Brien, M. and Penna, S. (2008) 'Social exclusion in Europe: some conceptual issues', *International Journal Social Welfare*, 17: 84–92.

Prottas, J. (1979) *The Street-level Bureaucrat in Public Service Bureaucracies*, Lexington: Lexington Books.

Smedley, A. and Smedley, B. (2005) 'Race as biology is fiction, racism as a social problem is real: anthropological and historical perspectives on the social construction of race', *American Psychologist*, 60(1): 16–26.

Torres, S. (2006) 'Elderly immigrants in Sweden: otherness under construction', *Journal of Ethnic and Migration Studies*, 32(8): 1341–1358.

Torres, S. (2019) *Ethnicity & Old Age: Expanding our Imagination*, Bristol: Policy Press.

Torres, S. (2020a) 'Racialization without racism in scholarship on old age', *Swiss Journal of Sociology*, 46(2): 331–349.

Torres, S. (2020b) 'Cultural diversity and aging: ethnicity, race and minorities', in G. Ritzer and C. Rojek (eds) *The Blackwell Encyclopedia of Sociology*, Hoboken: Wiley, https://doi.org/10.1002/9781405165518.wbeosc173.pub2.

Torres, S. and Lawrence, S. (2012) 'An introduction to "the age of migration" and its consequences for the field of gerontological social work', *European Journal of Social Work*, 15(1): 1–7.

Weber, M. (1961) 'Ethnic groups', in T. Parsons et al (eds) *Theories of Society*, Glencore: The Free Press.

Weber, M. (1978) *Economy and Society: An Outline of Interpretive Sociology*, Berkeley: University of California Press.

PART II

Applying the critical gerontological lens to social work research, policy and practice

8

Assessment, care planning and decision making

Anna Olaison and Sarah Donnelly[1]

In many European countries a climate of austerity and cuts to health and social care budgets, alongside issues of population ageing, are creating particular challenges in the provision of services for older people in the community (Lymbery and Postle, 2015; Donnelley, Begley and O'Brien, 2018). The introduction of neoliberalism into many European welfare states since the late 1990s has also meant challenges in terms of the reorganisation of social work policy and practice (Milner, Myers and O'Byrne, 2020). Budget cuts have taken place and standardisation has become commonplace, which has impacted on changing legislative and policy drivers for gerontological social work (Ray, Bernard and Phillips, 2018). Social workers have a key role to play in ensuring the participation of all older people in assessments, care planning and decision making in ways that uphold human rights, autonomy and self-determination. The application of a critical gerontological lens is particularly important in a context of neoliberalism and scarce resources, where social workers are increasingly reliant on informal caregivers, mainly family members, to provide care and support to older people, creating challenges and ethical dilemmas in practice situations.

---

[1] **Anna Olaison** is Associate Professor of Social Work at CESAR Centre for Social Work at Uppsala University in Sweden. Her programme of research aims to investigate how neoliberalism, changing social policies and standardisation of social services influence needs assessment practices. She has published on questions related to decision making and delivery of care and services for older people as well as social workers' abilities to use discretion in assessment meetings and documentation practices. Anna is a social worker and she leads several funded projects on the needs assessment practices of care services for older people. **Sarah Donnelly** is Assistant Professor of Social Work in the School of Social Policy, Social Work and Social Justice, University College Dublin, Ireland, and Co-convenor of the European Network for Gerontological Social Work (ENGSW). Sarah's research interests include ageing and dementia, adult safeguarding and capacity and decision making. Sarah is a registered social worker, an active member of the Irish Association of Social Workers (IASW) and a member of the Irish Gerontological Society.

As authors of this chapter, our writing has been influenced and shaped by our backgrounds as social work practitioners in the field of gerontological social work, and also as academics. Moreover, our experiences also originate from different social work traditions: Sweden (Olaison) and Ireland (Donnelly). This chapter will examine the impact that practice models and assessment instruments have on social work interventions within the context of the move towards a rights-based approach to care planning with older people and supported decision making. The chapter concludes with a helpful checklist for students and practitioners on 'Best practices in care planning meetings' with older people.

Assessment

Good-quality assessment has long been recognised as the cornerstone of effective social work practice and should be a dynamic process that is undertaken with the older person and their carer and/or significant others (Nelson Becker et al, 2020). Professional social work training in assessment has accordingly a strong focus on ecological systems theory (Bronfenbrenner, 2005), meaning that social workers pay attention to the microsystem at the level of the individual older person; the exosystem that encompasses their family, community and local services, the mesosystem that examines relationships and connections, the chronosystem that acknowledges changes over time and finally the macrosystem, including social and cultural values. Based on this theory, assessment is a central component in the coordination of care and services and is vital for the identification of needs, decision making and delivery of care and services for older people (Taylor, 2017). Effective assessment and support for carers are also pivotal in order to gauge stress levels, identify what support might be needed, and in reducing or preventing the use of expensive health and social care resources, including institutional care (Milne, 2020).

One challenge inherent in the assessment process that is similar for European countries is that the traditional biomedical model of assessment for older people has been criticised for having an overemphasis on an older person's presenting functional needs, which discourages a more holistic engagement with biographical, social and psychosocial needs and taking a lifecourse approach (Milne, 2020). A critical gerontological perspective questions the ways in which old age has been constructed and the conditions of ageing at micro and macro levels, including discriminatory and ageist policies where older people and their health and social care needs are constructed as a 'burden' to societies. As such, this perspective rejects stigmatisation of old age and the notion of ageing as a period of decline and dysfunction, and instead recognises the power in relation to the conditions of old age, and points to the fact that older people maintain capacities to learn, grow and change. A critical gerontological lens therefore encourages social workers to embrace an empowerment and strengths-based perspective (Saleeby, 1992) with a focus on 'ability' rather than 'inability'. Critical gerontology contends that social workers must advocate for a change in how population ageing is framed and portrayed, from primarily a social and economic burden to an opportunity for older people to 'make substantial social, economic, and cultural contributions, which can be enhanced by measures that improve their health and functional status' (Lloyd Sherlock et al, 2012, p 1295).

Social workers should recognise that every older person has strengths and that identifying and developing these strengths facilitates hope (Nelson-Becker et al, 2020), helping to safeguard autonomy and support meaningful participation in decision making. This is especially the case for social workers who are relying on the critical gerontological perspective outlined in Chapter 1. Taking a strengths-based approach to assessment means that older people are seen to have agency and to be the experts in their situation and should play an active part in the assessment process and any subsequent interventions. In the UK context, a strengths-based assessment sets out to identify:

- the older person's own strengths, wishes and priorities;
- the strengths of the older person's supporting network such as their family, friends and neighbours;
- their wider network of support, for example, local groups, voluntary organisations, corner shops, the local cafe or library. (Department of Health and Social Care, 2019, p 42)

Assessment entails a process of exploring a situation, which tends to consist of five stages:

1. preparing for the task;
2. collecting data;
3. applying professional knowledge (applying practice wisdom as well as theory);
4. making judgements;
5. deciding and/or recommending what needs to be done (about needs, risks, the seriousness of the situation and the older person's potential for coping and change) and making decisions/ recommendations (what is to be done and by whom, and when and how progress will be evaluated). (Taylor, 2017)

Care planning, on the other hand, may be defined as 'the process of developing an agreement between client and worker regarding problems identified, outcomes to be achieved, and services to be pursued in support of goal achievement' (Solan et al, 1986, p 30). In this respect, assessment can be viewed as part of a continuum of care planning for older people. There are, however, a wide variety of types of care planning and decision making that social workers assist with, including general care planning in relation to health and social care needs, advance care planning (financial and/or healthcare), planning for the possibility of a loss of decision making capacity and end-of-life care planning.

Assessment instruments

The introduction of 'needs assessments' in many European countries created a wide variety of types of assessment instruments (Lymbery and Postle, 2015). Policy debates in Europe since the 1990s identified the need to standardise the assessment process for older people, while at the same time arguing for the need for services to be more personalised (Milner, Myers and O'Byrne, 2020). These somewhat contradictory ideals about personalisation, evidence-based practice and standardisation have resulted in the implementation of different instruments for assessments (Taylor, 2017). For example, the Single Assessment Process (SAP) in the UK (Milner, Myers and O'Byrne, 2020) and the InterRai/Single Assessment Tool (SAT) have been used internationally for over 20 years (Hirdes et al, 2008). In the Nordic countries, several assessment instruments have been created that build on the ideas of SAP and SAT, for example Individens behov i centrum in Sweden (Swedish National Board of Health and Welfare, 2018), GERIX in Norway (Vabo, 2006) and Faelles Sprog in Denmark (Hansen and Vedung, 2005), to name a few. A common goal of these assessment instruments was to set out national service models and raise standards in assessments and in the way that services are provided for older persons, with the hope that it would enable them to make choices about their own care, whether at home or in institutional care. The original needs assessment models are rooted in systems theory (see earlier), in which organisational and administrative interests often dominate the assessment process (Milner, Myers and O'Byrne, 2020). Initially highlighting local flexibility within parameters of general policies (Lymbery and Postle, 2015), in recent years assessment has focused more on uniformity and standardisation, where the availability of services has a direct link to financial costs and tighter resource allocation (Olaison, 2017; Davies and Challis, 2018). The effective management of restricted resources has led to the development of assessment models that typically focus on dysfunction as a way of identifying 'eligible' needs. From a critical gerontological perspective, this approach is problematic as it can reinforce the tendency to consider older people who require support as being 'dependent', 'frail' or 'at risk' (Ray, Bernard and Phillips, 2018). Research has shown that these instruments have not fulfilled their objective, as it is hard for the standardised tools to be compatible with the parallel aspiration of personalisation of services (Lymbery and Postle, 2015). This development in assessment practice has resulted in social workers experiencing a considerable loss in relation to discretion in their professional role (Ellis, 2014; Olaison, Torres and Forssell, 2018), as they struggle to balance managerial pressures and professional approaches in relation to citizenship, social justice and human rights in order to protect the will and preferences of the older person (Evans, 2010; 2016). Social workers must therefore be aware of these tensions and strongly advocate that all older people, and particularly those with cognitive impairment, dementia or communication difficulties are actively involved in all stages of the assessment process and that their expressed wishes are sought, heard and acted on (Donnelley, Begley and O'Brien, 2018).

Challenges in assessment practice

In relation to personalisation of care, assessment practices pose two main challenges. The first relates to agency and the question of whether all older people have insight into their situation and needs. For example, can an older person with cognitive impairment fully understand and articulate their care needs, as well as identify possible ways of meeting their needs for support (Green and Sawyer, 2010; Österholm, Taghizadeh and Olaison, 2015)? The second relates to the possible conflicts that can occur between the older person and family members who are often conjoined with family ties and as care partners (Olaison and Cedersund, 2008; Nord and Nedlund, 2017). These challenges can be more visible in families that include late-in-life immigrants, where social workers report that they communicate more often and intensely with those relatives. The same relatives often expect and demand more support (Forssell, Torres and Olaison, 2014). Gerontological social workers are likely therefore to experience ethical dilemmas when upholding the human rights and expressed will and preference of the older person; from a critical gerontological perspective these include:

- the fact that the loyalty of social workers is often in the middle of conflicting interests, for example, what an older person wants versus what their family wants;
- the fact that social workers function as both helpers and controllers, particularly in situations where the older person has lost capacity or where there are safeguarding issues;
- the conflicts between the duty of social workers to protect the interests of the older people with whom they work and societal or organisational demands for efficiency and utility;
- the fact that resources in society are limited (International Federation of Social Workers, 2014) and often this impacts on social workers'

> ability to action an older person's will and preference. For example, an older person who needs home supports to age in place, but none are available. (Donnelly, 2021)

In negotiating this complex territory, it is important for gerontological social workers, regardless of what instruments they apply in assessment, to bear some fundamental principles in mind: working in partnership with older people, reflective practice, respecting agency and autonomy and ethical decision making (Hood, 2016). There is a need for mutually respectful interactions with the older person, a sense of shared involvement and responsibility as well as a need to consider the power dynamics within the process. Differences in socioeconomic status, gender, culture, disability, race, ethnicity and class identity are likely to be prominent in relationships between social workers and older people, and being able to communicate and understand information across cultures is, therefore, a crucial skill in assessment work (Hood, 2016). Recognising heterogeneity is also critical, as treating all older people as a homogeneous group overshadows the diversity among them and flatlines patterns of inequality (Ayalon and Tesch-Römer, 2018). In addition to core social work skills, practitioners, students and policy makers in this area need to have a sound knowledge base and understanding of the impact of ageing through a lifecourse perspective among diverse groups of older people (Nelson-Becker et al, 2020). Adopting a critical gerontological lens to assessment allows for a more reflexive and empowering practice for social workers, characterised by an awareness of the macro systems in which they operate. A critical gerontological perspective can also strengthen social workers' understanding that an advocacy and social justice perspective is something they can, and should, apply in practice in order to maximise the functional ability and quality of life of each older person.

Supported decision making (SDM)

In recent years in Europe, there has been a move towards a more human rights-based approach to the issue of supported and assisted decision making, with legislative changes strengthening the formal right for older people to participate. According to the United Nations Convention on the Rights of People with Disabilities (UNCRPD), 'persons with disabilities enjoy legal capacity on an equal basis with others in all aspects of life' (UNCRPD, Article 12; and see Chapter 3, which is entirely dedicated to human rights). Decision making becomes more complex for older people with multiple health and care needs, as the capacity to self-manage is affected by the cumulative effects of long-term conditions (Bunn et al, 2018). This raises important questions, however, about how decisions are currently made and experienced *in practice* (Larsson and Österholm, 2014), throwing up critical considerations for social workers who will be required to assist and support older people whose decision-making capacity may be impaired.

SDM is viewed as a key mechanism for upholding the human rights of persons with disabilities, with several commentators highlighting its potential for older people and people living with dementia (Sinclair et al, 2021). Many jurisdictions have ratified the Convention by establishing a specific legal framework for SDM. A supported decision-making approach applies a functional approach to determining decision-making capacity that is time, issue and context specific. It also introduces a model of will and preferences, where people's values must be central to all decision making and 'unwise' decisions are to be respected. It contains a presumption that all individuals have decision-making capacity and shall not be deemed to lack such capacity unless all reasonable steps have been taken, without success, to assist them (Davies et al, 2019). Despite a growing recognition of the importance of person-centred, inclusive and integrated approaches to care planning, research suggests that older people are frequently excluded from decisions (Donnelley, Begley and O'Brien, 2018).

The legacy of the paternalistic culture of care and the biomedical model has led to the mistaken belief that once a person is diagnosed with dementia, their abilities, autonomy and decision-making capacity are gone (Walsh et al, 2020). This is frequently used to justify surrogate decision making by health and social care professionals, who may engage in professional paternalism and institutional self-interest and demonstrate risk aversion in practice contexts (Baker, 2017). A critical gerontological lens helps us to recognise the clear tensions for the social work profession between our commitment to upholding 'will and preference' and professional codes of ethics and legislation that state that social workers must make decisions and interventions based on the 'best interests' of older people. The 'best interest' principle, it is often argued, is out of date, risk averse, ageist and contrary to the requirements of the UNCRPD (Donnelly, 2021), and gerontological social workers must collectively challenge and oppose this approach.

Promoting agency and autonomy

Emirbayer and Misches' (1998) model of agency can be seen as central to SDM, as it moves beyond classic ideas of human action as habitual and embedded within past experiences. The model distinguishes that people (in this case, older people) do not only act out of routine; rather, agency is oriented towards future possibilities and a person's capacity to reflect upon and assess their situation. It is the ability to exercise agency that is central to self-determination and a core aspect of developing a sense of identity (Hitlin and Johnson, 2015). Agency is also closely linked to autonomy and is discussed in greater detail in Chapter 4. The concept of relational autonomy is particularly important, as it defines human agency as an individual phenomenon, conceptualising it as fundamentally relational, which means that interaction in meeting with older persons can be both active and inactive, powerful and yet vulnerable to different degrees (Burkitt, 2016). According to Burkitt (2016, p 335), relational autonomy means seeing individuals as interactants who 'act in multiple webs of interdependence in which no one is ever completely independent or dependent but always somewhere in the continuum between these two abstractions'. Relational agency means that an older person's capacity to make choices occurs in relational webs of interdependence, which is why an ecological systems approach (Bronfenbrenner, 2005) is invaluable.

From a critical gerontological perspective, in order for SDM to be fully actualised in practice settings, social workers have a key role in supporting the older person's voice, autonomy and participation in decision making, as well as establishing a purposeful, supported decision-making environment. Early engagement with and elicitation of the older person's values and preferences is regarded as enhancing the decision-making process (Davies et al, 2019). Given the progressive nature of dementia, its impact on cognitive capacity and the ability to communicate at later stages, advance care planning is vital, and social workers have been recognised as being well positioned to take a leadership role in this task (Otis-Green et al, 2019).

Care planning meetings

A key part of the social work role with older people is care planning, which brings together the principles of involvement, supported decision making and person-centred care, which often culminates in what is referred to as a care planning meeting (or CPM). Although their original function was to respond to crisis situations (Loupis and Faux, 2013), CPMs are now routinely used in some European countries in a more anticipatory manner. When carried out well, they are thought to build important organisational bridges between hospital and community care for older people (Donnelly, Cahill and O'Neill, 2018). They are often conducted in a hospital setting and require multidisciplinary team (MDT) collaboration between the professional care providers, older people and their family/ caregivers. The desired outcome of the CPM is that all participants are satisfied with the amount of information exchanged; that decisions are made with clarity; and that ultimately the older person feels a sense of control and empowerment.

Although CPMs are an increasingly common part of gerontological social work, it is uncertain how, and by whom, the voice and wishes of older people are given due priority. The aims and outcomes of CPMs are not always clear, and older people tend not to be prepared and often lack essential knowledge about the CPM decision-making process and care options (Efraimsson et al, 2006; Donnelly, Cahill and O'Neill, 2018). The physical involvement of older people in CPMs does not necessarily guarantee genuine involvement and it is not uncommon for older people to be talked '*about*' rather than talked '*to*' (Donnelly et al, 2013). An added challenge is the often diverse and conflicting range of perspectives held by the MDT and other family members (Donnelly, Cahill and O'Neill, 2018). The formality of CPMs and the overuse of technical language tend to prevent opportunities for participation (Efraimsson et al, 2006). MDT members often control discussions and steer the focus of the CPM to their own or the institutional agenda (Donnelly et al, 2013). Past events and contemporary family dynamics may impact in these contexts and the preferences of older people and family members can often diverge, with excessive demands placed on family caregivers resulting in the older person feeling like a burden (Bångsbo, Duner and Linden, 2014).

From a critical gerontological perspective, there are significant challenges for practitioners in balancing competing agendas, for example, discharge-planning pressures leading to hurried decision making or balancing the autonomy and agency of the older person with that of their family members (Donnelly, Cahill and O'Neill, 2018). Research also indicates that an inverse relationship frequently exists in CPMs whereby if family member participation is high, participation of the older person is low (Donnelly et al, 2013). This has been especially noted in assessment and CPM meetings concerning late-in-life immigrants, where relatives often have a strong voice and these meetings are often experienced as more complex to navigate by social workers (Forssell, Torres and Olaison, 2015). Social workers must therefore strongly advocate for a social citizenship approach (Bartlett and O'Connor, 2010), which means promoting the agency of the individual, the routine inclusion of all older people in CPMs and challenging organisational, MDT or family member opposition to this. Particular challenges exist when there are risk issues or when the necessary community supports such as home care, equipment or housing cannot be accessed. In these circumstances, social workers must oppose premature or unnecessary admission to nursing home care and defend the older person's human right to age in place, advocating not only at the micro level, in relation to each older person they are working with, but also at the macro level for longer-term policy reform and equality of access to resources for all older people. As concerns have been expressed about the inadequacy of the knowledge base about how the participation of older people in CPMs is best accomplished in practice (Bångsbo, Duner and Linden, 2014), we have compiled a best practice checklist for CPMs in Table 8.1 (see Donnelly, 2013; Donnelly et al, 2013; and Donnelly, Cahill and O'Neill, 2018).

Table 8.1: Care planning meetings for older people: best practice checklist

Pre-meeting stage	A social citizenship approach should be adopted, which assumes that an older person has the ability to participate at some level, regardless of their cognitive ability.
	Time: establish what time of day the older person functions best and is cognitively most alert. **Environment**: establish the environment in which the older person functions best and is most comfortable. **People**: establish the people whom the older person trusts and with whom they communicate best and involve them in the communication process.
	Fostering of a therapeutic relationship should be a prerequisite: it will create an emotionally secure environment, enhancing the meaningful participation of the older person.
	Consideration should be given to the number of people in attendance at the CPM; smaller numbers are usually preferable. Issues of potential conflict should be identified in advance.
	The older person should be encouraged to identify any issues/topics they would like to be discussed during their CPM and to write down any questions they would like to ask/ to be asked on their behalf during the meeting.
During the CPM	CPMs should have a clear agenda, goal setting should occur, with good time management, skilled facilitation/chairing and a clear emphasis on decision making.
	CPMs involving older people with cognitive or communication difficulties may need additional consultation time within the CPM to ensure that shared/supported decision making occurs.
	Use simple, clear language and avoid the use of medical or other technical (discipline-specific) language; if used, an explanation of its meaning should be provided.
	Maintain good eye contact and turn to face the older person when you are speaking to them. Avoid the use of the third person, that is, 'she/he'; instead use the first person 'we', 'us' or 'you'. This will help to encourage more active participation.
	The use of scaling questions/diagrams can help to elicit the importance of an issue to an older person and can be a useful tool to help determine will and preferences.
	Use the 'teach-back method' to check understanding. Ask the older person to repeat what you have told them in their own words. *Do you understand everything we have been talking about?* *Would you like the information to be explained again?*
After the CPM	Provide a written summary of key decisions reached to all CPM participants in clear, easily understandable, accessible language.
	Debrief with the older person and their family members in relation to their CPM experience and address any issues arising. Debriefing with MDT members may also be required for CPMs where there was a great deal of emotion or conflict.

Source: Donnelly, 2013; Donnelly et al, 2013; and Donnelly, Cahill and O'Neill, 2018.

Conclusion

In this chapter we have highlighted opportunities and challenges inherent in assessment, care planning and decision making for gerontological social workers. While the introduction of standardised assessment instruments can be welcomed, they have also created ethical tensions for social workers trying to balance the conflicting aims of needs assessments and personalisation in an environment of reduced resources and increased managerialism and bureaucracy.

In applying a critical gerontological lens to practice, social workers must adopt an empowering, strengths-based, ecological systems approach to assessment and SDM. We must enable older people to make informed decisions wherever possible and in circumstances that respect their dignity, beliefs, individual choice and privacy. The participation of older people in assessment and decision-making processes must be considered in relation to a holistic perspective and their expressed will and preferences being established and acted on, and social workers must take on a strong advocacy role in relation to this. In addition, social workers must ensure that they are not pressured to abandon a human rights-based approach to SDM in favour of risk-based legalistic and procedural approaches that are often encouraged by employing organisations (Donnelly, 2021). Social work students, practitioners as well as policy makers need to understand the importance of the concepts of social justice, agency and autonomy for developing a critical understanding of the discourses that underpin different parts of assessment practice in order to develop a more affirming understanding of older persons' rights to care.

In CPMs, more attention must be given to pre-meeting preparation and information-sharing processes to ensure that decisions are communicated clearly. At the same time, the older person must be empowered to make supported decisions and enact self-determination, and be enabled to develop an awareness of their strengths and abilities as well as their care and support needs. We contend that active participation is possible in CPMs when a therapeutic relationship has been fostered and supportive and communicative approaches are adopted by social workers and MDT members. Social workers must create a culture for CPMs which safeguards the relational autonomy of the older person and supports their decision making while also making sure that the views of all meeting participants are heard. When CPMs are well prepared and carefully structured there are opportunities to tilt the balance of power in favour of the older person and to help them to maximise control over decisions affecting their lives.

One way forward in order to safeguard autonomy and promote the human rights of older people can be by creating an environment that encourages social workers to use their relational competence more (Nilsson and Olaison, 2020). Ultimately, we must remember, however, that it is not simply enough to include older people in assessment, care planning and decision-making processes, it must also be conveyed to them that their participation matters.

In sum, in a climate where neoliberal financial measures are likely to reinforce the dominance of more institutional and standardised priorities, the adoption of a critical gerontological lens to policy and practice is fundamental to ensure a strong focus on social justice and human rights for all older people.

References

Ayalon, L. and Tesch-Römer, C. (2018) 'Introduction to the section: ageism, concept and origins', in L. Ayalon and C. Tesch-Römer (eds) *Contemporary Perspectives on Ageism*, New York: Springer Open, pp 1–10.

Baker, D. (2017) 'How to achieve best practice in supported decision-making', *Community Care*, [online], Available from: www.communitycare. co.uk/2017/02/27/achieve-best-practice-supported-decision-making. [Accessed 12 January 2021].

Bångsbo, A., Duner, A. and Liden, E. (2014) 'Patient participation in discharge planning conference', *International Journal of Integrated Care*, 14(4): 1–11.

Bartlett, R. and O'Connor, D. (2010) *Broadening the Dementia Debate: Toward Social Citizenship*, Bristol: Policy Press.

Bronfenbrenner, U. (2005) *Making Human Beings Human: Bioecological Perspectives on Human Development*, Thousand Oaks: Sage Publications.

Bunn, F., Goodman, C., Russell, B., Wilson, P., Manthorpe, J., Rait, G., Hodkinson, I. and Durand, M.A. (2018) 'Supporting shared decision making for older people with multiple health and social care needs: a realist synthesis', *BMC Geriatrics*, 18(1): 1–16.

Burkitt, I. (2016) 'Relational agency: relational sociology, agency and interaction', *European Journal of Social Theory*, 19(3): 322–339.

Davies, B. and Challis, D. (2018) *Matching Resources to Needs in Community Care: An Evaluated Demonstration of a Long-term Care Model*, London: Routledge.

Davies, C., Fattori, F., O'Donnell, D., Donnelly, S., Ní Shé, E., O Shea, M., Prihodova, L., Gleeson, C., Flynn, A., Rock, B., Grogan, J., O'Brien, M., O'Hanlon, S., Cooney, M.T., Tighe, M. and Kroll, T. (2019) 'What are the mechanisms that support healthcare professionals to adopt assisted decision-making practice? A rapid realist review', *BMC Health Services Research*, 19(1): 960.

Department of Health and Social Care (2019) *Strengths-based Approach: Practice Framework and Practice Handbook*, London: Department of Health and Social Care, [online], Available from: www.gov.uk/government/publications/ strengths-based-social-work-practice-framework-and-handbook [Accessed 10 January 2021].

Donnelly, S. (2013) *Care Planning Meetings: Best Practice Guidelines for Healthcare Professionals: An Individualised Approach to Patient Participation*, [online], Available from: http://hdl.handle.net/10147/617561 [Accessed 12 January 2021].

Donnelly, S. (2021) 'The Assisted Decision-making Capacity Act, 2015: reflections for the profession of social work', in M. Donnelly and C. Gleeson (eds) *Towards a New Frontier for Human Rights: The Assisted Decision-Making (Capacity) Act 2015 Personal and Professional Reflections*, Dublin: Health Service Executive, [online], Available from: https://t.co/Lnita17M43?amp=1 [Accessed 10 January 2022].

Donnelly, S., Begley, E. and O'Brien, M. (2018) 'How are people with dementia involved in care planning and decision-making? An Irish social work perspective', *Dementia*, 18(7–8): 2985–3003.

Donnelly, S., Cahill, S. and O'Neill, D. (2018) 'Care planning meetings: issues for policy, multi-disciplinary practice and patient participation', *Practice*, 30(1): 53–71.

Donnelly, S.M., Carter-Anand, J., Cahill, S., Gilligan, R., Mehigan, B. and O'Neill, D. (2013) 'Multiprofessional views on older patients' participation in care planning meetings in a hospital context', *Practice*, 25(2): 121–138.

Efraimsson, E., Sandman, P.O., Hyden, L-C. and Rasmussen B.H. (2006) ' "They were talking about me": elderly women's experiences of taking part in a discharge planning conference', *Scandinavian Journal of Caring Sciences*, 20(1): 68–78.

Ellis, K. (2014) 'Professional discretion and adult social work: exploring its nature and scope on the front line of personalisation', *The British Journal of Social Work*, 44(8): 2272–2289.

Emirbayer, M. and Mische, A. (1998) 'What is agency?' *American Journal of Sociology*, 103(4): 962–1023.

Evans, T. (2010) 'Professionals, managers and discretion: critiquing street-level bureaucracy', *The British Journal of Social Work*, 41(2): 368–386.

Evans, T. (2016) *Professional Discretion in Welfare Services: Beyond Street-level Bureaucracy*, London: Routledge.

Forssell, E., Torres, S. and Olaison, A. (2014) 'Anhörigomsorg mot betalning: Biståndshandläggare om sent-i-livet-invandrares önskemål', *Socialvetenskaplig tidskrift*, 21(2): 114–137.

Forssell, E., Torres, S. and Olaison, A. (2015) 'Care managers' experiences of cross-cultural need assessment meetings: the case of late-in-life immigrants', *Ageing & Society*, 35(2): 576–601.

Green, D. and Sawyer, A.M. (2010) 'Managing risk in community care of older people: perspectives from the frontline', *Australian Social Work*, 63(4): 375–390.

Hansen, M.B. and Vedung, E. (2005) *Fælles sprog i ældreplejens organisering. Evaluering af et standardiseret kategorisystem*, Odense: Syddansk Universitetsforlag.

Hirdes, J.P., Ljunggren, G., Morris, J.N., Frijters, D.H., Soveri, H.F., Gray, L., Björkgren, M. and Gilgen, R. (2008) 'Reliability of the interRAI suite of assessment instruments: a 12-country study of an integrated health information system', *BMC Health Services Research*, 8(1): 277.

Hitlin, S. and Kirkpatrick Johnson, M. (2015) 'Reconceptualizing agency within the life course: the power of looking ahead', *American Journal of Sociology*, 120(5): 1429–1472.

Hood, R. (2016) 'Assessment for social work practice', in K. Davies and R. Jones (eds) *Skills for Social Work Practice*, Basingstoke: Palgrave Macmillan, pp 82–101.

International Federation of Social Workers (2014) *Global Social Work Statement of Ethical Principles*, [online], Available from: www.ifsw.org/global-social-work-statement-of-ethical-principles/ [Accessed 11 January 2021].

Larsson, A.T. and Österholm, J.H. (2014) 'How are decisions on care services for people with dementia made and experienced? A systematic review and qualitative synthesis of recent empirical findings', *International Psychogeriatric*, 26(11): 1849–1862.

Lloyd-Sherlock, P., McKee, M., Ebrahim, S., Gorman, M., Greengross, S., Prince, M., Pruchno, R., Gutman, G., Kirkwood, T., O'Neill, D., Ferrucci, L., Kritchevsky, S.B. and Vellas, B. (2012) 'Population ageing and health', *Lancet*, 379: 1295–1296.

Loupis, Y.M. and Faux, S.G. (2013) 'Family conferences in stroke rehabilitation: a literature review', *Journal of Stroke and Cerebrovascular Diseases: The Official Journal of National Stroke Association*, 22(6): 883–893.

Lymbery, M. and Postle, K. (2015) *Social Work and the Transformation of Adult Social Care: Perpetuating a Distorted Vision?*, Bristol: Policy Press.

Milne, A. (2020) *Mental Health in Later Life: Taking a Lifecourse Approach*, Bristol: Policy Press.

Milner, J., Myers, J.S. and O'Byrne, P. (2020) *Assessment in Social Work* (5th edn), London: Red Globe Press.

Nelson-Becker, H., Lloyd, L., Milne, A., Perry, E., Ray, M., Richards, S., Sullivan, M.P., Tanner, D. and Willis, P. (2020) 'Strengths-based social work with older people: a UK perspective', in A. Mendenhall, and M. Mohr-Carney (eds) *Rooted in Strengths: Celebrating the Strengths Perspective in Social Work*, Kansas: University Press of Kansas, pp 327–346.

Nilsson, E. and Olaison, A. (2020) 'Needs assessment in social work with older people in times of Covid-19: initial ideas from an empirical study', *Relational Social Work*, 4(2): 52–60.

Nordh, J. and Nedlund, A.C. (2017) 'To coordinate information in practice: dilemmas and strategies in care management for citizens with dementia', *Journal of Social Service Research*, 43(3): 319–335.

Olaison, A. (2017) 'Processing older persons as clients in elderly care: a study of the micro-processes of care management practice', *Social Work in Health Care*, 56(2): 78–98.

Olaison, A. and Cedersund, E. (2008) 'Home care as a family matter? Discursive positioning, storylines and decision-making in assessment talk', *Communication and Medicine*, 5(2): 145–158.

Olaison, A., Torres, S. and Forssell, E. (2018) 'Professional discretion and length of work experience: what findings from focus groups with care managers in elder care suggest', *Journal of Social Work Practice*, 32(2): 153–167.

Österholm, J.H., Taghizadeh Larsson, A. and Olaison, A. (2015) 'Handling the dilemma of self-determination and dementia: a study of case managers' discursive strategies in assessment meetings', *Journal of Gerontological Social Work*, 58(6): 613–636.

Otis-Green, S., Thomas, J., Duncan, L., Walling, A., Lieto, C., Kung, J., Pietras, C. and Wenger, N. (2019) 'Advance care planning: opportunities for clinical social work leadership', *Clinical Social Work Journal*, 47(3): 309–320.

Ray, M., Bernard, M. and Phillips, J. (2018) *Critical Issues in Social Work with Older People*, Basingstoke: Palgrave Macmillan.

Saleebey, D. (ed) (1992) *The Strengths Perspective in Social Work Practice*, White Plains: Longman.

Sinclair, C., Bajic-Smith, J., Gresham, M., Blake, M., Bucks, R.S., Field, S., Clayton, J.M., Radoslovich, H., Agar, M. and Kurrle, S. (2021) 'Professionals' views and experiences in supporting decision-making involvement for people living with dementia', *Dementia*, 20(1): 84–105.

Solan, E., Grannemann, M., Carter, E., Wells-Hunter, H., Decker, P., Bulvanoski, S., Coleman, C., Kluxen, M.E. and Johnson, T. (1986) *Assessment and Care Planning for the Frail Elderly: A Problem Specific Approach*, Office of the Assistant Secretary for Planning and Evaluation US Department of Health and Human Services, [online], Available from: https://aspe.hhs.gov/system/files/pdf/74016/asmtcare.pdf [Accessed 10 April 2021].

Swedish National Board of Health and Welfare (2018) *Individens behov i centrum. Lägesavstämning för 2017 – Äldreområdet*, Stockholm: Swedish National Board of Health and Welfare.

Taylor, B.J. (2017) *Decision Making, Assessment and Risk in Social Work*, London: Sage.

Vabø, M. (2006) 'Caring for people or caring for proxy consumers?', *European Societies*, 8(3): 403–422.

Walsh, S., O'Shea, E., Pierse, T., Kennelly, B., Keogh, F. and Doherty, E. (2020) 'Public preferences for home care services for people with dementia: a discrete choice experiment on personhood', *Social Science & Medicine*, 245: 112675.

9

Elder abuse

Lorna Montgomery and Gemma M. Carney[1]

Over the last 20 years, increased public and political awareness has developed alongside research, policy and professional developments to advance our understanding of the abuse of older people in families, communities, hospitals and institutional settings. In 2002, the World Health Organization (WHO) argued that elder abuse was a distinct social problem, defining abuse as 'a single, repeated act or lack of appropriate action, occurring within any relationship where there is an expectation of trust which caused harm or distress to an older person' (WHO, 2002).

In 2007, the first United Kingdom (UK) prevalence study of elder abuse reported that 4% of older people living in the community were subject to abuse or neglect (O'Keefe et al, 2007). In 2010, a prevalence study of elder abuse in Germany, Greece, Italy, Lithuania, Portugal, Spain and Sweden found that 19.4% of older people aged 60–84 years were exposed to psychological abuse; 2.7% to physical abuse; 0.7% to sexual abuse; and 3.8% to financial abuse (Soares et al, 2010). Pillemer et al (2016), in reviewing the international literature, found that, globally, elder abuse prevalence rates for older people living in the community, encompassing all forms of abuse, ranged from 2.2% to 36.2%, with a mean of 14.3%. The highest combined

[1] **Lorna Montgomery** is Senior Lecturer in Social Work in the School of Social Sciences, Education and Social Work, Queen's University Belfast, UK, and is Director of Practice Learning. She practised as a social worker/manager in the adult sector for 20 years, and has also worked for five years in a non-governmental organisation in Uganda, East Africa, conducting research on cross-cultural bereavement practices. Her teaching and research interests include adult safeguarding, mental health, parenting and cross-cultural practice. Her latest contributions include articles in *The Journal of Adult Protection* and *Practice*. **Gemma M. Carney** is a critical gerontologist and Senior Lecturer in Social Policy and Ageing at the School of Social Sciences, Education and Social Work at Queen's University Belfast, UK. She is a member of the editorial board of *Ageing & Society* and, with Paul Nash, University of Southern California, is author of *Critical Questions for Ageing Societies* (Policy Press, 2020). She leads a range of interdisciplinary studies of ageing at Queen's and is currently Co-Investigator on an AHRC-funded project, Dementia in the Minds of Characters and Readers.

prevalence was reported in China (36.2%) and Nigeria (30%), followed by Israel (18.4%), India (14%), Europe (10.8%), Mexico (10.3%), United Sates (9.5%) and Canada (4%).

As is apparent from the wide diversity in prevalence rates noted here, determining the extent of abuse is problematic, with prevalence studies often utilising differing definitions of abuse, different target populations and different methods (Cooper et al, 2008; Pillemer et al, 2016). However, it is widely recognised that elder abuse is increasing and that it often goes unreported, with official numbers most likely underestimating the extent of the problem (Iborra, Garcia and Grau, 2013).

A developing social problem

The abuse of older people is understood within a broader spectrum of family violence (Phelan, 2020) in which, as discussed in Chapter 8, an ecological systems approach (Bronfenbrenner, 2005) is generally adopted. However, policies and legislation that focus on the protection of older people have not achieved the same recognition as those within child protection (Chisnell and Kelly, 2019). The physical abuse of older people was first officially recognised in the UK in 1975 (Baker, 1975), with protection policies introduced in the Health and Social Care sector in the 1980s and 1990s, although Australia, the United States and Canada had begun to recognise 'elder abuse' as a distinct concept in the 1970s (Phelan, 2013). Such limitations in recognition and response to elder abuse have been directly attributed to the predominance of ageist attitudes (Biggs and Haapala, 2013; Gullette, 2017).

The development of theories that attempt to understand and explain elder abuse has also been slow, tending to focus more on individualistic reasoning and micro factors, with little regard given to structural issues. However, one important recent step in terms of policy recognition of elder abuse is to frame it as a common, structural problem for ageing societies, rather than as a personal issue for individual older people (Teaster et al, 2020). Critical gerontologists identify this shift in recognition of elder abuse as a systemic problem as a sea change of similar significance as the recognition of women's rights as necessary to the proper functioning of society in the 1970s (see Carney and Gray, 2015).

There is no globally accepted definition of elder abuse, due to the fact that elder abuse is a diverse, socially constructed phenomenon, with ambiguity and debate around what constitutes abuse. The WHO's definition, noted earlier, is not without challenge. There is a lack of clarity around the interface between elder abuse and intimate partner violence, and the ability to distinguish mistakes and accidents from negligence, abuse or suspected crimes is also problematic (CPEA, 2020).

In the 1990s, in an effort to standardise the way abuse was understood across countries, a typology of abuse was established (Phelan, 2013). This typically includes sexual, physical, financial, psychological, institutional and discriminatory abuse, and neglect. Elder abuse is often understood within the broad framework of 'adult safeguarding', referring to a range of processes and interventions offered to adults who, because of personal characteristics or life circumstances, require help to protect themselves (MacIntyre et al, 2017). The term 'adult protection' is often used synonymously with adult safeguarding; however, the remit of the former tends to be narrower and relates to legislation and protocols developed to respond when harm has occurred.

Legislation and policy

While all citizens, regardless of age or disability, are afforded the protection of criminal and civil laws, a number of global initiatives have placed specific duties on governments to provide additional protections for their older citizens. For example, the European Convention on Human Rights places obligations on governments to safeguard all adults (Donnelly et al, 2017). Additionally, a key aim of the 2012–20 WHO Strategy and Action Plan for Healthy Ageing in Europe is the prevention of elder abuse, including the need to ensure that quality regulations, standards, protocols and guidelines are in place for preventing elder abuse (WHO, 2012; Yon, 2020). Internationally, the 2030 WHO Agenda for Sustainable Development includes the prevention of elder abuse as a key target (WHO, 2015). Increasingly, governments have enacted specific laws and accompanying protocols to protect their older citizens and respond to abuse (Stewart, 2012). The focus of this legislation is often 'adult protection', which is generic; while it includes the abuse of older people, it incorporates all adults at risk, regardless of age or nature of impairment.

Arguably, an effective legal or policy framework should give older people equal access to justice while promoting their safety and autonomy. There are, however, variations in legislation across jurisdictions, with differences in the definitions of abuse and the powers and duties afforded to professionals (Montgomery et al, 2016). Taking the UK as an example, since 2007, each of the four UK countries has revised their elder abuse policy/legislation, definitions of abuse and statutory responses. Underpinning these changes is a move towards person-centred and consent-driven practice, a stronger emphasis on prevention and public engagement. However, while legislative advances are being made in many countries to promote a human rights response to elder abuse, arguably, 'much work remains to be done to crystallize aspirational laws and declarations and parlay them into (measurable) action and outcomes' (Teaster et al, 2020 p 70).

Elder abuse and mental capacity

As an adult, having the capacity to make decisions about your own life normally determines whether or not you are subject to state intervention (Stewart, 2012). Responses to alleged abuse should be made in the context of the older person's capacity to make an informed choice, including the choice about whether or not to accept help. Intervening in the lives of adults who have decision-making capacity may compromise an individual's right to self-determination (Preston-Shoot and Cornish, 2014). However, there are complexities in seeking to balance an individual's right to autonomy with a statutory duty to protect that individual, and to do so within the context of their decision-making capacity. Mackay (2017) suggests that assessing someone's safeguarding ability must be broader than just addressing binary capacity issues, and the context of one's life and relationships need to be considered. Additionally, many countries require mandatory reporting[2] of abuse in specific contexts (Donnelly, 2019).

Internationally, different legal frameworks have developed to identify and manage issues relating to mental capacity. Increasingly, the trajectory is towards developing rights-based legislative frameworks that support the principle of individual autonomy and assume capacity unless proven otherwise (see Chapter 8 for a more in-depth discussion of capacity and decision making). One of the biggest questions in terms of elder abuse is the extent to which age plays a role in adults being assumed not to have mental capacity. In taking a critical gerontological approach, it is essential that social workers identify and challenge age discrimination in these contexts.

Applying critical gerontological perspectives to social work practice

In considering elder abuse from a critical gerontology perspective we will begin by reflecting on three examples from practice; the first of these is a real case that is already in the public domain (see Smith, 2003), consequently, the full name of the older person has been used. The remaining two case

---

[2] Mandatory reporting refers to a mechanism in which individuals with reasonable suspicion that an older person is being subject to abuse or harm are required to report this either to the police or to social services. The scope and powers of mandatory reporting vary across different jurisdictions. Universal mandatory reporting requires all individuals, including the general public, to report suspected abuse, harm or neglect, while mandatory reporting may be limited to requiring reporting from designated categories of people, such as those with statutory responsibility (Donnelly, 2019).

scenarios, identified as Mr P and Ms X, are fictitious, although they have been adapted from practice.

Case 1: Societal ageism and elder abuse

Kathleen Grundy was an 81-year-old woman who, in June 1998, was found dead at her home in England. Her general practitioner, Harold Shipman recorded her cause of death as 'old age'. On investigation of an inauthentic-looking 'will', leaving £386,000 to Dr Shipman, Dr Shipman was arrested and subsequently found guilty of her murder. Mrs Grundy was not the first of Dr Shipman's elderly patients to die unexpectedly. A major independent public inquiry followed; a total of 250 murders of patients, the large majority of whom were older and female, were ascribed to Shipman over a 23-year period. The inquiry concluded that Shipman had been allowed to continue killing his patients because he attributed their deaths to natural causes such as 'old age' (Smith, 2003).

While this case is clearly extreme, arguably it should be considered an incidence of elder abuse, occurring because of the age of the victim and societal failure to recognise and respond to abuse of older people. Critical older people themselves have identified a link between social representations of old age and their vulnerability to abuse (Iborra, Garcia and Grau, 2013; Välimäki et al, 2020). The ability of Shipman to murder 250 victims undetected points to a society that on some level did not see the deaths of these older people as worthy of attention.

If we do not connect the personal experience of abuse with the political, social and cultural norms that allow it to happen, we are unwittingly attempting to contain elder abuse within a framework that privileges individualistic explanations (Harbison, 2012). This gives rise to 'an aspiration of pathology' (Penhale, 2010 p 240), a view that the characteristics of the older person are the fundamental problem. The broader context and potential impact of structural factors, such as the segregation or social isolation of older people on the basis of their age, tantamount to age discrimination, are ignored (Carney and Nash, 2020).

Case 2: Definitions and choice

Mr P is an 82-year-old man who was referred to social services by his general practitioner, as he was unable to pay his rent, was reported to be malnourished and had deteriorating mental health. Mr P admitted to giving the majority of his large pension to his son to pay off debts linked to his granddaughter's dowry. He disclosed that his son had pressured him to do so but also said that he felt that it was his duty to provide for his family. Mr P was resistive to any social work intervention and, while he acknowledged significant difficulties relating to the pressure from his son, he did not consider this as abuse. In seeking to find a way forward for Mr P, his social worker developed an ongoing supportive relationship, engaging with Mr P over time in order to assess the potential of coercive control,[3] assessing capacity in the context of Mr P's lifecourse and seeking to negotiate a culturally sensitive and rights–driven response (see Mackay, 2017).

The critical gerontology perspective suggests that there has been a narrow focus on how we conceptualise elder abuse (Biggs and Goergen, 2010). It is mainly through the efforts of health and social care professionals that elder abuse has begun to be recognised as a social problem (Biggs, 1996; Garnham and Bryant, 2017). However, in the course of defining elder abuse as a problem requiring professional intervention, the dominant narrative is a clinical, professional discourse that, despite the best intentions of those involved, can be reductive, underplaying the personal and interrelational significance of the abuse to the people who are experiencing it (Harbison et al, 2012). As with Mr P, the consequences of this discourse are far-reaching for older people in terms of their willingness to report abuse and the likelihood of that action leading to positive change.

When older people have been asked to describe what they see as abusive behaviour, abuse is often perceived in ways that are excluded from formal definitions and professional indicators (Taylor et al, 2014; Killick et al, 2015). As with Mr P, the way financial abuse is understood is implicitly intertwined with cultural values and beliefs, and this has had an inevitable impact on reporting, detection and intervention (Phelan, 2020).

Case 3: Mental capacity and residential care

Ms X is a 94-year-old woman diagnosed with dementia and recently admitted to a residential care home. Although her memory and communication were poor, she conveyed to her family that she did not feel safe in the home. She had a particular fear of night-time, and it later transpired that male residents would come into her bedroom and, on occasion, try to get into bed beside her. Ms X's family raised concerns over these fears and about the standard of personal care provided for her. The family felt that their concerns were not taken seriously.

Ms X was subsequently admitted to hospital due to general deterioration in her mental and physical health. Once in hospital, Ms X disclosed a range of concerns in relation to potential physical and emotional abuse.

---

[3] Coercive control or controlling patterns of behaviour include social isolation, extreme surveillance and threatening behaviour to control the victim-survivor (Wydall et al, 2018).

The significant risk of abuse to people living with dementia is a concern (Lelkes and O'Sullivan, 2020), with, in 2015, an estimated 47 million people worldwide living with dementia – a number projected to triple by 2050 (Livingston et al, 2017; see Chapter 10 for a more in-depth discussion on dementia). Individuals living with dementia are more likely to be subject to abuse than those without (McCausland et al, 2016), with dementia representing a particular risk factor for sexual abuse in residential settings (Burgess et al, 2000). High levels of dependency and communication difficulties increase vulnerability to abuse, which is also associated with poor quality of professional care (MacIntyre et al, 2017; Cooper and Livingstone, 2020). Moreover, from a critical gerontological perspective, it is evident that quality of care is also impacted upon by societal views of ageing, which are embedded within health and social care policies and institutions and internalised by staff and older people themselves (Wellin, 2018).

Critical gerontology approaches to practice

In our discussion thus far, we have suggested that elder abuse is rooted in harmful stereotypes and a negative social construction of old age, which can provide the perfect conditions for abuse to thrive. In the following section, we make some suggestions about how social work practice might be informed by a critical gerontology perspective. In promoting a lifecourse approach, we encourage social workers to view the older person's life holistically in order to understand the complex, multifaceted, interpersonal features of abuse. As discussed in Chapter 2, we also encourage social work practitioners and policy makers to consider how age intersects with gender, disability, inequality, poverty, ethnicity and race in ways that cause the accumulation of disadvantage over the lifecourse. While challenging, we argue that this intersectional, lifecourse approach to elder abuse will allow social workers to determine where abuse intervention should best be focused (Chonody and Teater, 2017).

International studies indicate, for example, that gender is a risk factor for elder abuse, with women more likely to experience it (Pillemer et al, 2016). Women have a greater life expectancy than men, and our frailest and oldest service users are most likely female. Moreover, the vast majority of carers of older people are female and are therefore vulnerable to poverty or gender inequality. Gender is also significant in structuring the quality of life experienced by older people, particularly women. Calasanti (2010) argues that gender inequalities are established within power relations in both local and global contexts, influencing paid labour, pension policies and family life in ways that restrict opportunities for older women and magnify gender issues throughout the lifecourse. Feminism, described as an investigation of women's subordination in order to understand how to change it (Goldner,

1993), understands violence as a reflection of unequal and oppressive power relations between the sexes. Older people's conceptualisations of abuse confirm that gender roles, family obligations and marital fidelity are all influential in contributing to abusive relationships (Martin, 2019).

Issues relating to gender-based violence can often be overlooked by health and social care providers; when women become 'older' their gender may be forgotten or hidden (Penhale, 2020). In a context where the abuse of older people is unrecognised by professionals, by the wider public and by older people themselves, older women are placed at increased risk (Martin 2019). Social work practitioners and policy makers are encouraged to:

- think about the intersection of elder abuse with gender-based violence. Identify gender-based violence and abuse and understand the particular experiences, needs and rights of older women within their socioeconomic context (Crockett et al, 2018; Penhale, 2020);
- consider the obstacles older women might face in help-seeking. For example, consider establishing peer-to-peer referral processes and help-seeking pathways that address barriers to disclosure for older women (Martin, 2019);
- consider campaigns like the Northern Ireland Women's Aid 'Older But No Safer'[4] awareness-raising initiative targeting a range of audiences to increase awareness of elder abuse, and dispelling the myth that domestic abuse does not affect older women.

As discussed in Chapter 5, in all societies it is women, children and older people who are most vulnerable to poverty, in large part because they are dependent on others for income (O'Rand et al, 2010). Poverty is known to exacerbate the potential for abuse and has been identified as the main contributor to elder abuse in developing countries (Podnieks et al, 2010). Older people may be impacted upon by poverty through poor nutrition, inadequate housing and clothing or social isolation. These are problems in their own right but may also lead to stress (Penhale, 2020). Moreover, in the context of austerity, neoliberal cost-cutting measures have impacted on health and social care provision, leading to a rise of inequality and weakening of welfare provision. The rapid ageing of increasingly globalised societies over the past 30 years provides a perfect storm in terms of increased demand for care, decreased provision of community care (Manthorpe et al, 2014) and continued pressure on women to provide eldercare, despite their increased labour force participation rates. Social work practitioners and policy makers are encouraged to:

---

[4] https://womens-aid.org.uk/older-but-no-safer/

- be poverty aware across the whole social work practice continuum, from elder abuse prevention to protection;
- consider how socioeconomic factors impact on older people and households and influence individuals' capacity to change (Morrison et al, 2018);
- consider the potential for increased dependency of the older person who may be dependent on the abuser for care in the context of neoliberal policies.

Racial and ethnic-based differences have been identified in elder abuse prevalence studies (Hernandez–Tejada et al, 2020), with, for example, high prevalence rates of psychological abuse and neglect found in many ethnic minority communities (Moon, 2000). Abuse may be exacerbated, as individuals from ethnic minority communities have been reluctant to complain about poor care, indicating a limited sense of their entitlement to services and fair treatment (Moon, 2000; Bowes et al, 2011). Much of our understanding of elder abuse is based on Western philosophy and practice, and, as such, the universal application of individualistic Western models of practice across cultures is problematic. For example, in some cultures, older people have a strong, collective moral code, promoting a sense of communal allegiance over individual well-being (Montgomery and Owen-Pugh, 2018), which will arguably influence an individual's willingness to report abuse and the suitability of responses. Social work practitioners and policy makers are encouraged to:

- consider the extent to which generic models of elder abuse investigation and interventions are applicable to a range of cultures;
- be alert to a history of discrimination that may shape expectations of fair treatment by ethnic minority groups;
- work with ethnic minority communities to help them define elder abuse and develop community expectations for services that are culturally sensitive and helpful (Moon, 2000).

Accumulation of disadvantage across the lifecourse

Throughout the lifecourse, it is well recognised that women are more likely than men to experience intimate partner violence, to be a victim of sexual assault and to have reduced access to healthcare. As women get older, the persistent and accumulative effects of these differences become more significant (Crockett et al, 2018). Studies of older people's experiences of abuse indicate that lifecourse factors are crucially important in understanding and responding to abuse (see Figure 9.1). For example, McDonald and Thomas (2013) conducted a pilot study of lifecourse factors in older people's experience of abuse in Canada. Their findings suggest that while the history of abuse is often not considered by professionals or researchers in the context of elder abuse, a childhood history of abuse had a determining influence on later mistreatment, over and above what happened later in life. Taking a lifecourse approach, Chisnell and Kelly (2019) suggest that grooming, exploitation and abuse can occur in some relationships across the life span. Common themes associated with abuse throughout the lifecourse include exploitation and power, the role of grooming by a perpetrator, the role of social deprivation, the over-simplification of categories of abuse and the coexistence of multiple types of abuse that often include an emotional or psychological element (Chisnell and Kelly, 2019). Moreover, there is frequent interdependency in abusive situations, especially in cases of family abuse where the older person is dependent on the abuser for care or support. Social work practitioners and policy makers are encouraged to:

- consider ways in which the older person might have experienced cumulative disadvantage over the lifecourse;
- consider that abuse and neglect might be part of a continuing pattern of mistreatment that has begun in early relationships;
- recognise the sustained nature of the abusive experiences and identify and respond to the intersectionality of gender, age, disability, race and other cumulative disadvantages.

Figure 9.1: Elder abuse: a holistic view on lifecourse and cumulative disadvantage

Prevention and intervention strategies

Finally, in promoting a critical gerontology approach, social workers are encouraged to act as advocates for social change, promoting a preventative agenda and encouraging consent-driven, rights-based, empowering and person-centred approaches to elder abuse investigation and intervention. Consideration is needed of the obstacles older men and women, including those from ethnic minority groups and those with a physical or cognitive disability, might face in seeking help. Such obstacles have not been sufficiently acknowledged and are not fully understood or addressed (Penhale, 2010). Awareness-raising initiatives should be prioritised and targeted at specific groups, developed within communities through co-production.

Preventative approaches should also target social factors that contribute to abuse and have the potential to be improved. For example, Hernandez-Tejada et al (2020) found that the most important predictive factors for all forms of elder abuse in the United States were lack of social support and poor health. Social workers should advocate for resources to address structural inequalities, for example, to enhance social support or improve health for older citizens, particularly for low-income groups with disproportionate minority group representation.

Additionally, education, communication training and support offered to paid carers have been found to reduce psychological abuse (McCausland et al, 2016). The support and training needs of carers should be prioritised, in particular, for those caring for someone with a physical or cognitive disability.

Finally, social workers should promote a personalisation agenda in safeguarding interventions to ensure that interventions do not predominate over the older person's will and preferences. For example, the Making Safeguarding Personal approach that provides the framework for safeguarding processes in England seeks to prioritise the needs and preferred outcomes of the older person over outcomes dictated by the professionals involved (Cooper et al, 2018). Social workers should maintain a positive and engaging working relationship with the older person in order to determine and promote their preferred outcome in situations of abuse.

Conclusion

Throughout this chapter, we have suggested ways in which professional discourses might be challenged and practice shaped by a critical gerontology perspective. This perspective recognises and challenges the influence of societal ageism on professionals and the public, giving consideration to the broader social framework that structures the relationship between social work and older women and men who have been subject to elder abuse.

Adopting a critical gerontological lens to examine these experiences should position the older person at the centre of the analysis. Their experience should be placed within a lifecourse context with consideration of wider societal issues relating to ageism, gender, race and ethnicity, disability and poverty. Adopting this holistic approach implies that vulnerability is largely situational; it is not the characteristics of the older person that result in their vulnerability, but rather it is how their lives are impacted upon by other situational and circumstantial factors such as poverty or gender-based violence that increase the risk of abuse (Penhale, 2010). Age is not the problem per se, rather, it is how chronological age is used to place a greater or lesser value on a person's life that provides the conditions in which elder abuse can flourish (Carney and Gray, 2015). As such, the critical gerontological approach thrusts power dynamics and structural inequalities between older people and perpetrators of abuse into the limelight (Doheny and Jones, 2020). Given that the professional voice has been privileged in defining elder abuse and creating a regulatory framework in response, the next stage in the battle against elder abuse calls on social workers and professionals to consider how older people might be empowered to shape policies that directly influence their lives.

References

Baker, A.A. (1975) 'Granny bashing', *Modern Geriatrics*, 8: 20–24.

Biggs, S. (1996) 'A family concern: elder abuse in British social policy', *Critical Social Policy*, 16(47): 63–88.

Biggs, S. and Goergen, T. (2010) 'Theoretical development in elder abuse and neglect', *Ageing International*, 35(3): 167–170.

Biggs, S. and Haapala, I. (2013) 'Elder mistreatment, ageism, and human rights', *International Psychogeriatrics*, 25(8): 1299–1306.

Bowes, A., Avan, G. and Macintosh, S. (2011) 'Dignity and respect in residential care: issues for black and minority ethnic groups', *Report to the Department of Health*, [online], Available from: www.scie-socialcareonline.org.uk/dignity-and-respect-in-residential-care-issues-for-black-and-minority-ethnic-groups/r/a11G000000533X4IAI

Bronfenbrenner, U. (2005) *Making Human Beings Human: Bioecological Perspectives on Human Development*, California: Sage Publications.

Burgess, A.W., Dowdell, E.B. and Prentky, R.A. (2000) 'Sexual abuse of nursing home residents', *Journal of Psychosocial Nursing and Mental Health Services*, 38(6): 10–18.

Calasanti, T. (2010) 'Gender and ageing in the context of globalization', in D. Dannefer and C. Phillipson (eds) *The SAGE Handbook of Social Gerontology*, London: Sage Publications, pp 137–149.

Carney, G.M. and Gray, M. (2015) 'Unmasking the "elderly mystique": why it is time to make the personal political in ageing research', *Journal of Aging Studies*, 35: 123–34.

Carney, G.M. and Nash, P. (2020) *Critical Questions for Ageing Societies*, Bristol: Policy Press.

Chisnell, C. and Kelly, C. (2019) *Safeguarding in Social Work Practice: A Lifespan Approach*, Learning Matters, London: Sage Publications.

Chonody, J.M. and Teater, B. (2017) *Social Work Practice with Older Adults: An Actively Aging Framework for Practice*, Los Angeles: Sage Publications.

Cooper, A., Cocker, C. and Briggs, M. (2018) 'Making safeguarding personal and social work practice with older adults: findings from local-authority survey data in England', *British Journal of Social Work*, 48(4): 1014–1032.

Cooper, C. and Livingston, C. (2020) 'Elder abuse and dementia', in A. Phelan (ed) *Advances in Elder Abuse Research*, New York: Springer International Publishing, pp 137–147.

Cooper, C., Selwood, A. and Livingston, G. (2008) 'The prevalence of elder abuse and neglect: a systematic review', *Age and Ageing*, 37(2): 151–160.

CPEA (2020) *Independent Whole Systems Review into Safeguarding and Care at Dunmurry Manor Care Home*, CPEA: Belfast

Crockett, C., Cooper, B. and Brandl, B. (2018) 'Intersectional stigma and late-life intimate-partner and sexual violence: how social workers can bolster safety and healing for older survivors', *British Journal of Social Work*, 48(4): 1000–1013.

Doheny, S. and Jones, R.I. (2020) 'What's so critical about it? An analysis of critique within different strands of critical gerontology', *Ageing & Society*, 1–21, doi:10.1017/S0144686X20000288.

Donnelly, S. (2019) 'Mandatory reporting and adult safeguarding: a rapid realist review', *The Journal of Adult Protection*, 21(5): 241–251.

Donnelly, S., O'Brien, M., Walsh, J., McInerney, J., Campbell, J. and Kodate, N. (2017) *Adult Safeguarding Legislation and Policy Rapid Realist Literature Review*, Dublin: HSE National Safeguarding Office/Trigraph Limited.

Garnham, B. and Bryant, L. (2017) 'Epistemological erasure: the subject of abuse in the problematization of "elder abuse"', *Journal of Aging Studies*, 41: 5–59.

Goldner, V. (1993) 'Feminist theories', in P. Boss, W.J. Doherty, R. LaRossa, W.R. Schumm, and S.K Steinmetz (eds) *Sourcebook of Family Theories and Methods: A Contextual Approach*, New York: Springer Science & Business Media, pp 623–626.

Gullette, M. (2017) *Ending Ageism, or How not to Shoot Older People*, Chicago: Chicago University Press.

Harbison, J., Coughlan, S., Beaulieu, M., Karabanow, J., Vanderplaat, M., Wildeman, S. and Wexler, E. (2012) 'Understanding "elder abuse and neglect": a critique of assumptions underpinning responses to the mistreatment and neglect of older people', *Journal of Elder Abuse & Neglect*, 24(2): 88–103.

Hernandez-Tejada, M.A., Frook, G., Steedley, M., Watkins, J. and Acierno, R. (2020) 'Demographic-based risk of reporting psychopathology and poor health among mistreated older adults in the national elder mistreatment study wave II', *Aging & Mental Health*, 24(1): 22–26.

Iborra, I., Garcia, Y. and Grau, E. (2013) 'Spain', in A. Phelan (eds) *International Perspectives on Elder Abuse*, London: Routledge, pp 168–188.

Killick, C., Taylor, B.J., Begley, E., Carter Anand, J. and O'Brien, M. (2015) 'Older people's conceptualization of abuse: a systematic review', *Journal of Elder Abuse & Neglect*, 27(2): 100–120.

Lelkes, J. and O'Sullivan, E. (2020) 'Elder abuse and adult safeguarding', *Medicine*, 49(1): 62–65.

Livingston, G., Sommerlad, A., Orgeta, V., Costafreda, S.G., Huntley, J., Ames, D., Ballard, C., Banerjee, S., Burns, A., Cohen-Mansfield, J., Cooper, C., Fox, N., Gitlin, L.N., Howard, R., Kales, H.C., Larson, E.B., Ritchie, K., Rockwood, K., Sampson, E.L., Samus, Q., Schneider, L.S., Selbaek, G., Teri, L. and Mukadam, N. (2017) 'Dementia prevention, intervention, and care', *Lancet*, 390(10113): 2673–2734.

MacIntyre, G., Stewart, A. and McCusker, P. (2017) *Safeguarding Adults: Key Themes and Issues*, London: Palgrave.

Mackay, K. (2017) 'Choosing to live with harm? A presentation of two case studies to explore the perspective of those who experienced adult safeguarding interventions', *Ethics and Social Welfare*, 11(1): 33–46.

Manthorpe, J., Klee, D., Williams, C. and Cooper, A. (2014) 'Making safeguarding personal: developing responses and enhancing skills', *The Journal of Adult Protection*, 16(2): 96–103.

Martin, E. (2019) *Exploring a Hidden Population at the Intersection of Gender, Ageing, Domestic Violence and Substance Use*, unpublished PhD thesis, Queen's University, Belfast.

McCausland, B., Knight, L., Page, L. and Trevillion, K. (2016) 'A systematic review of the prevalence and odds of domestic abuse victimization among people with dementia', *International Review of Psychiatry*, 28(5): 475–484.

McDonald, L. and Thomas, C. (2013) 'Elder abuse through a life course lens', *International Psychogeriatrics*, 25(8): 1235–1243.

Montgomery, L. and Owen-Pugh, V. (2018) 'Therapeutic interventions for bereavement: learning from Ugandan therapists', *International Social Work*, 61(6): 988–999.

Montgomery, L., Anand, J., McKay, K., Taylor, B., Pearson, K.C. and Harper, C.M. (2016) 'Implications of divergences in Adult Protection legislation', *Journal of Adult Protection*, 18(3): 149–160.

Moon, A. (2000) 'Perceptions of elder abuse among various cultural groups: similarities and differences', *Generations: Journal of the American Society on Aging*, 24(2): 75–80.

Morrison, A., McCartan, G., Davidson, G. and Bunting, L. (2018) *Anti-poverty Practice Framework for Social Work in Northern Ireland*, Belfast: Department of Health UK.

O'Keefe, M., Hills, M., Doyle, C., McCreadie, S., Scholes, R., Constantine, R., Tinker, A., Manthorpe, J., Biggs, S. and Erens, B. (2007) *UK Study of Abuse and Neglect of Older People Prevalence Survey Report*, London: Department of Health UK.

O'Rand, A., Isaacs, K. and Roth, L. (2010) 'Age and inequality in global context', in D. Dannefer and C. Phillipson (eds) *The SAGE Handbook of Social Gerontology*, Los Angeles: Sage Publications, pp 127–136.

Penhale, B. (2010) 'Responding and intervening in elder abuse and neglect', *Ageing International*, 35(3): 235–252.

Penhale, B. (2020) 'Gender issues in Elder Abuse', in A. Phelan (ed) *Advances in Elder Abuse Research*, New York: Springer International Publishing, pp 165–181.

Phelan, A. (ed) (2013) *International Perspectives on Elder Abuse*, London: Routledge.

Phelan, A. (ed) (2020) *Advances in Elder Abuse Research*, New York: Springer International Publishing.

Pillemer, K., Burnes, D., Riffin, C. and Lachs, M.S. (2016) 'Elder abuse: global situation, risk factors, and prevention strategies', *The Gerontologist*, 56(Suppl 2): S194–S205.

Podnieks, E., Anetzberger, G.J., Wilson, S.J., Teaster, P.B. and Wangmo, T. (2010) 'WorldView environmental scan on elder abuse', *Journal of Elder Abuse & Neglect*, 22(1–2): 164–179.

Preston-Shoot, M. and Cornish, S. (2014) 'Paternalism or proportionality? Experiences and outcomes of the Adult Support and Protection (Scotland) Act 2007', *Journal of Adult Protection*, 16(1): 5–16.

Smith, J. (2003) *The Shipman Enquiry*, London: The Stationery Office, [online], Available from: https://assets.publishing.service.gov.uk/governm ent/uploads/system/uploads/attachment_data/file/273227/5854.pdf [Accessed 1 February 2021].

Soares, J., Barros, H., Torres-Gonzales, F., Ioannidi-Kapolou, E., Lamura, G. and Lindert, J. (2010) 'Abuse and health in Europe', as cited in I. Garcia and E. Grau (2010) *Abuse and Health Among Elderly in Europe*, Kanus: Lithuanian University of Health Sciences Press.

Stewart, A. (2012) *Supporting Vulnerable Adults: Citizenship, Capacity, Choice*, Edinburgh: Dunedin.

Taylor, B.J., Killick, C., O'Brien, M., Begley, E. and Carter Anand, J. (2014) 'Older people's conceptualisation of elder abuse and neglect', *Journal of Elder Abuse and Neglect*, 2(3): 223–243.

Teaster, P.B., Lindberg, B.W. and Zhao, Y. (2020) 'Elder abuse policy, past, present, and future trends', in A. Phelan (ed) *Advances in Elder Abuse Research*, New York: Springer International Publishing, pp 53–71.

Välimäki, T., Mäki-Petäjä-Leinonen, A. and Vaismoradi, M. (2020) 'Abuse in the caregiving relationship between older people with memory disorders and family caregivers: a systematic review', *Journal of Advanced Nursing*, 76(8): 1977–1987.

Wellin, C. (ed) (2018) *Critical Gerontology Comes of Age: Advances in Research and Theory for a New Century*, London: Routledge.

World Health Organization (WHO) (2002) *The Toronto Declaration on the Global Prevention of Elder Abuse*, Geneva: World Health Organization, [online], Available from: www.who.int/ageing/projects/elder_abuse/alc_ toronto_declaration_en.pdf [Accessed 1 February 2021].

WHO (2012) *Strategy and Action Plan for Health Ageing in Europe, 2012–2020*, [online], Available from: www.euro.who.int/en/health-topics/Life-stages/ healthy-ageing/publications/2012/strategy-and-action-plan-for-healthy- ageing-in-europe,-20122020 [Accessed 1 February 2021].

WHO (2015) *Transforming our World: The 2030 Agenda for Sustainable Development*, [online], Available from: https://sdgs.un.org/publications/ transforming-our-world-2030-agenda-sustainable-development-17981 [Accessed 1 February 2021].

Wydall, S., Clarke, A., Williams, J. and Zerk, R. (2018) 'Domestic abuse and elder abuse in Wales: a tale of two initiatives', *British Journal of Social Work*, 48(4): 962–981.

Yon, Y., Lam, J., Passmore, J., Huber, M. and Sethi, D. (2020) 'The public health approach to elder abuse prevention in Europe: progress and challenges', in A. Phelan (ed) *Advances in Elder Abuse Research*, New York: Springer International Publishing, pp 223–237.

10

Dementia: a disability and a human rights concern

Suzanne Cahill[1]

Dementia is a broad clinical term used to describe a group of illnesses that have common symptoms but different origins. There are hundreds of different types of dementia, but by far the most common is Alzheimer's disease (Winblad et al, 2016). Age is the single strongest risk factor for dementia (WHO, 2019), but some rarer types of dementia, such as frontotemporal dementia, can occur in younger to middle-aged adults (Jefferies and Aggrawal, 2009). Around the world, about 50 million people have dementia, of whom about 10 million live in Europe (WHO, 2019). However, population ageing means that over the next 30 years the numbers of people likely to develop dementia will reach 131 million. The biggest increase will be among people living in low- to middle-income countries, as this is where population ageing is happening fastest (WHO, 2015a). Dementia does not only incur emotional and social costs; its economic cost is very considerable. For example, in 2018 the global cost of dementia was estimated to be circa \$1 trillion (ADI, 2015). Accordingly, the magnitude of dementia should not be underestimated.

In this chapter, a critical gerontological lens will be used to help interrogate and better understand several of the challenges and complexities that gerontological social workers face because of dementia and the pivotal position the biomedical model has had in framing dementia since the latter half of the 20th century. The specific aim of this chapter, therefore, is to apply a critical gerontological lens to challenge the dominant discourse and put forward alternate frameworks for broadening the debate on dementia,

---

[1] **Suzanne Cahill** is Adjunct Professor of Social Work and Social Policy at Trinity College Dublin, Ireland. She holds an honorary professorship in Dementia Care at the National University of Ireland Galway and is an affiliated Professor in Health and Welfare at the Institute of Gerontology in Jönkoping University in Sweden. Most of her academic career has been spent researching and campaigning for the rights of people living with dementia and their family caregivers. Her most recent book is *Perspectives on the Person with Dementia and Family Caregiving in Ireland* (Peter Lang, 2021).

improving practice and giving agency, choice and control back to the individual and their family members. By applying this lens and framing dementia as a disability and a human rights issue, social workers can help to enhance practice, inform policy and create a more inclusive society for all. Questions to be answered in this chapter will include: (1) how the critical gerontological lens can be used to extend social workers' understanding of the complexities of dementia; (2) how social workers can help to maximise and support capacity and decision making for people living with dementia; and (3) how they can balance the rights of people living with dementia, and of their family carers, against the backdrop of neoliberal policies that may result in reliance on family members for the individual's home support.

The biomedical model and how dementia defies biomedical thinking

Dementia is a progressive and usually irreversible condition characterised by symptoms that include memory loss, cognitive decline, impairment in motor skills and a deterioration in behavioural, emotional, psychological and social skills. In young people, and for most of the 20th century, dementia was labelled Alzheimer's disease (Alzheimer, 1907); it was considered rare and abnormal and was not amenable to treatment. In older people, dementia was labelled as senility and was considered a normal part of ageing (Kahn, 1975). So, to be forgetful, disorientated and exhibit irregular behaviour was not unusual, and doting and senility were an expected part of the ageing process. The alleged normality of senility was finally challenged in the late 1960s by scientists (Blessed et al, 1968) who showed that both young people and some older people previously labelled as 'senile' could develop Alzheimer's disease, the most common type of dementia. This work led to the disease or biomedical model that is the conventional perspective most of us are familiar with.

Proponents of the biomedical model argue that dementia is a progressive, irreversible, neurodegenerative brain disorder. It is characterised by intellectual deterioration and by a deterioration in mental and physical functioning (NICE/SCIE, 2007). The focus here is on aetiology (the causes of the disease), pathology (the disease), prognosis (expectation of disease trajectory) and pharmacology (drug treatments for disease). The biomedical framing (Finnema et al, 2000) focuses mainly on deficits, plaques and tangles, the diseased and atrophied brain. Increasingly the person is seen as a patient whose personhood (identity and social standing) and scope to engage in decision making is significantly impaired and whose actions and behaviour (even regular) are often interpreted as pathological. The model has the potential to reduce the person to a non-person, an isolated patient or a passive recipient of care. Dementia becomes the individual's defining features and all emotional, relational and social bonds are disregarded. Drug treatments are the ultimate solution to all medical problems and, until a cure is found, the condition is regarded as tragic. A doom and gloom nihilistic discourse prevails. In short, the biomedical model views dementia as an impairment that needs to be treated, cured and fixed (Garcia Iriarte et al, 2016).

But, in many ways, dementia defies conventional and biomedical thinking (Hughes, 2011). First, as a syndrome, it cannot be 'diagnosed' but only 'recognised', since, in of itself, dementia is not a disease. For example, a medical doctor can suspect that dementia is developing in a patient, but until a full battery of tests, including brain scans, blood tests, neuropsychological testing and, at times, psychiatric assessment, are undertaken, the disease or diseases that cause dementia – that is, the dementia sub-type – cannot be identified. Knowing the dementia sub-type is important, as the latter determines drug treatments. Second, no blood or urine-based biomarkers (the characteristics by which diseases can be identified) are available clinically for dementia. Third, drug treatments are ineffective in the majority of cases and there is no consistent evidence from clinical trials and systematic reviews that anti-dementia drugs improve quality of life (Cooper et al, 2013). Fourth, there is no direct causal pathway between brain pathology and dementia symptoms. For example, traditionally, plaques (clusters of abnormal proteins that form between nerve cells in the brain) and tangles (knotted abnormal proteins that form inside brain cells) identified on autopsy were considered the hallmarks of Alzheimer's disease but more recent research as cited by Vernooij-Dassen (2020) has shown that some people whose brain autopsies demonstrate plaques had no symptoms of the condition when alive. Others, whose brain autopsies show normal brain structure and functioning (no plaques and tangles), had symptoms of dementia when alive. The nuns' study, a United States-based longitudinal study (Snowdon, 1997) of a large group of Notre Dame Catholic nuns, designed to investigate causes of Alzheimer's disease, also revealed similar findings, with no clear causal pathway found between symptom presentation in life and brain pathology following death.

Dementia as a disability

There is merit therefore in applying a critical lens to help broaden the debate on dementia and challenge more conventional thinking, and in recent years a number of different lenses have been successfully applied. These include personhood (Kitwood,1997), citizenship (Bartlett and O'Connor, 2010), a population-health approach (Travers et al, 2015), disability (Gilliard et al, 2005; Shakespeare et al, 2017) and human rights (Kelly and Innes, 2012; Cahill, 2018). In particular, the disability lens holds appeal for gerontological social work where the principles of respect for diversity, autonomy, self-determination, equality, social justice and social inclusion must at all times be upheld. These same principles align well with social work principles and values. Although the disability framing has gained traction since the 1990s, some laypeople, including those living with dementia, have eschewed this labelling (Mental Health Foundation, 2015). People from different cultural backgrounds also define the meaning of dementia and its associated stigma differently and the condition does not always have negative connotations (Cipriani and Borin, 2015). Therefore, we must start by asking the question whether dementia can be regarded as a disability. This is a different question from another one often posed: do people with dementia consider themselves as disabled?

Nobody would refute the fact that dementia is a disability, since the diseases that cause it create inabilities. Take for example Alzheimer's disease; it causes inabilities in rational thinking, memory, problem solving, judgement and so on. But, unlike physical disabilities that are often visible and sometimes congenital, many of the inabilities associated with dementia are not readily apparent and develop over time. These impairments may fluctuate and in the long term are not amenable to rehabilitation. Nor have we witnessed dementia activists campaigning for non-discriminatory policies or staging riots calling for appropriate welfare entitlements. For these reasons, along with others such as the power of the medical fraternity, the motivation of pharmaceutical companies to find the rubber bullet and the influence of the media, many people, including those who have dementia, have been disinclined to think about dementia as a disability.

Yet there are benefits associated with challenging the biomedical model and applying a critical gerontological lens to consider dementia as a disability. First, the disability framing reminds us that the everyday experiences of an older person with dementia are shaped not only by the impairment(s) but also by broader societal and political factors. Disability is a problem located in society, and it is society, through its institutions and unhelpful environments, and not the impairment, that disables the person. Applying the critical gerontological lens, social workers must consider what society can do to help the older person to live well with dementia and what they can do to promote the older person's agency, autonomy, independence and quality of life.

For example, at diagnosis, the social worker needs to be involved in advising the older person and their family members about issues pertinent to that stage of the illness trajectory. This includes empowering the older person and giving advice on (i) advanced care planning tools, including making healthcare directives and appointing enduring powers of attorney; (ii) access to home technologies, to promote more independent living; (iii) access to cognitive rehabilitation and cognitive stimulation therapy and so on. The emphasis here should not be on 'prescribed disengagement', a term used to describe the unfair paternalistic and sometimes oppressive ways some older people are treated at the time of a dementia diagnosis (Lee-Fay et al, 2018) but, rather, on mobilising all of the resources necessary to empower the individual to take control over their own life. This includes supporting that person to participate in future care planning and other important decision making relevant to their life; see Chapter 8. In other words, in applying the critical gerontological lens, social workers need to realise that solutions to dementia can be found not in eliminating the impairments (a biological solution) but, rather, in dismantling the social, attitudinal and environmental barriers society sometimes erects against those who have a disability like dementia (a sociopolitical solution) (Degener, 2014).

Extrapolating from this, social workers need to understand the term 'excess disability'. This is defined as 'the discrepancy that exists when a person's functional incapacity is greater than that warranted by the actual impairment' (Sabat, 1994, p 158), and can be eliminated through the manipulation of the built environment and psychosocial environment. For example, by adapting the physical environment through cueing, signage, assistive technology and so on and making it more accessible, a cognitively impaired person's autonomy can be promoted. Likewise, by challenging negative stereotypes and eliminating the pejorative language often surrounding dementia, a person's self-esteem and sense of worth may be enhanced and that person may be helped to lead a more normal life. This model gives agency, power and control back to the person who is the expert by experience and whose rights should always be placed at the centre stage.

Consider for a moment the current situation where many government-led home care services have been temporarily discontinued due to COVID-19. As I write, many daycare centres in Ireland remain closed because of the pandemic and respite care and other post-diagnostic services critical to promoting quality of life have been temporarily discontinued. This is despite evidence that service closure has resulted in significant deskilling and a deterioration in the health and well-being of some people living with dementia, along with their primary caregivers (Alzheimer Society of Ireland, 2020; Hennelly and Cahill, 2020). Also consider the harsh restrictions imposed on some family members regarding visits to care homes and nursing homes, where visiting times are limited and monitored and the residents' privacy rights may not always be strictly upheld. Although understandable when first introduced, several of these restrictions have continued during a period when hairdressers, gastronomic pubs, sports clubs and other public amenities have reopened.

Gerontological social workers must question, challenge and play a key role in revoking several of these unfair and discriminatory policies and practices. Are such policies and practices inclusive and in keeping with the promotion of human rights, including the older person's right to a family life? Who advocates for the resident with severe dementia, who is unable to speak for herself and whose family caregiver may be silenced, frightened to complain for fear of recrimination? For those living in care homes or nursing homes because of dementia, do their healthcare needs receive the same attention as the healthcare needs of other residents who are cognitively intact? Are care home residents who have dementia and who develop COVID-19, offered specialist medical treatment, including a critical-care bed in a hospital setting if required? Gerontological social workers must be trained to look not only at how dementia may disable the older person but also at how unfair systems and structures may further disable them and render them vulnerable. At all times they must be cognisant of the need to apply both a micro and macro level of analysis in their everyday social work practice.

There are many other examples of discriminatory policies that make life all the more difficult for the individual living with dementia and where gerontological social workers can play a critical key role, highlighting service deficits and lobbying for policy reform. For example, in some Western countries, because of age and the absence of age-appropriate services, it can be extremely difficult for a cognitively impaired person to obtain a diagnosis of dementia or qualify for post-diagnostic services (Fox et al, 2020). We also know that knowledge about Alzheimer's disease seems to vary between ethnic groups, suggesting a lack of uptake of service use by minorities (Ayalon and Areán, 2004) and dependence on statutory services being seen as a source of shame (Rauf, 2011). Lengthy delays in obtaining general practice or memory clinic test results can add further distress for people worried about their cognitive and memory symptoms. The negative attitude of some employers toward dementia and their inability to provide reasonable accommodation, adjusting employment arrangements for a person diagnosed with mild dementia, are further examples of discrimination. Professor Sube Bannerjee's UK-based research showed the harmful effects that antipsychotic medication can have when prescribed to many people with dementia. His review suggested that antipsychotic medication was effective in only about 20 per cent of all cases yet accounted for as many as about 1,800 cases of excess mortality per year in the UK and about 1,600 cases of stroke (Bannerjee, 2009). Yet, why are so many older people in nursing homes given this type of medication for agitation and other challenging behaviours, despite evidence of the often-deleterious effects of these drugs?

The ubiquity of neoliberal policies across many European countries and the absence of adequate government support to enable people living with dementia to remain at home in the community is a real challenge for gerontological social workers. For example, the European Union RightTimePlaceCare study (Bökberg et al, 2015), which collected data on community services across eight European countries, showed a significant absence of dementia specialist services across Europe and a major gap between service use and service provision. In this same study, specialist services considered vital to the sustainability of home care were seldom available, and even when they were, they were seldom used, probably because these services were inappropriate. Boyle (2010) has argued that failure on the part of the UK government to expand home care services for older people has created a barrier, denying older people the right to exercise autonomy and to continue living at home. Gerontological social workers need to challenge inequities in service provision such as these and address older people's rights against the backdrop of what constitute at times harsh neoliberal policies.

Dementia as a human rights issue

Many of these earlier questions and concerns have a human rights dimension, and the corollary to applying a critical gerontological lens and contextualising dementia as a disability is that dementia should also be seen as a human rights issue. It is a human rights issue, since those living with the condition are at heightened risk of injustice, discrimination, exclusion and inequality (Mittler, 2015). They are at heightened risk because of their age – being older, the person is often subjected to ageist attitudes and policies; and because of gender – more women than men develop dementia. They are at heightened risk because of their socioeconomic status – women who in some Western European countries have never worked in the labour market are often financially disadvantaged in later life. They are at increased risk too because of ethnicity – about 40 per cent of dementia is preventable (Livingston et al, 2020), but knowledge of protective factors for dementia remains poor among racial and ethnic minority groups (Cahill et al, 2015). For example, a study that examined ethnic differences in female dementia caregivers' knowledge, attitudes and beliefs about Alzheimer's disease showed that Hispanics and Chinese, compared to the White group, were more likely to believe that the condition is a normal part of ageing and that it can be diagnosed by a blood test (Gray et al, 2009). In this way, age, gender, socioeconomic status and ethnicity, either independently or jointly, place some older people at heightened risk of developing dementia, and having dementia can often compromise that person's human rights (Mittler, 2015; see Chapter 3).

Many people also conflate mental capacity and legal capacity. Mental capacity refers to one's decision-making ability and skills. It is usually assessed by a health service professional such as a doctor, social worker or psychologist. To have mental capacity a person must demonstrate that they can understand, retain, use and weigh up information and options to make and communicate a decision. On the other hand, legal capacity is usually determined by a lawyer and refers to the recognition that a person is both a holder and executor of legal rights (Flynn, 2018). The right to legal capacity means the right to be recognised as a person before the law on an equal basis with others, and for that individual to have rights and responsibilities (Flynn, 2018).

Often the assessment of mental capacity is used by health and social care professionals as a justification to deny a person's legal capacity, and indeed in several European countries today this practice is supported by outdated mental health legislation that favours substituted over supportive decision making (Alzheimer Europe, 2016). In Ireland, the law has (under the 2015 Assisted Decision-Making Capacity Act) been updated to reflect a presumption of capacity. This means that in Ireland a person shall not be deemed as being incapable of engaging in decision making unless all practical steps have first been taken and have failed to help that person to do so. In this way, the new mental health legislation in Ireland enshrines a legal right to autonomy for a person whose mental capacity may be compromised (Cahill, 2018). One of the difficulties in Ireland, however, is that this new legislation is still not being fully implemented by many health and social care professionals, who continue to adhere to the old system. This is another area where gerontological social workers must question practices that serve to disempower older people.

Gerontological social workers also need to keep in mind that people with dementia come within the United Nations Convention on the Rights of People with Disabilities (UNCRPD) definition of people with disabilities and therefore have access to all the rights contained in that Convention (CRPD, 2006). The latter is a useful tool for practitioners to use when applying a critical gerontological lens to interrogate practice. Each of the Articles contained in the UNCRPD has direct application to the lives of people living with dementia and their family members. Gerontological social workers need to familiarise themselves with these Articles and use them to challenge injustices and discrimination. They are the gold standards against which compliance must be measured: respect for the full range of the person's rights, will and preference must remain at the heart of every legal system and must be achieved by social workers, irrespective of the existence of any disability including dementia. Article 12 is especially important, as it states that people living with a disability have a right to enjoy legal capacity on an equal basis with others and will be provided with the support required to exercise this capacity. This Article explicitly forbids mental capacity to be used as a justification for the denial of legal capacity, even with respect to important decisions. Accordingly, substituted decision making is a violation of human rights and should never be permitted.

In the context of the person living with dementia, some other salient rights contained in the UNCRPD include the right to live independently and be included in the community (Article 19), the right to privacy (Article 22), the right to health, including a diagnosis (Article 25) and the right to rehabilitation (Article 26). Framing dementia as a rights issue also means that at a local level a country's Human Rights and Equality Acts should be invoked to protect the individual. At an international level, all policies, legislation and guidelines need to comply with various treaties and conventions, including the European Convention on Human Rights. Interestingly, the International Federation of Social Workers (IFSW) considers social work to be a human rights profession and social workers are well positioned to ensure that people's fundamental rights are at all times respected and upheld (IFSW, 2018).

Finally, understanding dementia as a human rights issue means adopting a human rights approach in everyday gerontological social work practice. This is an operational way of working in the field from a social model perspective (Garcia Iriarte, 2016). The social model considers dementia as a problem located in society. By and large, it is society, not the individual, that disables and oppresses individuals with dementia. Likewise, it is society through its well-formulated social policy that can overturn oppressive practices. The human rights approach means training practitioners in human rights principles and applying these principles, namely, participation, accountability, non-discrimination, empowerment and legality in everyday practice (WHO, 2015b). Participation refers to the fact that everyone has a right to participate in decisions that affect their own lives. Accountability means that human service organisations must monitor human rights standards and have remedies in place to address standard breaches. Non-discrimination refers to the fact that all forms of discrimination are prohibited, prevented and eliminated, with priority given to the most vulnerable. Empowerment means that all individuals and communities should understand their rights and be supported to participate in the development of policies and practices that affect their lives. Legality refers to the recognition that rights are legally enforceable entitlements linked to national and international law.

These principles align well with social work principles and can build on social workers' professional ethics. These human rights principles are also in line with most people's fundamental values, for example, empathy, fairness, equity, compassion and so on. A human rights approach ensures that a person is treated with maximum dignity and respect and is fully involved in all important decision making about their support and care. All too often health and social care practitioners, including social workers, are trained to assess and consider human needs but not human rights. Human rights training can help to build on elements of social work training and person-centred care training (Cahill, 2018). It provides a more robust framework for social work practitioners, as it offers the potential for legal protection, service entitlement and a positive shift in how dementia is understood and responded to. Most importantly, gerontological social workers can use a human rights approach to enhance their practice, obtain additional resources, empower others and protect themselves.

Facilitators and obstacles to using a human rights-based approach

The biomedical model has traditionally influenced the dominant discourse on dementia and has influenced practitioners', policy makers' and researchers' understanding and response to dementia. Recent years have witnessed a shift in the tone of the dominant discourse; slowly, dementia is being understood as a disability with a human rights dimension. What has helped to shape this shift is the powerful voice of the individual living with dementia; an authentic voice that for so long has been silenced. What has also helped is the collective voice of persons directly affected by dementia, through organisations like the Dementia Alliance International (DAI, 2016). Our understanding of and response to dementia have also been hugely broadened by the work of the WHO, especially their development and implementation of the global action plan on dementia, a policy document heavily embedded in human rights (WHO, 2017). It has also been influenced by the excellent work of Alzheimer Disease International and Alzheimer Europe, organisations committed to empowering people with dementia and ensuring their rights are upheld.

On the other hand, obstacles still remain that continue to make it difficult for service providers, including gerontological social workers, to use a human rights-based approach in their practice. These include a fear of whistleblowing by front-line workers, the lack of focus on human rights training in many undergraduate degree courses and the absence of severe penalties being imposed on those who breach human rights. These obstacles need to be overcome and the rights of people diagnosed with dementia must be driven from all directions and be led by the top levels of organisations.

Conclusion

Dementia poses key challenges for gerontological social workers because of its complexity and because of the way in which the illness affects every aspect of an individual's cognitive, physical, social, emotional and behavioural health. It is a particular challenge since public and professional understandings of dementia have traditionally been influenced by the biomedical model, a model that, although useful, has, as argued in this chapter, significant limitations. However, gerontological social workers are often employed in clinical settings where this disease model remains dominant and is seldom challenged. This model, with its emphasis on plaques and tangles, drugs, custodial care and an atrophied brain, tends to pathologise the individual, seeing the person as 'being the disease' rather than 'having the disease'.

By applying a critical gerontological lens, social workers have within reach the tools necessary to look beyond the biomedical model, expand thinking and use different prisms to challenge some of the artificial barriers some people with dementia and their family members encounter. For example, at diagnosis, the primary care/community-based social worker can play a key role in advising the older person and family members on topics such as driving, financial support, banking, accessing appropriate legal support such as advanced care planning and so on. What is critically important here is that the older person is given ample opportunity and support to engage in decision making on matters directly relevant to their life. Later and at a more advanced stage of the illness, for example when the move from home into a care home is being considered, the critical gerontological lens can again be applied by the social work practitioner, committed to ensuring that all possible support services have been exhausted before that person enters long-term residential care. At this more advanced stage, the gerontological social worker continues to play a key role in advocating for the individual, ensuring that any decision making undertaken always respects the person's will and preference. This may mean, for example, reminding multidisciplinary team members or palliative care staff about the detailed content of an advanced healthcare directive.

In this chapter a critical gerontological lens has been applied to interrogate dementia from a practice and policy perspective. It is argued that, for gerontological social workers, this lens broadens the debate on dementia and challenges the dominant discourse or conventional way of thinking about dementia. It allows for a deeper and more holistic understanding of a condition that has traditionally been seen in a nihilistic way and it reinforces the need for social work practitioners to work at both a personal/individual and a wider societal level. By applying the critical gerontological lens and by contextualising dementia as a disability and a human rights concern, gerontological social workers can help to enhance practice, inform policy and create a more inclusive society for everyone. By using this framework, social work practice underpinned by values such as fairness, equity, respect and dignity can be promoted. The lens also ensures that human rights principles such as participation, accountability, non-discrimination, empowerment and legality are operationalised in everyday social work practice with older people. The values of the social work profession mean that it is ideally positioned to uphold older people's rights, and this chapter has argued that contextualising dementia as a disability and human rights concern provides fresh insights and new frameworks for interrogating practice and policy.

References

Alzheimer, A. (1907) 'Über eine eigenartige Erkrankung der Hirnrinde: Allgemeine Zeitschrift für Psychiatrie und Psychisch-Gerichtliche Medizin, 64', in D.A. Rottenberg and F.H. Hochberg (eds) *Neurological Classics in Modern Translation*, New York: Hafner Press, pp 146–148.

Alzheimer Europe (2016) *Dementia in Europe Yearbook: Decision-making and Legal Capacity Issues in Dementia*, Luxembourg: Alzheimer Europe.

Alzheimer's Disease International (2015) *The World Alzheimer Report 2015: The Global Impact of Dementia: An Analysis of Prevalence, Incidence, Cost and Trends*, London: Alzheimer's Disease International, [online], Available from: www.alz.co.uk/research/world-report-2015 [Accessed 8 April 2020].

Alzheimer Society of Ireland (2020) *COVID-19: Impact and Need for People Living with Dementia and Family Carers*, [online], Available from: https://alzheimer.ie/wp-content/uploads/2020/07/ASI-Follow-Up-Covid-Report-Final.pdf [Accessed 8 April 2020].

Ayalon, L. and Areán, P.A. (2004) 'Knowledge of Alzheimer's disease in four ethnic groups of older adults', *International Journal of Geriatric Psychiatry*, 19(1): 51–57.

Banerjee, S. (2009) *The Use of Antipsychotic Medication for People with Dementia: Time for Action. A Report for the Minister of State for Care Services*, London: Department of Health, [online], Available from: www.rcpsych.ac.uk/pdf/Antipsychotic%20Bannerjee%20Report.pdf [Accessed 8 April 2017].

Bartlett, R. and O'Connor, D. (2010) *Broadening the Dementia Debate: Towards Social Citizenship*, Bristol: Policy Press.

Blessed, G., Tomlinson, B.E. and Roth, M. (1968) 'The association between quantitative measures of dementia and of senile change in the cerebral grey matter of elderly subjects', *The British Journal of Psychiatry*, 114(512): 797–811.

Bökberg, C., Ahlström, G., Leino-Kilpi, H., Soto-Martin, M.E., Cabrera, E., Verbeek, H., Saks, K., Stephans, A., Sutcliffe, C. and Karlsson, S. (2015) 'Care and service at home for persons with dementia in Europe', *Journal of Nursing Scholarship*, 47(5): 407–416.

Boyle, G. (2010) 'Social policy for people with dementia in England: promoting human rights?' *Health & Social Care in the Community*, 18(5): 511–519.

Cahill, S. (2018) *Dementia and Human Rights*, Bristol: Policy Press.

Cahill, S., Pierce, M., Werner, P., Darley, A. and Bobersky, A. (2015) 'A systematic review of the public's knowledge and understanding of Alzheimer's disease and dementia', *Alzheimer Disease & Associated Disorders*, 29(3): 255–275.

Cipriani, G. and Borin, G. (2015) *Understanding Dementia in the Sociocultural Context: A Review* (2), 198, [online], Available from: https://login.e.bibl.liu.se/login?url=https://search.ebscohost.com/login.aspx?direct=true&AuthType=ip,uid&db=edsbl&AN=RN367352897&lang=sv&site=eds-live&scope=site [Accessed 23 September 2021].

Cooper, C., Mukadam, N., Katona, C., Lyketsos, C.G., Blazer, D., Ames, D., Rabins, P., Brodaty, H., de Mendonça Lima, C. and Livingston, G. (2013) 'Systematic review of the effectiveness of pharmacologic interventions to improve quality of life and well-being in people with dementia', *The American Journal of Geriatric Psychiatry*, 21(2): 173–183.

CRPD (2006) *Convention on the Rights of Persons with Disabilities*, New York: United Nations.

Degener, T. (2014) 'A human rights model of disability', in P. Blanck and E. Flynn (eds) *Routledge Handbook of Disability Law and Human Rights*, London and New York: Routledge, pp 31–51.

Dementia Alliance International (2016) *The Human Rights of People Living with Dementia: From Rhetoric to Reality*, Ankeny: Dementia Alliance International.

Finnema, E., Droes, R.M., Ribbe, M. and van Tilburg, W. (2000) 'A review of psychosocial models in psychogeriatrics: implications for care and research', *Alzheimer Disease and Associated Disorders*, 14(2): 68–80.

Flynn, E. (2018) 'Legal capacity for people with dementia: a human rights approach', in S. Cahill (ed) *Dementia and Human Rights*, Bristol: Policy Press, pp 157–174.

Fox, S., Cahill, S. and Kilty, C. (2020) *A Review of Diagnostic and Post-diagnostic Processes and Pathways for People Living with Young Onset Dementia*, Tullamore: Health Service Executive.

Garcia Iriarte, E., McConkey, R. and Gilligan, R. (2016) *Disability and Human Rights*, New York: Palgrave Macmillan.

Gilliard, J., Means, R., Beattie, A. and Daker-White, G. (2005) 'Dementia care in England and the social model for disability-lessons and issues', *Dementia: The International Journal of Social Research and Practice*, 4(4): 571–586.

Gray, H.L., Jimenez, D.E., Cucciare, M.A., Hui-Qi, T. and Gallagher-Thompson, D. (2009) 'Ethnic differences in beliefs regarding Alzheimer disease among dementia family caregivers', *American Journal of Geriatric Psychiatry*, 17(11): 925–933.

Hennelly, N. and Cahill, S. (2020) *The Impact of COVID-19 on People Living with Dementia in Ireland, Long Term Care Covid*, [online], 6 June, Available from: www.ltccovid.org/2020/06/06/new-report-the-impact-of-covid-19-pandemic-on-people-living-with-dementia-in-ireland/ [Accessed 28 April 2021].

Hughes, J. (2011) *Thinking through Dementia: International Perspectives in Philosophy and Psychiatry*, Oxford: Oxford University Press.

International Federation of Social Workers (2018) *Global Definition of Social Work*, [online], Available from: www.ifsw.org/what-is-social-work/global-definition-of-social-work/ [Accessed 11 January 2021].

Jefferies, K. and Agrawal, N. (2009) 'Early-onset dementia', *Advances in Psychiatric Treatment*, 15(5): 380–388.

Kahn, R.L. (1975) 'The mental health system and the future aged', *The Gerontologist*, 15(1, Part 2): 24–31.

Kelly, F. and Innes, A. (2012) 'Human rights, citizenship and dementia care nursing', *International Journal of Older People Nursing*, 8(1): 61–70.

Kitwood, T. (1997) *The Concept of Personhood and its Relevance for a New Culture of Dementia Care*, London: Routledge.

Lee-Fay, L., Swaffer, K., McGrath, M. and Brodaty, H. (2018) 'Do people with early-stage dementia experience prescribed disengagement? A systematic review of qualitative studies', *International Psychogeriatrics*, 30(6): 807–831.

Livingston, G., Huntley, J., Sommerlad, A., Ames, D., Ballard, C., Banerjee, S., Brayne, C., Burns, A., Cohen-Mansfield, J., Cooper, C., Costafreda, S.G., Dias, A., Fox, N., Gitlin, L.N., Howard, R., Kales, H.C., Kivimäki, M., Larson, E.B., Ogunniyi, A., Orgeta, V., Ritchie, K., Rockwood, K., Sampson, E.L., Samus, Q., Schneider, L.S., Selbæk, G., Teri, L. and Mukadam, N. (2020) 'Dementia prevention, intervention, and care: 2020 report of the Lancet Commission', *Lancet*, 396(10248): 413–446.

Mental Health Foundation (2015) *Dementia Rights and the Social Model of Disability: A New Direction for Policy and Practice*, London: Mental Health Foundation.

Mittler, P. (2015) 'Time for action: asserting our rights', *Journal of Dementia Care*, 23(6): 10.

NICE/SCIE (2007) *Dementia: A NICE-SCIE Guideline on Supporting People with Dementia and their Carers in Health and Social Care, National Clinical Practice Guideline No 42*, The British Psychological Society and Gaskell, London: NICE/SCIE.

Rauf, A. (2011) *Caring for Dementia: Exploring Good Practice on Supporting South Asian Carers*, Bradford: Bradford Metropolitan District Council.

Sabat, S. (1994) 'Excess disability and malignant social psychology: a case study of Alzheimer's disease', *Journal of Community & Applied Social Psychology*, 4(3): 157–166.

Shakespeare, T., Zeilig, H. and Mittler, P. (2017) 'Rights in mind: thinking differently about dementia and disability', *Dementia*, 18(3): 1075–1088.

Snowdon, D.A. (1997) 'Aging and Alzheimer's disease: lessons from the Nun Study', *The Gerontologist*, 37(2): 150–156.

Travers, C., Lie, D. and Martin Khan, M. (2015) 'Dementia and the population health approach: promise, pitfalls and progress: an Australian perspective', *Reviews in Clinical Gerontology*, 25(1): 60–71.

Vernooij-Dassen, M., Moniz-Cook, E., Verhey, F., Chattat, R., Woods, B., Meiland, F., Franco, M., Holmerova, I., Orrell, M. and de Vugt, M. (2020) 'Bridging the divide between biomedical and psychosocial approaches in dementia research: the 2019 INTERDEM manifesto', *Aging & Mental Health*, 25(2): 206–212.

World Health Organization (WHO) (2015a) *World Report on Ageing and Health*, [online], Available from: www.who.int/ageing/events/world-report-2015-launch/en/ [Accessed 10 December 2020].

WHO (2015b) *Ensuring a Human Rights-based Approach for People Living with Dementia*, Geneva: WHO, [online], Available from: www.who.int/mental_health/neurology/dementia/dementia_thematicbrief_human_rights.pdf [Accessed 10 December 2020].

WHO (2017) *Global Action Plan on the Public Health Response to Dementia 2017–2025*, Geneva: WHO.

WHO (2019) *Risk Reduction of Cognitive Decline and Dementia*, WHO guidelines, Geneva: WHO.

Winblad, B., Amouyel, P., Andrieu, S., Ballard, C., Brayne, C., Brodaty, H., Cedazo-Minguez, A., Dubois, B., Edvardsson, D., Feldman, H., Fratiglioni, L., Frisoni, G.B., Gauthier, S., Georges, J., Graff, C., Iqbal, K., Jessen, F., Johansson, G., Jönsson, L., Kivipelto, M., Knapp, M., Mangialasche, F., Melis, R., Nordberg, A., Rikkert, M.O., Qiu, C., Sakmar, T.P., Scheltens, P., Schneider, L.S., Sperling, R., Tjernberg, L.O., Waldemar, G., Wimo, A. and Zetterberg, H. (2016) 'Defeating Alzheimer's disease and other dementias: a priority for European science and society', *The Lancet Neurology*, 15(5): 455.

11

User involvement

Peter Beresford[1]

User involvement and critical gerontology are two key concepts and approaches for social work and related services with older people in the early 21st century. Yet, so far exploration of their interrelations seems to be at an early stage. For this reason, the aim of this chapter, to look more closely and critically at the role of user involvement in relation to critical gerontology in a European context, is likely to be both especially timely and productive. The praxis of user involvement is likely to be maximised through a critical gerontological lens and, in turn, critical gerontology is unlikely to fulfil its promise unless united with an in-depth understanding of the theory and practice of participation. The chapter will address user involvement in policy, practice, learning and research and conclude with a case study offering implications for practice.

It is because such a focus on the involvement of older people is not only consistent with a critical gerontological approach but is also likely to be a key feature in its development that we need to get beyond the rhetorical appeal of such involvement to examine the ideological, practical and discriminatory constraints operating on it and how these may be unpicked and overcome. While my work on participation has mainly been located in the United Kingdom (UK), it has also involved numerous cooperation and international studies and activities with a wide range of European countries, which will be drawn on in this discussion. Worth noting is also that this chapter offers valuable contributions to ongoing debates on user involvement.

---

[1] **Peter Beresford OBE** is Visiting Professor at the University of East Anglia, UK, and Co-Chair of Shaping Our Lives, the national disabled people's and service user-led organisation. He is a long-term user of mental health services and Emeritus Professor at Brunel University London and the University of Essex, UK. He has a long-standing track-record of involvement in the issue of participation as writer, researcher, activist and educator. His latest book is *Participatory Ideology: From Exclusion to Involvement* (Policy Press, 2021).

Conflicting approaches to involvement

While participatory developments in relation to social work and beyond have been different and have taken place at different speeds and to different degrees in different countries, there is no question that the move to greater user and carer involvement, including that of older people, has been an international and pan-European one (Cox and Pawar, 2006; Bastiaens et al, 2007; Borg et al, 2015; Chiapparini, 2016; Beresford, 2018). The pressure for such involvement has come from both those shaping policy and those on the receiving end of it.

The ideological position underpinning welfare service user calls for greater involvement and empowerment can best be described as based on a liberatory and democratising approach. Service users have campaigned explicitly for the right to speak for themselves, to have more control over their lives and the policies impacting on them and to have more equal access to political processes. This, however, stands in some contrast to the parallel and contemporaneous pressure for user involvement coming from the service system and governments over this same period. This period, from the 1980s onwards, has been typified by a shift to the political right in Europe and internationally and an increasing distrust of state intervention and public welfare, and a shift to the private market and voluntarism. Pressure here for involvement has been framed primarily in consumerist terms of the public service 'customer' having more choice and involvement in the same sense as consumers in relation to private goods and services (Beresford, 2019).

This is a far cry from the democratic imperative advanced by service users and their movements. So, while they press for a progressive redistribution, for example, in relation to public policy and services, the prevailing managerialist/consumerist model bears a much closer relation to market ideas of listening to the voice of the consumer in order to maximise markets and increase cost-effectiveness. Such a supermarket model of involvement bears little relation to what older people and other service users have pressed for, but the same terminology has tended to be applied to these contrasting models and motivations. Sadly, as we have seen, older people are both a disparate and fragmented constituency with limited market pull and an under-developed pressure group, largely spoken for by other interests. This helps us both to understand and to explain their very limited capacity to exert policy and political influence in relation to their rights and needs.

Involving older people

First, it needs to be said that older people are one of the groups that have been highlighted historically as tending to be marginalised and often poorly served in schemes and initiatives for user involvement. This seems to be related to their acquired impairments, lowered expectations and the ageist discrimination they experience. Thus, while there seems to be general agreement that many older people welcome being involved and that it can benefit their lives (Age UK, 2011; Soares et al, 2019), and they are the largest group of adult social work service users, efforts to involve them have tended to be less effective than with other groups, like disabled people and mental health service users, although there is much experience to show how limitations can be overcome (Carter and Beresford, 2000; Fudge et al, 2007). The largest government-funded research study of exclusions in user involvement in the UK again highlighted the marginalisation of older people as have studies in other areas like health, and this seems to reflect a wider international situation (Beresford, 2013; Omeni et al, 2014; Altwegg-Boussac and Ward, 2019).

We can gain a helpful historical perspective from an early large-scale survey of North Battersea in south London, which highlighted that older people were the group least likely to get involved in local calls for involvement and, when asked, were less likely to want more say – less than half, compared with two-thirds of the total sample (N: 580 households). They seem to have lower expectations and to be less demanding, particularly compared to families with small children (Beresford and Croft, 1978). They made comments like: 'I'm past it now. It's up to younger people now. They have to stick together', and '[I'm] too old. It doesn't matter what you say anyway, the council takes no notice' (Beresford and Croft, 1978, p 74).

The diversity of older age

Not only are older people as an overall constituency often ill-served by participatory schemes and requirements, but these often also fall short in relation to particular groups of older people and through the failure to take adequate account of significant issues of intersectionality as well as heterogeneity in the older population. Thus, we know that older lesbian, gay, bisexual, transsexual and queer (LGBTQ) and BAME people (which is the UK abbreviation for people of Black, Asian and minority ethnic descent), older women and disabled people can all expect to face additional barriers and exclusions in the way of their equal involvement. Class is also an important issue in relation to ageing, since while some older people may have been economically and socially privileged in their younger lives, others may not have been, and disadvantages in relation to income, physical and mental health and social security generally increase with age. There are also considerable inequalities in relation to retirement preparation, opportunities and age (Hoban et al, 2013). Thus, older people are a large but very heterogeneous population and, to complicate matters further, definitions of older age vary massively, with some official definitions starting at age 50 even as retirement ages recede into the late 60s internationally. Many older people in Europe are now surviving into their 90s, with a second generation in their 60s and 70s often being called upon to look after them (Sargeant, 2011).

All these factors highlight the importance of the inclusive involvement of older people, yet this is far from the routine reality. Thus, the formal political process tends to access more conservative views related to older age, associated particularly with older White voters – for example, in UK countries, support for Brexit, harsh welfare reform and anti-immigration policies – but it has not resulted in support for public service spending, for example on social care, support for family carers or long-term health conditions (Inman, 2019). This is also a broader issue reflected in the rise of right-wing populist parties across Europe. At the same time, this is not adequately compensated for by existing arrangements for user and public involvement in public policy and services because of their limited ability, as we have seen, to include and reflect the views of older people. Given the continuing increase in the proportions and absolute numbers of older people in Western societies linked with broader demographic change, this is an increasingly important political and policy issue (Goerres, 2009). Yet, while this population change has often been acknowledged, this has often been in unhelpful, negative terms, framing it as a 'time bomb' and 'old age crisis'. Little has been done to address it progressively.

Certainly, efforts to involve older people effectively have not kept pace with such developments. The reasons for this seem to be complex and multifactorial. One of the biggest pressures for user involvement grew out of the emergence of welfare user movements like the international disabled people and mental health service user/survivor movements. Developing particularly from the 1980s, encouraged by and learning from the new social movements based on identity – the women's, Black civil rights and LGBTQ movements – they challenged the stigma, barriers, inequality and segregation significantly imposed upon them in and by mainstream society. There have been some equivalent developments among older people, including movements like the United States Grey Panthers and the UK National Pensioners Convention, but on nothing like the same scale, or with the same impact representing an international older people's movement. Instead, older people have largely continued to be represented or at least spoken for, by traditional charitable organisations, and the problems they face depoliticised and presented in charitable, dependency and welfare terms.

While there are lessons to learn for the present discussion from all the service user movements that have emerged particularly over the last quarter of the 20th century, perhaps the most significant insights are offered by the disabled people's movement. Not only has this been the most prominent and probably most developed welfare user movement both in Europe and globally; it is also the one with closest ties and most cross-overs with the population under consideration here – older people – since they are most likely to need support because of their increasing physical, sensory and intellectual impairments (Charlton, 1998).

While older people make up the largest proportion of disabled people, the latter movement has tended to reflect the concerns of working-age disabled people. In addition, many older people do not identify as disabled and seem instead frequently to see this as another stigmatising rather than liberatory label (Carter and Beresford, 2000). This may be seen as a loss, since, while the achievements of the international disabled people's movement should not be overstated, they have had an important political, social and cultural impact, leading significantly to renewed understandings of disability, more liberatory and inclusive policy approaches and a new emphasis on the rights and participation of disabled people. The latter has highlighted the importance of disabled people being able to have more say and control over their lives and the policies and services impacting on them.

User involvement and research

User involvement has developed in social work and beyond in a range of contexts, including professional education, standard setting, regulation, planning and practice. Social work has been the site of some of the biggest innovations in this area, and within that professional education has emerged as a particularly significant site and opportunity for change (McLaughlin et al, 2020). Service users have seen it as having the potential to 'change the culture' of practice by changing the socialisation of new practitioners. By 2003, such user and carer involvement was a requirement in all aspects and stages of UK social work, and in England, in addition, central government funding continues to be provided to underpin this. The emergence and expansion of the European network for user and carer involvement in social work learning, PowerUS, offers broader evidence of this (Askheim et al, 2017).

One of the other key domains where such involvement has been advanced, by both mainstream organisations and service users, has been in research and knowledge production. This is now both a Europe-wide and global development (McLaughlin et al, 2020). Organised service user interest in research first emerged from the disabled people's movement, although it has subsequently gained much wider interest across groups. Its impetus was the sense disabled people felt of being victimised by conventional research. They saw it as biased and over-medicalised and, as a result, they wanted to develop a different kind of research – one which they saw as relevant, helpful and empowering (Barnes and Mercer, 1997; Barnes et al, 2002). The emancipatory disability research which they developed – and other expressions of user-controlled research which followed it, like mental health service user/survivor research – place an emphasis on research which:

- equalises research relationships between researchers and researched;
- involves service users fully and equally in the research process;
- works to support the empowerment of service users;
- is committed to making broader social and political change (Beresford and Croft, 2012; McLaughlin et al, 2020).

Again, ideological tensions have emerged between the 'public, patient involvement and engagement' that has developed in conventional research and the demands for user-led and co-produced research advanced by service users, service user researchers and their movements. In significant ways, conflicts have reflected broader differences between consumerist and democratic approaches to participation, with mainstream research emphasising the value of learning from what service users know to advance their agendas and service users increasingly drawing distinctions between existing knowledge processes and sources and their own 'experiential knowledge', increasingly wary of merely informing other people's plans and proposals (McLaughlin et al, 2020).

   This is because not all research rests on the same principles and not all research is necessarily seen by service users and their movements as in their interests or advancing their rights. Crucially, service users have been concerned with pioneering research which supports the development of their/our own knowledge(s). These issues, highlighted by involvement in research, have broader significance for older people's participation and critical gerontology and the relationship between the two.

Challenging inequalities in knowledge production

To take a step back, research is of far more than academic importance because of the key role it is seen as having in the production of knowledge. It tends to be identified as the most rigorous, reliable and systematic method of knowledge production (Pollitt, 2003). This leads us to the issue of the knowledge base of social work – as well as of health and welfare more generally and critical gerontology specifically – and also ultimately to why it is so important that the perspectives of older people as service users, and indeed of practitioners, are taken into equal account.

   Traditional positivist research has emphasised values of neutrality, objectivity and distance. By claiming to eliminate the subjectivity of the researcher, the credibility of the research, the rigour, reliability and replicability of its findings are seen to be optimised. Service users and their organisations, however, have challenged this. They have questioned the 'unbiased value-free' position, based on the professional expertise of the researcher, which is seen as a central tenet of such research. User involvement in research, particularly user-controlled research, calls this into question, with its commitment to making change, involving service users and valuing their subjective knowledge. Moreover, while there has been widespread policy and research support for such participation, it has itself come in for significant methodological attack for breaching these principles of traditional positivist research (Beresford, 2012). Central to this is its introduction of and valuing of what has come to be called experiential knowledge; that is to say, knowledge based on people's subjective and lived experience, rather than professional training or research and experiment. Such experiential knowledge has been granted less value and credibility under the operation of traditional research values and principles. Instead, a hierarchy of knowledge has been seen to exist, with that generated through research randomised trials seen as the gold standard and first-hand accounts seen as having the lowest status (Glasby and Beresford, 2006; Fricker, 2007). The knowledge claims of researchers without such direct experience are seen to be stronger.

Revaluing experiential knowledge

However, service users have upended these arguments, suggesting instead that by devaluing experiential knowledge we lose a key knowledge source. They also highlight that this means, crucially, that if an individual has direct, lived experience of problems like disability or poverty, or of oppression and discrimination, of cuts and 'austerity', of ageism, racism and sexism, when such traditional positivist research values are accepted, what they say – their accounts and narratives – will be seen as having less legitimacy and authority. Because people experiencing hardship will be seen as 'close to the problem', they cannot claim that they are 'neutral', 'objective' or 'distant' from it. So, in addition to any discrimination and oppression they already experience, they are likely to be seen as a less reliable and a less valid source of knowledge. By this logic, if someone has experience of discrimination and oppression, they can expect routinely to face further discrimination and be further marginalised by being seen as having less credibility and being a less reliable source of knowledge (Beresford, 2003).

At the same time, the devaluing of experiential knowledge has increasingly come to be seen as problematic. This has unfortunately been a role historically played by much social research, where problems come to be seen as 'real' only when they are reported by 'experts' like researchers. Then it is their interpretations and versions of issues and phenomena which are accepted. This issue of marginalising the knowledge of particular vulnerable groups has begun to be talked about in terms of 'epistemic violence' (Liegghio, 2013) or 'epistemic injustice' (Fricker, 2007), meaning devaluing and marginalising the knowledge of people who suffer abuse, discrimination and oppression (Westwood, 2019). Increasing international interest in what has come to be called 'public, patient involvement' in research thus raises the uncomfortable issue of including experiential knowledge centrally and on equal terms with other kinds of knowledge. At the same time, it means working towards achieving epistemic equality and ensuring that everybody can contribute to creating a general knowledge base and that perspectives of entire social groups are no longer excluded from that process. We are beginning to see the real involvement of ordinary and disadvantaged people in research; for example, people with learning difficulties who communicate differently or older people who experience dementia (Faulkner, 2004). There is also a growing body of work and discussion about user-controlled research where people who have traditionally been the objects of research are now carrying out their own research and so restoring their epistemic existence (Beresford and Croft, 2012). All this can also be seen as part of the project and inseparable from the development of critical gerontology.

Including practitioner knowledge in the equation

There is also an additional aspect to this that is of importance to critical gerontology and older people themselves. Recognition of the role of experiential knowledge also highlights important issues about the involvement of *practitioners* in knowledge formation. It brings us back to the issue of the frequent exclusion of current practitioners from mainstream social work discourse and the potentially negative consequences this can have. One psychiatric system survivor researcher, Jasna Russo, has developed this discussion. She argues that it is essential for the service user to foster their first-person perspective and sees talking in the third person as the privilege of the non-service user, non-abused or oppressed person. But Russo has also worked as a social worker and, while she believes it is crucial for accounts from the first person (the service user/older person) to be valued and prioritised, she has also introduced the second person into the discussion – the you – and for her, here the you is the social worker. If there is to be work and a meaningful, equal relationship between service user and practitioner, she suggests, the practitioner must recognise themselves as the second person in the relationship; they must be aware of themselves and bring themselves to it (Russo, 1997; 1999; 2013).

Thus, as a person has their unique experiential knowledge as a service user, so does the worker as a practitioner. This has also been described as 'practice wisdom' – what you learn from doing the job – and while it should certainly not be substituted for user knowledge, it is an experiential knowledge of its own – underpinning the other half of the relationship between service user and practitioner. In addition, just as service users argue that they are much more than passive recipients of care and support – they may be parents, partners, students, volunteers, community activists, workers and so on – so social workers are much more than the sum of their professional learning and identity. We all have complicated and multiple identities. We only have to think of all the different roles and relationships we each may have. None of us has monolithic or uniform identities. Identities are complex, although sometimes we are made to simplify them. Thus, social workers are much more than their professional socialisation and learning. They have their own subjectivity, their own experiential as well as professional knowledge.

I want to stress here the value of social workers drawing on *all* of themselves, not to have to deny parts of who they are in their work. This could include their own experience of ageing. Otherwise, they reduce themselves to a narrow understanding of their professional role and a status of alienation, 'othering' and inequality. As has been seen, we should remember that there isn't a specific or discrete group of 'service users'. While any of us may be in many different places and relations to it, needing help and support is something that in our increasingly harsh and unequal world can happen to anyone, including social workers themselves. Moreover, another of the valuable benefits of user involvement has been that people with lived experience of hardship, loss, abuse, discrimination and using services are now increasingly being recruited to become social workers, with that experience coming to be seen as a strength, rather than a deficit.

Participation and critical gerontology

As this book highlights, a critical gerontological approach rejects a narrow medicalised understanding of ageing and old-age inequality and instead investigates its ideological and social construction. But in its fully developed form it demands more than focusing an external lens on older people and their older age. Here it is suggested that it must also mean supporting older people to advance their own knowledge and develop their own critiques based on their direct lived experience, and for these to be granted equal value with traditional knowledge sources. It is difficult to see how a critical gerontological approach, with its commitment to making sense of and challenging old-age inequalities, could be consistent with research or practice which was not inclusive of older people on equal terms.

A case study for critical gerontology

A case study of the gains to be got from this and its significance for critical gerontology is offered by the findings of a large research and development project, Shaping Our Age, supported by the UK Big Lottery research programme and jointly led by the author of this chapter. While it was a specifically UK-wide project, it offers broader European and international insights. The project had two interrelated concerns; to improve older people's 'well-being' (an established focus for policy makers' interest) and to involve them equally in the process. It sought to do this by:

- exploring with a diverse range of older people their understanding of their well-being;
- identifying five local sites where they could be supported to be involved in development and action projects;
- developing participatory ways through local activities in which older people could help each other to improve their well-being;
- providing the learning that could help to enable and support older people to improve their and other people's well-being (Hoban et al, 2011; 2013).

In retrospect, we can see that this project was positioned within a critical gerontological framework. Crucially, it 'sought to move older people from the margins to the centre of debates surrounding their well-being by supporting their active contributions to society (Hoban et al, 2013, p 7). This was reflected in its process as well as its focus and aims. The aim was to establish a truly participatory project which included both a principal investigator (PI) and project worker who were disabled (and in one case older) and committed to the principles and values of emancipatory disability research and the participatory commitments of social action research; and to establish a diverse and active group of 15 older people from the four nations of the UK, recruited through a transparent application and interview process. Older people in the project were involved in all its aspects, including:

- an initial consultation in advance of the project
- staff recruitment
- setting the parameters of the research
- its ongoing development
- selecting the local projects
- designing the research
- developing the local projects
- information collection
- analysis of findings
- evaluating findings
- reporting, communicating and disseminating findings

In the development sites, the skilled local involvement workers worked alongside older people for over a year individually and collectively, taking their lead from them and seeking to develop 'meaningful conversations' with them to support them to do what they wanted to.

Key findings of the case study

As well as highlighting aspects of personal well-being like health, personal finances, being free from pain, loving life and being contented, 'social connectedness' was by far the most strongly voiced and commonly mentioned characteristic associated with well-being by older people in the project. They highlighted relationships and social contacts with family and friends and within communities as essential to well-being. As well as offering practical support, these connections brought to older people a sense of belonging and feeling valued. They also offered the well-being benefits gained from fun, good conversation and laughter. The contribution of groups and clubs to well-being was frequently mentioned, along with volunteering and supporting others. Older people also made clear that the 'doing to' approach – the traditional approach to working with older people – while meeting important needs, was not necessarily conducive to improving their well-being, but could instead feel paternalistic and increase passivity and dependency. Some complained about being patronised and not being sufficiently involved or valued. We also heard from people outside services who did not want to be associated with what they saw as traditional and stereotypical models of delivery or with services specifically targeting older people.

In contrast, many older people preferred a working with and *involvement-led* approach to practice, which they felt created and sustained a humanistic process that could enhance social and personal well-being. For them, this meant starting with older people's own knowledge, skills and experience, spending time with them, individually and in small groups, listening and supporting rather than leading and directing – and talking *with* them. Involvement and improved well-being were clearly related. We heard from older people that being involved in a process of personal development and small group interactions contributed most to their personal and social well-being. The involvement workers were able to help this happen through small-group work, creating supportive settings and opportunities, working alongside older people to listen, encourage and prompt, building rapport and trust, and through 'meaningful conversations'. What became clear in the developmental part of the project was that it was not the particular activities that older people took part in that were important for their well-being, but that they had a say in what they were doing (Hoban et al, 2013, p 10).

The project also highlighted the barriers that continue to obstruct older people's involvement, and particularly the involvement of some groups of older people. The project:

> discussed ways to address these barriers with black and minority ethnic communities and identified a need for direct contact and

outreach in their environment, to build partnerships and to engage these communities in meaningful consultations. We also explored methods for engaging older disabled people and found success when using an approach that focused on the individual, their capabilities and interests. When working with people with dementia we found value in meaningful conversations, creative activities and games and valuing the person as an individual. (Hoban et al, 2013, p 10)

Additional consultations were held with four specific groups of older people to test out the project's findings with them. These included older BAME people, older people from the LGBTQ community, older people living in residential care and a group of older disabled women. They confirmed the findings from Shaping Our Age as well as adding further insights and emphases (James et al, 2012; James et al, 2013). The project reported two overall conclusions. These were that:

• Older people's involvement in all aspects of the project reveals the potential that exists for their greater contribution more generally. This requires a shift in mindset away from notions of personal 'deficit' (what people cannot do) to one which focuses on people's collective and individual capacities to shape their own well-being. The findings from this project support an *involvement-led approach* that values the potential of older people, their aspirations and strengths.
• Major barriers exist to well-being for specific groups of older people. However, an involvement-led approach offers new possibilities for tackling these barriers and issues of exclusion.

These findings also have major implications for the critical gerontology project and wider work in Europe. Not only do they highlight the philosophical complementarity of critical gerontology and democratic participatory approaches to work with older people. They also strengthen not only the view that critical gerontology is consistent with participatory approaches to work with older people but that such participation needs to be further advanced, explored and evaluated in critical gerontology itself and in its application to social work and other services, to make possible the maximum benefit. They also have clear take-home messages for social work policy and practice. The aspiration must be to co-production rather than imposition. The experiential knowledge of service users and carers combined with the practice wisdom of social workers are the essential ingredients for the kind of participatory, co-produced social work that we know people value from social work (Beresford et al, 2007).

We can still have hope for it for the future, but the policy crisis following from COVID-19 in the UK and globally means that much ground seems to have been lost in some settings. While some countries like, for example, Taiwan and New Zealand have adopted more participatory and effective policy responses to the pandemic, the opposite has been true from the UK policy response. As service users, their organisations and allies have highlighted, instead of drawing on the lived experience/experiential knowledge of groups like Black and minoritised older and disabled people in developing responses and shaping the research agenda, there has instead been a tendency to act as if user involvement was an unaffordable luxury in times of health emergency (Beresford et al, 2021; Williams et al, 2021). If some commentators – and this author was not one of them – thought there was an increase in the meaningful involvement of and co-production with older people during the last decade, the emergence of COVID-19 and the nature of policy responses to it seem to have put paid to that hope, and older people have been among the most numerous victims dying from the virus, at least partly because of the inadequacy of health and social care systems (Beresford, 2021).

References

Age UK (2011) *Engaging with Older People: Evidence Review*, London: Age UK, [online], Available from: www.scie-socialcareonline.org.uk/engaging-with-older-people-evidence-review/r/a11G000000PYxqrIAD [Accessed 29 August 2021].

Altwegg-Boussac, C. and Ward, C. (2019) 'Innovations and participation of service users, a European dynamic: lessons from a major conference', *Vie Sociale*, Eres, 25–2(1–2): 27–42.

Askheim, O.P., Beresford, P. and Heule, C. (2017) '"Mend the gap": strategies for user involvement in social work education', *Social Work Education*, 36(2): 128–140.

Barnes, C. and Mercer, G. (eds) (1997) *Doing Disability Research*, Leeds: Disability Press.

Barnes, C., Oliver, M. and Barton, L. (eds) (2002) *Disability Studies Today*, Cambridge: Polity.

Bastiaens, H., Van Royen, P., Pavlic, D.R., Raposo, V. and Baker, R. (2007) 'Older people's preferences for involvement in their own care: a qualitative study in primary health care in 11 European countries', *Patient Education and Counselling*, 68(1): 33–42.

Beresford, P. (2003) *It's Our Lives: A Short Theory of Knowledge, Distance and Experience*, London: Citizen Press in association with Shaping Our Lives.

Beresford, P. (2013) *Beyond the Usual Suspects: Towards Inclusive User Involvement*, research report, London: Shaping Our Lives.

Beresford, P. (2018) 'Service user involvement in social work and beyond: exploring its origins and destinations', *Zeszyty Pracy Socjalnej*, 23(1): 5–20.

Beresford, P. (2019) 'Public participation in health and social care: exploring the co-production of knowledge, policy and practice review article', *Frontiers in Sociology*, 3: 41.

Beresford, P. (2021) 'What are we clapping for? Sending people to die in social care – why the NHS did this and what needs to happen next', in P. Beresford, M. Farr, G. Hickey, M. Kaur, J. Ocloo, D. Tembo and O. Williams (eds) *COVID-19 and Co-production in Health and Social Care Research, Policy, and Practice Volume 1: The Challenges and Necessity of Co-production*, Open Access eBook, Bristol: Policy Press, pp 89–98.

Beresford, P. and Croft, S. (1978) *A Say in the Future: Planning, Participation and Meeting Social Need*, London: Battersea Community Action.

Beresford, P. and Croft, S. (2012) *User Controlled Research: Scoping Review*, London: NHS National Institute for Health Research (NIHR) School for Social Care Research, London School of Economics.

Beresford, P., Adshead, L. and Croft, S. (2007) *Palliative Care, Social Work and Service Users: Making Life Possible*, London: Jessica Kingsley.

Beresford, P., Farr, M., Hickey, G., Kaur, M., Ocloo, J., Tembo, D. and Williams, O. (eds) (2021) *COVID-19 and Co-production in Health and Social Care Research, Policy, and Practice Volume 1: The Challenges and Necessity of Co-production*, Open Access eBook, Bristol: Policy Press.

Borg, M., Johnson, T.A., Bryant, W., Beresford, P. and Karlsson, B. (2015) 'Flerstemt forskningssamarbeid innen psykisk helse: erfaringer fra Storbritannia og Norge', *Tidskrift for Psykisk Helsearbeid*, 12(1): 61–70.

Carter, T. and Beresford, P. (2000) *Age and Change: Models of Involvement for Older People*, Joseph Rowntree Foundation, York: York Publishing.

Charlton, J.I. (1998) *Nothing About Us without Us: Disability, Oppression and Empowerment*, Oakland: University of California Press.

Chiapparini, E. (ed) (2016) *The Service User as a Partner in Social Work Projects and Education*, Germany: Verlag Barbara Budrich.

Cox, D. and Pawar, M. (2006) *International Social Work: Issues, Strategies and Programs*, California: Sage.

Faulkner, A. (2004) *Capturing the Experience of those Involved in the TRUE Project: A Story of Colliding Worlds*, Eastleigh: NIHR Involve.

Fricker, M. (2007) *Epistemic Injustice: Power and the Ethics of Knowing*, New York: Oxford University Press.

Fudge, N., Wolfe, C.D.A. and McKevitt, C. (2007) 'Involving older people in health research', *Age and Ageing*, 36(5): 492–500.

Glasby, J. and Beresford, P. (2006) 'Who knows best? Evidence-based practice and the service user contribution, commentary and issues', *Critical Social Policy*, 26(1): 268–264.

Goerres, A. (2009) *The Political Participation of Older People in Europe: The Greying of our Democracies*, London: Palgrave Macmillan.

Hoban, M., James, V., Pattrick, K., Beresford, P. and Fleming, J. (2011) *Voices on Wellbeing: A Report of Research with Older People*, Cardiff: Shaping Our Age, WRVS.

Hoban, M., James, V., Beresford, P. and Fleming, J. (2013) *Shaping Our Age – Involving Older Age: The Route to Twenty-First Century Well-being*, Final Report, Cardiff: Royal Voluntary Service.

Inman, P. (2019) 'Age, not class is now what divides British voters most', *The Guardian*, [online], 21 December, Available from: www.theguardian.com/politics/2019/dec/21/age-not-class-is-what-divides-british-voters-most [Accessed 29 August 2020].

James, V., Hinchliffe, D., Hoban, M., Fleming, J. and Beresford, P. (2012) *Shaping our Age: Local Report Sheffield: Consultations with Service Users and Carers*, Unpublished report: Cardiff: WRVS.

James, V., Meakin, B. and Andrews, E. (2013) *Involving Older Age: The Route to Twenty-First Century Well-being: Post Launch Consultations with People from Diverse Communities*, Cardiff: Shaping Our Lives.

Liegghio, M. (2013) 'A denial of being: psychiatrization as epistemic violence', in B.A. LeFrancois, G. Reaume and R.J. Menzies (eds) *Mad Matters: A Critical Reader in Canadian Mad Studies*, Toronto: Canadian Scholar's Press.

McLaughlin, H., Beresford, P., Cameron, C., Casey, H. and Duffy, J. (eds) (2020) *The Routledge Handbook of Service User Involvement in Human Services Research and Education*, London: Routledge.

Omeni, E., Barnes, M., MacDonald, D., Crawford, M. and Rose, D. (2014) 'Service user involvement: impact and participation: a survey of service user and staff perspectives', *BMC Health Services Research*, 14: 491.

Pollitt, C. (2003) 'Public management reform: reliable knowledge and international experience', *OECD Journal on Budgeting*, 3: 3.

Russo, J. (1997) 'Reden in der dritten person, privileg der nicht-betro enen', in V. Wildwasser Bielefeld (ed) *Der Aufgestörte Blick. Multiple Persönlichkeiten, Frauenbewegung und Gewalt*, Bielefeld: Kleine Verlag, pp 286–289.

Russo, J. (1999) 'Keine sonderbehandlung: besonders bin ich schon', in C. Brügge (ed) *Frauen in Ver-rückten Lebenswelten*, Bern: eFeF Verlag, pp 126–138.

Russo, J. (2013) 'From empowerment to emancipation: situating first person knowledge', general opening lecture at *Tenth International Conference of the European Network For Mental Health Service Evaluation (ENMESH)*, Verona, Italy, 3–5 October.

Sargeant, M. (2011) *Age Discrimination and Diversity: Multiple Discrimination from an Age Perspective*, Cambridge: Cambridge University Press.

Soares, C.C., Marques, A.M., Clarke, P., Klein, R., Koskinen, L., Krasuckiene, D., Lamsodiene, E., Piscalkiene, V. and Küçükgüçlü, O. (2019) 'Older people's views and expectations about the competencies of health and social care professionals: a European qualitative study', *European Journal of Ageing*, 16: 53–62.

Westwood, S. (ed) (2019) *Ageing, Diversity and Equality: Social Justice Perspectives*, Abingdon: Routledge.

Williams, O., Tembo, D., Ocloo, J., Kaur, G., Hickey, M., Farr, M. and Beresford, P. (eds), (2021), *COVID-19 and Co-production in Health and Social Care Research, Policy, and Practice Volume 2: Co-production: Methods and Working Together at a Distance*, Open Access eBook, Bristol: Policy Press.

12

Opportunities and future prospects for gerontological social work with a critical lens

Marjaana Seppänen and Mo Ray[1]

Although the status and role of gerontological social work varies locally (Pajunen et al, 2009) and by country (see Chapter 5), it has commonly been regarded as a low-status area of practice with poor professional potential (Lymbery, 2005). Arguably, the low status afforded to gerontological social work and the older population it serves has contributed to its limited success in developing its identity and visibility as a distinct speciality. A tendency for social work to focus on meeting 'care' and 'health' needs in old age means that it has often occupied a more marginal space in its ability to fully respond to the diversity of ageing experience. The variable presence, visibility and purpose of gerontological social work has arguably been reinforced by managerialist approaches in public service and welfare policy. Increased pressure to reduce public sector funding is common in most developed countries (Pentaraki, 2018). The impact of austerity measures over the past decade has increased the strain on public service professionals, including social work. For example, in Greece and Spain, but echoed to varying

---

[1] **Marjaana Seppänen** is Professor of Social Work at the University of Helsinki, Finland. Her background is in social sciences (especially social work) and she has extensively studied and published on questions connected to gerontological social work, ageing, well-being and the living conditions of older adults. Marjaana is part of several international research networks in gerontology and social work. **Mo Ray** is Professor of Health and Social Care in the School of Health and Social Care, University of Lincoln, UK. After qualifying as a social worker in 1990, she worked as a social worker/care manager in adult teams, specialising in practice with older people. Her interest in long-lasting relationships and the impact of ill health and disability led to Mo completing a part-time PhD at Keele University, UK, on marriages that last a lifetime. She subsequently secured an ESRC Fellowship which led to a social work lectureship at Keele University. She worked in a number of roles, including Director of Social Work Studies. Mo was awarded a personal Chair in Gerontological Social Work in 2014. Her research interests focus on experiences of ageing, ageing and care, and social relationships in older age.

degrees throughout Europe, the impact of cuts to health and other public sector organisations has exacerbated challenges for social workers coping with the implications of long waiting lists for services, rapid and inappropriate discharge from hospital, social work shortages and increased pressures on older people to cope alone with deteriorating and difficult circumstances or to rely on families, assuming the older person has one (Ioakimidis et al, 2014; Verde-Diego et al, 2018; Deusdad, 2020).

A unifying goal of this edited collection is to advance the development of gerontological social work by contributing theoretical, conceptual and practical understanding of age and ageing. Each chapter has presented examples of the ways in which a critical gerontology lens can enhance and further the goals of an ethical social work practice with older people. To this end, this book creates an important space for practitioners, scholars and educators to consider and reflect on the challenges, possibilities and spaces gerontological social work might have or be able to create, to develop gerontological social work. The purpose of this concluding chapter is not to simply repeat arguments already made throughout the book, but to attempt to consider the scope for the future development of gerontological social work. Drawing on the contributing authors, we start by identifying the key challenges that gerontological social work education and practice face, before considering the opportunities that may be available to develop gerontological social work.

The status of gerontological social work and the challenges it faces

The opening chapter in this book (see Chapter 1) highlighted the core mandates for social work: promoting human rights, social change, development, social cohesion and the empowerment and liberation of people, as defined by the International Federation of Social Workers (IFSW) (IFSW, 2014). The Federation includes in its definition the importance of a social work critical consciousness through 'reflecting on structural sources of oppression and/or privilege, on the basis of criteria such as race, class, language, religion, gender, disability, culture and sexual orientation' (IFSW, 2014). The observant reader will notice the omission of age in this statement. This is problematic, given the commitment of the IFSW to challenging structural sources of oppression and inequalities. Arguably, the absence of age in the Federation's statement reflects societal ageism, considered the most pervasive form of discrimination, which remains more accepted and challenged less often than other forms of discrimination (World Health Organization, 2021). The omission of age also means that opportunities to analyse the intersections between age and other structural criteria are overlooked.

It is perhaps unsurprising that the development of gerontological social work has not been considered to have reached its potential. Although gerontological social work is recognised in countries such as Australia, Canada and the United States (US), there is variability in the extent to which the term is used to convey a specialist area of practice, informed by critical social work and gerontological theory and research. In the US, gerontological social work has been significantly influenced by geriatric medicine and a focus on health/illness (see Chapter 5). By contrast, in the UK, gerontological social work is hardly a recognised specialism. Historically, social work with older people has occupied a peripheral role and the emphasis on social work as little more than arranging care, combined with the often glacially slow development of policy and service innovation, has reinforced its lack of desirability as a career option (Means and Smith, 1998; Richards et al, 2014).

Despite country-by-country variation in the establishment and operationalisation of gerontological social work, it is fair to say that, as a speciality, it has never had a 'golden age'. Uncertainty about the value of gerontological social work and what it should be is likely to have been reinforced by the persistently low status afforded to older people, especially those people most likely to use social work services. This is illustrated by Higgs (see Chapter 4), who points to the 'othering' of old age when labels such as 'clinical frailty' question 'the capacity of the person so categorised to be a 'competent social actor or have an agentic social identity'. In this context, assessment and decisions underpinned by an uncritical analysis of labels such as frailty, risk or vulnerability risk decisions being based on what is 'best' for an older person, rather than how an older person can be supported to identify what might be best for them. In reality, what is available is as, if not more, pertinent as what might be 'best' for the person. In any event, older people at the end of the 'what's best? what's available' paradox risk being excluded from crucial life decisions (for example, moving to a care home) likely to have a significant impact on the rest of their life (Larsson and Olsterholm, 2014; Donnelly Begley and O'Brien, 2018). Consequently, the potential to fully embrace and harness rights-based practice is squeezed by policies that, in most countries to varying degrees, concentrate on resource management and service-based responses to individual problems and the 'care needs' of (eligible) older people (Ray and Seppanen, 2014).

Welfare policies too often articulate a 'rhetoric of rights' (Harbison, Chapter 3) by emphasising the importance of, for example, individual autonomy, which is increasingly centred on self-management via 'personalised' support to achieve independence and preserve autonomy. In England, for example, the growth of so-called cash for care to choose and purchase support was identified as a key means to achieve these policy aspirations. This also has the impact of denuding both the purpose and potential value of social work as, arguably, anyone with the correct procedural training could broker arrangements for a direct payment. Research has found, though, that outcomes for older people are not improved by direct payments and have failed to lead to any significant improvements in living arrangements (Woolham et al, 2017). Older people in receipt of cash payments are typically awarded a lower spend when compared to other groups, which is invariably used for personal care rather than to access resources to support social connection, reduce social exclusion or promote well-being (Feltoe and Orellana, 2013).

Higgs (see Chapter 4) highlights the importance of 'choice-making ... as part of the bedrock of contemporary society'. But, in reality, choice is an illusory concept, as the care 'market' flounders in the mire of financial constraints, an undervalued and poorly rewarded workforce, unfilled care vacancies and care providers leaving the market altogether (Glasby, 2000). More importantly, Woolham et al (2017, p 980) conclude that

> the policy goal of independence is an inappropriate one for most frail elderly people ... rather than a renewed focus on ways of trying to make personal budgets and direct payments work for older people, it may be necessary to accept the need for policy change focused on developing specialist gerontological social work to enable the co-production of person-centred, non-personal budget-based forms of care and support.

Woolham's argument implies the importance of maintaining a focus on older people's rights and opportunities to participate in decisions about their own lives as well as offering important evidence-based arguments for challenging existing policy orientations.

Given the focus on family care and challenges in accessing services in many countries, most older people do not seek help from social workers and social service organisations unless their circumstances are complex (Donnelly, Begley and O'Brien, 2018; Pentaris et al, 2020). This suggests that resolution of the problems that older people experience is less likely to be amenable to individual, service-based solutions. But structural factors such as long-term poverty, insecure housing or living in a neighbourhood experiencing multiple deprivations have often been marginalised in traditional social work approaches with older people (see Chapter 5). Thus, social work has often been limited in its ability to highlight and influence change in the consequences of, for example, social exclusion (Walsh et al, 2021), which directly affects the capacity for supporting an isolated older person to remain at home and feel socially included. To do otherwise risks a life that amounts to basic survival, reinforces exclusion or limits social contact to care visits and, at worst, constitutes a form of 'house arrest' (Phillipson and Ray, 2016).

The biomedicalisation perspective common among health and social work practitioners reinforces the potential for the challenges that older people experience to be attributed to individual pathology or the 'problem' of old age, caused, for example, by factors such as increasing frailty or cognitive impairment. For example, Montgomery and Carney (see Chapter 9) have argued that the tendency to view abuse as a personal problem fails to take account of the political, cultural and social structures that allow it to happen, and reinforces negative views of older people as fundamentally vulnerable and dependent. Similarly, Grenier and Sussman (see Chapter 5) highlight that late-life homelessness should not, as it often is, be perceived or treated as an individual misfortune. Rather, critical analysis of structural inequalities across the lifecourse, such as poverty, racism or a lack of affordable housing, contributes to housing insecurity or homelessness in later life. Working effectively for older homeless people requires action from a variety of 'systems, levels and practices' which have 'not been the primary focus of dialogue, debate and scholarship in gerontological social work' (see Chapter 5).

The continued centrality of biomedical perspectives on ageing has reinforced the perception of old age as a problem per se. Burden narratives in the media, for example, often focus on the numbers of predominantly older people who will be affected by dementia, combined with concern about the 'cost' of old age to health and social care systems. These messages continue to inform and shape perceptions of 'the elderly' who need to use social care services as a homogeneous group characterised by the burden of dependency. In this analysis, their precarious position in the lifecourse both separates 'them' from the rest of 'us' while, at the same time, relying on 'us' to support them in their growing and inevitable dependency, frailty and risk (Estes and Binney, 1989; Seppanen, 2017; Pentaris et al, 2020). An emphasis on the sameness of older people using personal social services overshadows individual biographies as well as obscuring processes of discrimination, injustice and inequality, which both create and reinforce this view (Pentaris et al, 2020). There is a danger, in this analysis, that infringing an older person's human rights is normalised in the management of their needs. Cahill (see Chapter 10) argues that people living with dementia are at heightened risk of discrimination and exclusion, and a rights-based profession such as social work is critical in upholding basic rights that recognise people's inherent worth. For example, research with older Moroccan migrants living in Belgium highlighted that interactions between migration history and experience, culture and religion influenced the experience of dementia for older people and their informal carers (Chaouni and De Donder, 2019). Experiences of discrimination influenced participant reluctance to approach formal care, reinforced by 'invisible realities of, for example, dementia as a condition, sources of support and the role of family care'. Research in Denmark (see Nielsen et al, 2020) examining dementia coordinators' perceptions of minority ethnic groups' access to dementia services highlighted barriers including language, lack of suitable services and inadequate cultural sensitivity. As Torres argues (see Chapter 7), social work research, policy and practice needs to expand its imagination about what ethnicity and migrancy mean for older people, and how our failure to grasp their complexity can get in the way of how we conceive their impact over the lifecourse. The risk of exclusion is heightened among older migrants and people from ethnic minorities living with dementia.

In a health and social work context, standardised assessment tools may reinforce age-based assumptions based on the 'measurement' of functional ability and activities of daily living. The focus on functional abilities may mean that age-based stereotypes (older people are sexually inactive; abused older people are vulnerable and frail; older people in the 'fourth' age are bound to be depressed/lonely/isolated) remain unchallenged and reinforce the homogeneity of old age, which is not easily compatible with lifecourse approaches (see Chapter 8). A lifecourse approach (see Chapter 2) offers opportunities to surface experiences of inequality or marginalisation over time and for the individual perspective and unique experience of the older person to be visible, as well as being alert to the potential implications of inequalities and oppression over the course of a life. Willis and Hafford-Letchfield (see Chapter 6) critique 'equal-same treatment' in policy and practice as it prevents recognition of sexual lives and histories that fall outside of heterocentric norms. If gerontological social workers are to achieve a holistic understanding of an individual older person, then they must recognise, for example, the impact of accumulative experiences of homophobia and sexuality-based discrimination. A lifecourse perspective encourages analysis of the relationship between gender, sexual abuse and violence and other structural factors such as racism and poverty. It also challenges assumptions that traumatic life events, for example, are somehow less relevant as people age and become old. Traumatic events are widely understood to have long-term implications for people, and yet, for older adults, trauma is often disenfranchised or overlooked (Kusmaul and Anderson, 2018, p 355). The so-called, 'non-compliant' older person living with dementia who rejects personal care from a stranger may be doing so for any number of reasons, including understandable reluctance and fear associated with trusting another person to carry out intimate body care. But we must also keep in mind that older people may have experienced trauma, such as a history of intimate partner abuse, torture, trauma associated with migration or childhood abuse that engenders fear and mistrust, as well as the risk of being retraumatised by abrupt, insensitive and discontinuous approaches to care and care transitions. While trauma-informed practice has been slow to develop in respect of older people, there are signs that it is beginning to be recognised as crucial in processes such as assessment and decision making (Kusmaul and Anderson, 2018).

While there is a paucity of research that examines the experience of older people using social work services, Manthorpe et al (2008) found that older people were critical of social workers who concentrated their practice on administrative and bureaucratic procedures. An exploratory study in England examining the contribution of gerontological social work to older people and other professionals highlighted the value placed on social work skills such as relationship building and continuity with older people with complex needs and circumstances (Willis et al, 2021). Social workers will often work with the 'oldest old', whose circumstances are more likely to be complex and characterised by change, loss and uncertainty, and a detailed understanding of the unique way in which the person perceives and approaches changing and uncertain situations is critical (Tanner, 2016).

While there is increased attention on co-production and participatory methods in service transformation, policy development and research, Beresford (see Chapter 11) illustrates how older people have tended to be poorly served in the development of user-involvement initiatives, as well as how services fall short in recognising the diversity of ageing experience and contexts. Several chapters in this book have highlighted the ways in which older people are marginalised and their experiential knowledge and lived experience silenced or devalued. By devaluing experiential knowledge, we lose a valuable knowledge source and, more importantly, effectively silence older people who experience abuse, discrimination or oppression. Lived experiences of, for example, ageism and racism remain substantially absent in scholarly debates or policy relevant to social work and personal social services, as well as in research on old age (Torres, 2020). Gendron et al (2016, p 999) highlight that, despite the considerable expansion of research and commentary about microaggression in relation to ethnicity, sexism, heterosexism and sexuality, 'ageism in relation to microaggression is glaringly absent'.

Ageist stereotypes propagate anxieties about personal ageing, and this undoubtedly contributes to the fact that older people are the least preferred group to work with among social work students (Gutheil et al, 2009; Carey, 2021). Personal fears about ageing may be caused by and also reinforce a lack of opportunities for exposure to gerontological research, knowledge and practice during social work training, which in turn may reinforce ideas that practice with older people is less meaningful, complex and rewarding (Richards et al, 2013) and not 'real' social work (Duffy, 2017). Approaches to social work that foreground biomedical perspectives and individual 'dysfunction' are likely to perpetuate entrenched ageist stereotypes, which remain all too commonplace in health and social care systems (Duffy, 2017).

Opportunities for gerontological social work

Gerontological social work practice, education, policy and scholarship, as has been argued throughout this book, are well placed to have a pivotal role in challenging and changing entrenched negative and ageist practices associated with old age. The spaces for developing gerontological social work have historically been limited and, arguably, remain so in the context of welfare retrenchment and policies that advance autonomy and choice, which Lloyd (2006) has commented as representing a third-age narrative addressing a fourth-age audience.

But, we would argue that there was never a more critical time to focus on the contribution that gerontological social work can make to policy, practice, education and scholarship. Torres (see Chapter 7) has illustrated population ageing as a key demographic trend throughout Europe and beyond, characterised by increased heterogeneity (for example, the numbers of people ageing without children or having disruptive family relationships; international migration and fluid constructions of family and support networks). Population ageing should emphatically not be constructed as a 'bad news' story. But the nexus of persistent and growing lifecourse inequalities and its impact on experiences of ageing cannot be overlooked.

Despite differences in welfare models and service structures, there is a need to develop gerontological social work in a way that challenges and ultimately breaks out of an orientation to service-based responses to the needs of individual older people (Mendes, 2009). What might it mean to claim that gerontological social work makes a distinct difference to older people's lives when other health, allied health and social care practitioners may also legitimately claim to achieve similar outcomes? The authors in this book have argued the importance of the nexus between critical social work and critical gerontological theory and research, underpinned by human rights-based approaches and commitments to social justice. From a practice perspective, this means resisting 'proceduralised' approaches to practice in order to challenge and change systems that perpetuate and reinforce age-based stereotypes and assumptions. Willis and Hafford-Letchfield (see Chapter 6), for example, have highlighted the ways in which social work as a rights-based profession can effectively challenge heteronormative assumptions about sexual identity in older age as well as opening up discussion with older people about sexuality and intimacy and their potential implications for any interventions or services that are offered. Similarly, 'care' policies are built on assumptions of family care and that behind every older person there are adult children waiting in the wings to provide support and assistance. Older people who, for whatever reason, are ageing without children may be especially vulnerable to expectations to accept residential care in the absence of close family care. Social workers can be instrumental in supporting people who are ageing without children to discuss and make clear their preferences and aspirations if, for example, they need extensive support or they lose decision-making capacity. In other words, gerontological social workers should, as a key part of their role, be working to change systems rather than shoehorning individual older people into services which are, too often, based on assumptions that essentially 'dependent' and 'vulnerable' older people need, more or less, the same kinds of support.

Negative and ageist stereotypes inevitably shape older people's experiences of ageing, and gerontological social workers should have a role in challenging practices that propagate age-based discrimination and that pathologise older people's behaviour. This latter point is important in respect of people living with dementia, who may be defined as having 'challenging behaviour' without considering the feelings and experiences a person may be communicating by their behaviour. Ageist language and labels, such as 'poor historian', 'frequent flier' and 'premier league users', perpetuate stereotypes of the older person as the problem to services, rather than encouraging us to take a critical look at the ways in which policies are operationalised and services organised in ways that limit the potential to understand the interacting factors that impact on an older person's experience.

Social work education should include opportunities for social work students to understand the scale and impact of ageism, as well as opportunities to critically reflect on and discuss their attitudes to and perceptions of social work with older people. As practitioners, all social workers should be aware of the pervasive nature of ageism in health and social care and their own potential to behave in a way that reinforces ageist assumptions and age-based stereotypes.

Gerontological social workers should resist interventions that they believe will worsen a person's situation as a fundamental aspect of ethical practice. Maintaining openness and honesty with older people and their supporters about what is or is not possible is critical. Forming alliances and connections with national and international professional bodies is another way to encourage awareness of issues pertaining to social work with older people and to encourage organisations to identify and challenge age-based discrimination and ageism as strategic and policy priorities.

It is timely, too, that gerontological social work develops sufficient professional confidence to make judgements about, for example, the time it takes to complete a complex assessment. Milne (see Chapter 2) has reflected on the limitations of a social work approach that emphasises the importance of fast throughput and single visits even in situations of complexity. Montgomery and Carney (see Chapter 9) highlight the importance of privileging the voice and experience of older people who have been subjected to abuse and overlooked at the expense of more powerful commentators responsible for shaping policies and services that affect older people. This too has implications for approaches to practice and a recognition that long-standing and unrecognised trauma from abuse and the harm caused by abuse suggests complex, trauma–aware approaches.

A lack of gerontological expertise and content in the social work curriculum, combined with low motivation for gerontological social work among student social workers, has been significantly reported (Richards et al, 2014). However, research suggests that when social work students are exposed to practice with older people their attitudes are often transformed (Adler, 2006). While not all social work programmes will include gerontological expertise in their teams, those that do may be at the forefront in infusing gerontological research and theory into social work programmes and disseminating good practice. Drawing on the experience of older citizens to recruit and support the learning and teaching of social work students is likely to encourage students to become more aware of experiences of ageing.

Developing and sharing resources that promote gerontological social work could help to develop an awareness of this area of practice. For example, in England, an interactive case and accessible case study for gerontological social work was developed by an established special interest group of social work academics to encourage the development of critical perspectives and gerontologically informed practice (Gero (G8), 2016). The British Association of Social Work (BASW) has developed a professional capabilities framework for practice with older people, identifying the evolution of practice capabilities from student to strategic leadership roles (BASW, 2018). Many of the authors in this collection have highlighted the need to widen the gerontological social work research agenda. Collaborations between researchers, older people and practitioners can contribute significantly to making the voice and experience of older people more visible, as well as to how contemporary responses to old age may reinforce and perpetuate experiences of disadvantage, inequality and marginalisation.

Social workers, academics and educators have argued that it is critical to claim professional identity as a means of resisting challenges to social work that may erode, devalue or sideline its knowledge, skill and value base. But being able to confidently communicate what gerontological social workers do and how they contribute to and impact on the lives of older people, as well as contribute to interdisciplinary practice, remains a significant research gap (Moriarty and Manthorpe, 2016). A small-scale study in England by Willis et al (2021) exploring innovation in social work with older people highlighted, for example, the value of specialist knowledge, skills and values that impacted on other professionals and decision making, including the use of legal knowledge to protect the rights of older people and positive risk management. This resonates with the analysis of Richards et al (2014, p 2320), who argued that gerontological social workers should 'ally themselves not only with service users and carers but also with colleagues from other disciplines to address shared concerns and to make the case for social work with older people' as well as with gerontological social work scholars. Building such alliances means, for example, making visible older people's experiences of discrimination or sub-optimal services.

It is timely to find ways to communicate confidently what gerontological social work does and what the contribution is to the lives of older citizens as well as to inter- and multiprofessional work. This will assist gerontological social workers to develop a sense of professional confidence, cohesion and identity, as they are embarked on a similar mission, underpinned by rights-based practice and critical social work and gerontological approaches. The development of networks for gerontological social work, such as the special interest group represented in this collection (and mentioned in Chapter 1), may further contribute to the visibility of gerontological social work and its sphere of activity.

Conclusion

We need practice, research and education that make visible the social, economic and political forces that shape and influence the lives of older people. In promoting a shared understanding of the 'moral core' (Bisman, 2004) of gerontological social work, a rights-based approach, supported by theoretical perspectives identified throughout this collection, is crucial. Making the lives and experiences of older people visible and working to keep older people's perspectives and aspirations at the centre of gerontological social work is crucial. We need a shift in perspective from the older person being a problem to the older person having a problem. Being open and sensitive to the nature of the problem(s) should promote analysis and action that consider the ways in which structures create and reinforce oppression, how lifecourse experiences are likely to impact in older age and, crucially, the older person's experience. A focus on the individual is likely to reinforce stereotyped assumptions about old age and fail to lift analysis to an appropriate examination of the intersections of factors such as age, gender, poverty and ethnicity, overlaid by macro structures and their influence in shaping experiences of ageing and old age. It is important to challenge proceduralised approaches to practice that are unsatisfactory in resolving complex and interacting contexts with single service solutions.

Gerontological social work that is committed to a rights-based approach supports the importance of practice that preserves the dignity of older people. Inevitably, there are times when older people experience sub-optimal care that also transgresses the moral foundations of the social worker. Building relationships and collaborative alliances with older people should be central to the social work role, but a contemporary focus on single-visit assessment and rapid throughput of work, regardless of the complexity of a person's circumstances, may jeopardise relationship-based approaches.

While recognising regional and country differences, there is merit in working towards the development of a gerontological social work identity broadly characterised by key attributes. The importance of promoting and enhancing knowledge, skills and values that broaden the gerontological social work agenda is beginning to be recognised internationally, both in education and in practice. All social work education programmes should, as a core element of their offer, support learning that helps students to understand the importance of rights-based practice that encourages the development of a critical lens in order to appreciate the impact of structural inequalities across the whole lifecourse and the broader structural factors that impact on older people. We want to underline the importance of sharing examples of good practice, promoting gerontological social work via professional networks, researchers' cooperation and local support networks. We have promising examples of research that demonstrates the value of gerontological social work both to older citizens and to interdisciplinary colleagues. Notwithstanding significant challenges and an indifferent pathway to a coherent identity, gerontological social work remains on the agenda. Joining and being active in social work professional bodies such as the European Social Work Research Association and its special interest group for gerontological social work can create a space in which to develop an active role in critiquing policies aimed at practice with older people and advocating for policy reform that addresses the implications of research, the lived experience of older people who use services and the expertise of gerontological social workers.

References

Adler, G. (2006) 'Geriatric field education in social work: a model for practice', *Educational Gerontology,* 32(29): 707–719.

Berdai Chaouni, S. and De Donder, L. (2019) 'Invisible realities: caring for older Moroccan migrants with dementia in Belgium', *Dementia*, 18(7–8): 3113–3129.

Bisman, C. (2004) 'Social work values: the moral core of the profession', *British Journal of Social Work*, 34(1): 109–123.

British Association of Social Work (2018) *Capabilities Statement for Social Workers in England Who Work with Older People*, [online], Available from: www.basw.co.uk/resources/capabilities-statement-social-workers-england-who-work-older-people [Accessed 12 March 2021].

Carey, M. (2021) 'The neoliberal university, social work and personalized care for older adults', *Ageing & Society*, 1–15, doi:10.1017/S0144686X20001919.

Deusdad, B. (2020) 'COVID-19 y la crisis de las residencias de mayores en España: edadismo y precariedad', *Research on Ageing and Social Policy*, 8(2):142–168.

Donnelly, S., Begley, E. and O'Brien, M. (2018) 'How are people with dementia involved in care planning and decision-making? An Irish social work perspective', *Dementia*, 18(7–8): 2985–3003.

Duffy, F. (2017) 'A social work perspective on how ageist language, discourses and understandings negatively frame older people and why taking a critical social work stance is essential', *British Journal of Social Work*, 47(7): 2068–2086.

Estes, C. and Binney, E.A. (1989) 'The biomedicalisation of ageing: dangers and dilemmas', *The Gerontologist*, 29(5): 587–596.

Feltoe, E. and Orellana, K. (2013) *Making Managed Personal Budgets Work for Older People*, London: Age UK.

Gendron, T.L., Welleford, E.A., Inker, J. and White, J.T. (2016) 'The language of ageism: why we need to use words carefully', *The Gerontologist*, 56(6): 997–1006.

Gero (G8) (2016) *Supporting Social Work with Older People, Research into Practice for Adults*, [online], Available from: https://gsw.ripfa.org.uk/ [Accessed 8 March 2021].

Glasby, J. (2000) 'Taking the stress out of social work: a multidimensional model of occupational stress', *Practice*, 12(1): 29–44.

Gutheil, I.A., Heyman, J.C. and Chernesky, R.H. (2009) 'Graduate social work students' interest in working with older adults', *Social Work Education*, 28(1): 54–64.

International Federation of Social Workers (2014) *Global Definition of Social Work*, [online], Available from: www.ifsw.org/what-is-social-work/global-definition-of-social-work/ [Accessed 20 February 2021].

Ioakimidis, V., Santos, C.C. and Martinez Herrero, I. (2014) 'Reconceptualising social work in times of crisis: an examination of the cases of Greece, Spain and Portugal', *International Social Work*, 57(4): 285–300.

Kusmaul, N. and Anderson, K. (208) 'Applying a trauma-informed perspective to loss and change in the lives of older adults', *Social Work in Health Care*, 57(5): 355–375.

Lloyd, L. (2006) 'A caring profession? The ethics of care and social work with older people', *British Journal of Social Work*, 36(7): 1171–1185.

Lymbery, M. (2005) *Social Work with Older People*, London: Sage.

Manthorpe, J., Moriarty, J., Rapaport, J., Clough, R., Cornes, M., Bright, L. and Iliffe, S., OPRSI (Older People Researching Social Issues) (2008) '"There are wonderful social workers but it's a lottery": older people's views about social workers', *British Journal of Social Work*, 38(6):1132–1150.

Means, R. and Smith, R. (1998) *From Poor Law to Community Care: The Development of Welfare Services for Elderly People 1939–1971*, Bristol: Policy Press.

Mendes, P. (2009) 'Tracing the origins of critical social work practice', in J. Allan, L. Briskman and B. Pease (eds) *Critical Social Work*, Sydney: Allen and Unwin, pp 17–29.

Moriarty, J. and Manthorpe, J. (2016) *The Effectiveness of Social Work with Adults*, London: Kings College, [online], Available from: www.kcl.ac.uk/scwru/res/knowledge/effectiveness [Accessed 1 March 2021].

Nielsen, T.R., Nielsen, D.S. and Waldemar, G. (2020) 'Barriers to post-diagnostic care and support in minority ethnic communities: a survey of Danish primary care dementia coordinators', *Dementia*, 19(8): 2702–2713.

Pajunen, E., Seppänen, M. and Kuusinen-James, K. (2009) *Vanhussosiaalityö Päijät-Hämeessä*, Verson raportteja 2/2009, Lahti: Verso.

Pentaraki, M. (2018) 'Austerity common sense and contested understandings of the austerity measures within a leadership of a professional association of social workers', *European Journal of Social Work*, 22(6): 1–12.

Pentaris, P., Willis, P., Ray, M., Deusdad, B., Lonbay, S., Niemi, M. and Donnelly, S. (2020) 'Older people in the context of COVID-19: a European perspective', *Journal of Gerontological Social Work*, 63(8): 736–742.

Phillipson, C. and Ray, M. (2016) 'Ageing in urban environments: challenges and opportunities for a critical social work practice', in C. Williams (ed) *Social Work and the City*, Basingstoke: Palgrave Macmillan, pp 151–171.

Ray, M. and Seppänen, M. (2014) 'Rakenteellinen lähestymistapa vanhussosiaalityössä – kriittisen gerontologisen sosiaalityön näkökulma', in A. Pohjola, M. Laitinen and M. Seppänen (eds) *Rakenteellinen Sosiaalityö*, Kuopio: Unipress, pp 234–249.

Richards, S., Sullivan, M.P., Tanner, D., Beech, C., Milne, A., Ray, M., Phillips, J. and Lloyd, L. (2014) 'On the edge of a new frontier: is gerontological social work in the UK ready to meet twenty-first century challenges?' *British Journal of Social Work*, 44(8): 2307–2324.

Seppänen, M. (2017) 'Gerontologinen sosiaalityö', in A. Kananoja, M. Lähteinen and P. Marjamäki (eds) *Sosiaalityön Käsikirja*, Helsinki: Tietosanoma Oy, pp 260–270.

Taghizadeh Larsson, A. and Österholm H.J. (2014) 'How are decisions on care services for people with dementia made and experienced? A systematic review and qualitative synthesis of recent empirical findings', *Psychogeriatrics*, 26(11): 1849–1162.

Tanner, D. (2016) 'Sustaining the self in the "fourth age": a case study', *Quality in Ageing and Older Adults*, 17(3): 157–167.

Torres, S. (2020) 'Racialization without racism in scholarship on old age', *Swiss Journal of Sociology*, 46(2): 331–349.

Verde-Diego, C., Prado Conde, S. and Aguiar Fernandez, F.X. (2018) 'The impact of the financial crisis on families in Spain: the case of Ourense, Spain', *International Social Work*, 63(1): 42–54.

Walsh, K., Scharf, T., Van Regenmortel, S. and Wanka, A. (2021) 'The intersection of ageing and social exclusion', in K. Walsh, T. Scharf, S. Van Regenmortel and A. Wanka (eds) *Social Exclusion in Later Life: Interdisciplinary and Policy Perspective*, Open Access, Cham: Springer, pp 3–24.

Willis, P., Lloyd, L., Hammond, J., Milne, A., Nelson-Becker, H., Perry, E., Ray, M., Richards, R. and Tanner, D. (2021) 'Casting light on the distinctive contribution of social work in multidisciplinary teams for older people', *British Journal of Social Work*, bcab004, https://doi.org/10.1093/bjsw/bcab004.

Woolham, J., Daly, G., Sparks, T., Ritters, K. and Steils, N. (2017) 'Do direct payments improve outcomes for older people who receive social care? Differences in outcome between people aged 75+ who have a managed personal budget or a direct payment', *Ageing & Society*, 37(5): 961–984.

World Health Organization (2021) *Global report on ageism*, Geneva: World Health Organization, [online], Available from: www.who.int/teams/social-determinants-of-health/demographic-change-and-healthy-ageing/combatting-ageism/global-report-on-ageism [Accessed 1 March 2021].

Index

References to endnotes show both the
page number and the note number (231n3).

Ingram Content Group UK Ltd.
Milton Keynes UK
UKHW022324050423
419677UK00004B/278